Multicultural/ Multiracial Psychology

❖ ❖ ❖ ❖

Multicultural/ Multiracial Psychology

MESTIZO PERSPECTIVES IN PERSONALITY AND MENTAL HEALTH

❖   ❖   ❖   ❖

Manuel Ramirez III, Ph.D.

JASON ARONSON INC.
Northvale, New Jersey
London

The author gratefully acknowledges permission to reprint material from:

Aztec Thought and Culture: A Study of the Ancient Nahuatl Mind by M. Leon-Portilla. Copyright © 1963 by University of Oklahoma Press.

"Folk Healing for the Wounded Spirit: II. Medicine Men: Purveyors of an Ancient Art" by S. Fields, in *Innovations* 3:12–18. Copyright © 1976 by American Institutes for Research.

Indians of North America by H. E. Driver. Copyright © 1969 by University of Chicago Press.

The Psychological Sense of Community by S. B. Sarason. Copyright © 1974 by Jossey-Bass Publishers.

Production Editor: Elaine Lindenblatt

This book was set in 11 pt. Berling Roman by Alpha Graphics of Pittsfield, New Hampshire, and printed and bound by Integrated Book Technology of Troy, New York.

Library of Congress Cataloging-in-Publication Data

Ramírez, Manuel, 1937–
    Multicultural/multiracial psychology : mestizo perspectives in personality and mental health / Manuel Ramirez III.
        p.   cm.
    Includes bibliographical references and index.
    ISBN 0-7657-0073-5 (softcover : alk. paper)
    1. Personality and culture—North America.   2. Personality and culture—South America.   3. Psychiatry, Transcultural—North America.   4. Psychiatry, Transcultural—South America.
    5. Ethnopsychology.   6. Mestizos—Psychology—America.   I. Title.
BF698.9.C8R34   1997
155.8'40407—dc21   97-5664

Printed in the United States of America on acid-free paper. For information and catalog write to Jason Aronson Inc., 230 Livingston Street, Northvale, New Jersey 07647-1731. Or visit our website: http://www.aronson.com

To *el profe*, Alfredo Castañeda
mentor, friend,
and
father of my academic life

ABOUT THE AUTHOR

Born in Rio Grande City, Texas, **Manuel Ramirez III** was reared in the historic community of Roma, TX, in the United States-Mexico border region. He received a B.A. in psychology and a Ph.D. in clinical psychology from the University of Texas at Austin. He did a postdoctoral internship at Norfolk State Hospital and Outpatient Clinic in Norfolk, NE, and has taught at California State University at Sacramento, Rice University, Pitzer College of the Claremont Colleges, the University of California at Riverside, and the University of California at Santa Cruz. He is currently Professor of Psychology at the University of Texas at Austin and Clinical Professor of Psychology at the University of Texas Southwestern Medical Center at Dallas. Author of *Psychotherapy and Counseling with Minorities: A Cognitive Approach to Individual and Cultural Differences*, Dr. Ramirez has been named Distinguished Minority Researcher by the American Educational Research Association.

❖ CONTENTS ❖

❖ PREFACE ❖

Major portions of this book were originally published under the title *Psychology of the Americas: Mestizo Perspectives in Personality and Mental Health* (1983). That work reflected the reality of ethnic/racial and national groups at a time when these groups were considered to be more distinct and when class/race-ethnic and national lines were more rigidly construed. The content of this book reflects its title and focuses on the psychology of multicultural/multiracial peoples—*mestizo* being the synthesis or amalgamation of Native American Indian and European people, cultures, and lifestyles—and the diverse environments in which they live. It addresses contemporary conditions in which distinction of groups and nations have blurred. Although Latinos of Mexican descent and those of other nations of the Americas remain the primary focus here, the new edition expands coverage to include United States populations that have their origins in Puerto Rico, Cuba, and the Philippines as well as people of mixed ethnic/racial heritage including African Americans, whites, and Native American Indians.

The changes in the work reflect the changes I have come to understand as a result of influences of my private practice, research, teaching, and self-exploration. During the intervening time, however, a concept from the original Preface remains true: "In the context of an Americas/mestizo personality psychology and psychiatry, all people in the Americas (regardless of race, nationality, or ethnic group) are considered to be psychological mestizos because they have been socialized in mestizo environments" (Ramirez 1983, p. xiii).

The clients I work with in my private practice are coping with problems that arise in their relationships with people of other ethnic/racial or national groups, or they are themselves the products of mixed ethnic/racial relationships. Many are also struggling to understand how growing up in different sociocultural systems has divided loyalties within themselves; still others have to deal with the attitudes and perceptions of those around them who try to

pigeonhole them into rigid groups or categories, expecting stereotypical behaviors.

The experiences of many of my clients, students, and participants
in research projects have led me to appreciate the observation by
W. E. B. DuBois (1903) that the African American "ever feels his
two-ness—an American, a Negro, two souls, two thoughts, two un-
reconciled strivings, two warring ideals in one dark body, whose
dogged strength alone keeps it from being torn asunder." DuBois
stated that the history of the African American is the history of the
attempt to merge a double self into a better, truer self.

My experiences and observations have also validated Hall's (1992)
views concerning her research on people of mixed ethnic/racial
heritage:

> Americans of mixed racial/ethnic heritage must also live in two worlds.
> Mixed individuals who have minority and majority (ethnic and white)
> heritages have similar choices to those mentioned. . . . The choices are
> multiplied when the individual is in a dual-minority combination (e.g.,
> black Japanese). Ethnic identity for all racially mixed groups is exacer-
> bated by the fact that they are racially mixed in a non-mixed society.
> They are a numerical minority, have few role models, and are usually
> not totally accepted by either ethnic group with which they share
> heritage. [pp. 251–252]

Self-exploration has proved to be a powerful teacher. The seed had
first been planted when, as an adolescent, I visited family graves with
my father. As we left the cemetery of my hometown of Roma, Texas,
located on the United States–Mexico border region, I noticed a grave-
stone engraved with the family name of Jones. This, standing alone
among markers of exclusively familiar Latino names, prompted me
to ask, "Who are the Joneses? I didn't realize that there were Anglos
living in Roma." His response took me by surprise: "Oh, they are not
Anglos, that is the Hones family who lives down the street from us."
For the first time I realized that in the sociocultural environment of
the United States–Mexico border region of Texas, I had grown up
knowing the family but not realizing the Spanish language influence
had changed the pronunciation of their name from the English *j* sound
to the more familiar *h* sound, the Spanish pronunciation for that
spelling. "Jones" had gradually changed to "Hones." The transforma-

tion of the pronunciation of a last name reflected the family's transformation into cultural mestizos.

The seed of self-exploration had been planted many years before it sprouted fully in 1986 at the *Rinkeybe Konferense* held at Stockholm, Sweden, when I was asked to deliver a keynote address for a conference on multicultural education focusing on the people of various developing countries who had been encouraged to come to Sweden during the guest-worker program, and who had decided to remain as permanent residents. As I prepared for the conference I recalled that one of my ancestors was of Swedish descent. One of my great-great-grandfathers had immigrated from Sweden to the United States in 1840. He later settled in South Texas, where he and my great-great-grandmother, Juanita Zamorano, met and married. This was the history of the maternal side of my family.

My paternal genealogy also included mixed heritage: the Ramirezs were originally *conversos* (Jews who had converted to Christianity) who came to New Spain (Mexico) from either Spain or Portugal in the 1540s, settling first in what is now the Monterrey area in northern Mexico and migrating eventually to the Lower Rio Grande Valley of Texas. My heritage also included the Mexican mestizo (Native American and European) influences typical of most people who grow up in the Rio Grande Valley.

This self-exploration led me to realize that I myself am a person of mixed ethnic heritage. It is now clear to me why I had been so interested in the development of a mixed ethnic heritage/mestizo psychology and psychiatry and what drew me to the research and exploration that underlie this work and its precursor, *Psychology of the Americas: Mestizo Perspectives in Personality and Mental Health.* Like many of my clients, research participants, and students, I had been working within a framework of the mestizo worldview developed as a product of the sociopolitical events that were the experience of many in the Americas.

In the context of an Americas/mestizo personality psychology, all peoples in the Americas and many in the rest of the world are considered to be psychological mestizos, because they have been socialized in multicultural/multiracial (mestizo) environments. Although most of the impetus for the Americas/mestizo psychology has come from the cultures of Native Americans and research on Latino mestizos, the assumptions, models, concepts, methodologies, and approaches of the new psychology can be applied to most people of the Americas and of much of the world.

What is the mestizo worldview, vis-à-vis personality psychology and the helping professions? The answer can be found in what Julian Rappaport (1977) has referred to as the new paradigm in psychology—respect for human diversity and the right to be different, and the belief that human problems are those of person–environment fit, rather than of incompetent (inferior) people or inferior psychological and cultural environments. But it is much more than this; it is a belief in the importance of synthesizing and amalgamating diversity to arrive at multicultural/multiracial identities, perspectives on life, and new approaches to solutions of problems. In line with this view, this book offers some new models that are based on the paradigms of diversity and synthesis. Specifically, it presents a conceptual framework based on the relationship of value/belief systems to personality styles. The specific model discussed in the book focuses on individual development of pluralistic identities, on the mental health of families coping with acculturation stress, on person–environment fit of migrating individuals who are mismatched with institutions and agencies of the "new" community, and on intergroup relations in situations of conflict.

A review of research and development efforts of the last twenty-five years reveals that mestizo multicultural/multiracial psychology has had an effect on the social sciences and helping professions. This book provides guidelines for the continued development of these efforts. It advances a model for multicultural assessment and psychotherapy that encourages the development of pluralistic perspectives and lifestyles. Further it focuses on a way for conceptualizing issues faced by the Americas and the world as a whole: immigration, international trade, intercultural dependence, and multicultural personality development.

❖ ACKNOWLEDGMENTS ❖

The idea for the first edition of this book grew out of several conversations with Alfredo Castañeda before his untimely death in January 1981. My wife, Susanne Doell, read parts of the original manuscript and listened patiently as I attempted to put thoughts into words; many of her constructive criticisms and suggestions are incorporated into the text.

I owe a deep debt of gratitude to Terry Foster for her invaluable help with both the 1983 edition and this edition. Terry not only edited and prepared the manuscript, she also gave me suggestions that helped make the writing experience an epiphanous journey of self discovery.

The financial support for the research on multiculturalism and leadership was provided by the Organizational Effectiveness Branch of the Office of Naval Research, Contract No. N00014-79-C-0015. I am grateful to several persons who assisted me on the multiculturalism and leadership study, among them Raymond Buriel, Camilo Chavez, Barbara Goffingon Cox, Raymond T. Garza, Alexander Gonzalez, P. Leslie Herold, and Roque Mendez. I also owe a debt of gratitude to Robert Guthrie and Robert Hayles formerly of the Office of Naval Research for their help and guidance on the multiculturalism and leadership study.

❖ 1 ❖

A Psychology of the Americas: A Mestizo Multicultural/Multiracial Perspective

In spite of our efforts to create a science that is universal, culture-free and beyond the boundaries of time and space, psychology is still very much culture bound.

—Ruben Ardila (1982)

The concept of person-environment "fit" rather than inferior or superior people or cultures is beginning to take hold. Recognition and support for diversity is emerging.

—Julian Rappaport (1977)

Mental health care exerts an influence on the basis of its claim to scientific status, but the claim is false. Thus, mental health care has a place in our society that it does not deserve, and we think about it wrongly. What it actually does, I argue here, is induct people into understanding life in certain ways that are artifacts of the cultures of healing—that is, the schools of care—rather than facts about human nature. That is, it "enculturates" them.

—Robert T. Fancher (1995)

Why propose a psychology specific to one area of the world, to one hemisphere? After all, psychology is a science and, as such, it should be applicable to everyone. These thoughts could easily occur to the readers of this chapter, for we have all been encouraged to believe that scientific knowledge is universal. What I am proposing in this book, however, is that the definition of science represented in psychology and the other social sciences and helping professions is a product of the European worldview. That is, the social sciences and helping professions have not represented the worldview that emerged from the experience of the Americas—the mestizo worldview. The uniqueness of life in the Americas, vis-à-vis Europe, as observed by Tocqueville (1835) and Zea (1945), has not been assimilated into the consciousness and professional practice of many social scientists and mental health workers either in the Americas or the rest of the world.

Americans and other multicultural/multiracial people in the world are, therefore, being viewed, evaluated, and treated by means of theories, assessment instruments, research, and intervention methodologies that are based on a European perspective of life and health. In recent decades, increasingly greater discontent has been expressed concerning assumptions in psychology and the helping professions that are based on the European worldview (Cronbach 1975, Osborne 1982, Rappaport 1977). Rappaport traces the origins of professional psychology in the United States to Darwin's theory of evolution: "Here in the study of individual differences was the perfect combination of laboratory measurement methods developed in the German physiological tradition and philosophical ideas concerning how man 'ought' to be" (p. 9).

Rappaport also observed that Reigel (1972) had succeeded in tracing some of the origins of developmental psychology in America to Darwin's theory: "Darwin's notion of the 'struggle for survival' was supportive of a reemergence of the philosopher Hobbes' argument that man is essentially competitive and established social order only as a means for protection of self and property" (p. 39).

Ardila (1982) observed that the development of psychology in Latin America has been unduly influenced by psychology in the United States and thus ultimately by a European worldview. Diaz-Guerrero (1977) was one of the first Latino social scientists to criticize the European perspective as reflected in the research done by Fromm and Maccoby (1970), as well as that by Oscar Lewis in Mexico. Ramirez (1978) has also been critical of the use of European worldview-based theories and approaches to study people in Mexico and the United States.

This book urges social scientists and mental health practitioners to realize that the theories, instruments, methodologies, and approaches they use may ignore the realities of the people of mixed ethnic/racial heritage and of the cultural mestizos of the world. It encourages practitioners and researchers to recognize that as long as the European worldview bias exists in their professions and in their work, it will be difficult for multicultural/multiracial people—cultural and genetic mestizos—to understand themselves and their environments, resulting in a continuing drift toward misunderstanding and conflict.

TWO HISTORICAL TRADITIONS, WORLDVIEWS, AND PERSPECTIVES IN RESEARCH AND PRACTICE

The European Worldview in the Social Sciences and Mental Health Professions

The worldview that has had the greatest influence on the social sciences and mental health professions is the product of certain events that were significant in the evolution of cultures on the European continent. Perhaps the most important of these events was the extensive colonization efforts by France, England, and Spain. In particular, it was the detribalization and accompanying enculturation programs that so impacted the evolution of the European worldview vis-à-vis perspectives on pluralism, diversity, and individual differences.

The colonization programs reflected the colonizers' belief that their culture and lifestyle and, especially, their religious beliefs were superior to those of the colonized populations (Collins 1954). The detribalization and enculturation efforts of the colonization programs thus were attempts to break up loyalties and allegiances of members of the colonized populations to families, tribes, religions, regional areas, and countries. The principal objective of those efforts was to replace the old loyalties with total allegiance to the culture and religion of the colonizer. The enculturation program adopted by the British was particularly thorough, involving sending members of the native populations to England, where they learned English, were trained in Christianity, and were taught British history and culture. After several years, these people were returned to their native lands to assist in implementation of the enculturation programs.

Inherent in the belief that the colonized populations must replace their cultural identities, lifestyles, and religious beliefs with those of the colonizers was the assumption that the colonized cultures and peoples were psychologically deficient and primitive. Mannoni (1960), a French psychoanalyst, published a paper on the psychology of colonization in which he concluded that colonization was made possible by an inherent need in the participant populations to be dependent. He believed that this need for dependency was satisfied by the high degree of individualism and self-dependency characteristic of Europeans. In fact, Mannoni made it appear that the colonized

populations were characterized by an unconscious desire for colonization: "Where Europeans have founded colonies of the type we are
considering, it can safely be said that their coming was unconsciously
expected—even desired—by the future subject peoples" (p. 644).

Mannoni recognized the need to prepare young men for a colonial
career by giving them a "really modern psychology" that would allow
them to better understand the indigenous population and their relations to them. This emphasis on the use of knowledge of the social
sciences to ensure the success of colonization programs provided some
of the early impetus for the development of cross-cultural psychology in Europe. For example, Geza Roheim, a psychoanalytically
trained ethnologist, did psychoanalytic field studies from 1928 to 1931
in central Australia, Somaliland, and the Normanby Islands with the
support of Marie Bonaparate. The first report based on Roheim's
research was entitled "The Psychoanalysis of Primitive Culture Types"
(1932).

In general, the colonization programs followed by the European
countries and, in particular, the application of psychological concepts
to understand the behavior of members of the colonized populations
helped to shape a worldview, vis-à-vis peoples whose cultures and
lifestyles differed from those of the colonizers. In turn, this view had
a significant impact on the development of social sciences and mental
health professions with respect to individual and cultural diversity.

Other sociopolitical events that helped to shape the European
worldview were the Democratic and the Industrial Revolutions. The
extensive psychological and sociological impact of these revolutions
have been eloquently described by Robert Nisbet in his book *Tradition and Revolt* (1970). Nisbet observed that the Industrial and Democratic Revolutions led to the displacement of the traditional belief
system in Europe and to its replacement with a modernistic system
of values. That is, modern beliefs in individualism, egalitarianism, and
secularism replaced beliefs in the sacred origin of the universe, group
identity, and respect for ritual and tradition. Nisbet further asserted
that traditional beliefs came to be perceived as being incompatible
with technology and progress. Black (1972) observed that modernization eventually became identified with Europeanization or Westernization. Thus, from the perspective of the European worldview,
peoples and cultures identified with traditional values and belief systems are assumed to be psychologically underdeveloped and in need

of Europeanization or Westernization. The reasons behind Mannoni's (1960) conclusion that colonized peoples "unconsciously desired" colonization and that they needed the "high degree of individualism and self-dependency characteristic of Europeans" become clear. Similarly, Nisbet (1953) observed that the exaggerated emphasis of individualism in Western psychological theories of personality development, functioning, and adjustment could be attributed to the impact of the Industrial Revolution on the social sciences. It is no accident, then, that concepts emphasizing individual development and independence have figured so importantly in theories of personality and in the goals of psychotherapy, counseling, and education.

The third major series of sociopolitical events that helped to shape the European worldview as reflected in the social sciences and mental health professions was the separation of the domains of science and religion. The origin of the separation is dated to Galileo's assertion that the earth was not the center of the universe, in opposition to long-held Church doctrine. The introduction of Darwin's theory of evolution led to further separation between the domains of science and religion in Europe. In contrast to the European experience, science and religion remained conjoined in the cultures of the native peoples of the Americas. The polarization between the Church and the scientific community in Europe accounts for many of the crucial differences between the European and mestizo worldviews as reflected in the social sciences. For example, with few exceptions, such as Jungian theory, religion and spiritualism have not played a major role in the theories and intervention approaches of the mental health professions.

The three sets of sociopolitical events discussed above have influenced the development of some of the tenets of the European worldview, vis-à-vis personality, the social sciences in general, and the helping professions. These tenets are as follows:

1. The technological and economic development of a culture or society are synonymous with the degree of psychological development of its members. This belief states that cultures that are technologically underdeveloped are populated by peoples who are likewise psychologically underdeveloped and/or who are pathological. The writing of Mannoni (1960) concerning dependency complexes in colonized populations and McClelland's

(1961) cross-cultural speculations regarding need achievement are examples of how psychological development has been equated with technological development. Witkin and Berry (1975) concluded that members of non-Western cultures are undifferentiated psychologically; that is, they are field dependent in their cognitive style. Examples in the cross-cultural personality literature are numerous. In fact, a review of the culture/personality literature could easily lead to the conclusion that one of the primary goals of this area of study has been to prove the superiority of European cultures to cultures of non-European origin.

2. Psychological development and religious ideology are equated: the greater the adherence to European-Christian beliefs by a culture or a nation, the more civilized, sophisticated, and well-adjusted its inhabitants or members are assumed to be. Although science and religion were officially separated in Europe, Christianization and modernization came to be seen as synonymous because early colonization efforts by Spain and England emphasized Christianization of native populations. People whose religious beliefs were not based on the European-Christian ideology were believed to be superstitious and underdeveloped; belief in European-Christian ideals was seen as synonymous with a degree of psychological sophistication.

3. Darwin's theory of evolution nurtured a belief in genetic superiority. Certain people are believed to be genetically and/or biologically superior to others (Guthrie 1976). Specifically, people of Northern and Western European stock are believed to be genetically superior to Latinos and African Americans (Herstein and Murray 1994). Expression of this belief is reflected in the writings of Jensen (1969) and Shockley (1965), but this belief has a long history in European thought. Sir Francis Galton, a cousin of Charles Darwin, authored a book entitled *Hereditary Genius: Its Locus and Consequences*, published in 1869. The book sought proof for the hypothesis that eugenics and greatness followed family lines. Galton thus introduced a science of heredity, eugenics, which proposed "a program of racial improvement through selective mating and the sterilization of the unfit." Galton established the Eugenics Society of Great Britain and published the *Eugenics Review*, a monthly journal that

served as the chief medium of communication for eugenicists throughout the world. The works of Galton and other eugenicists eventually led to the recapitulation theory, which held that an individual organism, in the process of growth and development, passes through a series of stages representing phases of development appearing in the evolution of the species. A principal proponent of the recapitulation theory in the United States was G. Stanley Hall, the influential psychologist and president of Clark University. In his book *Adolescence* (1904) Hall described Africans, American Indians, and Chinese as members of "adolescent races." Hall argued that people who had not "recapitulated" beyond an inferior stage should be prevented from reproducing their kind. He believed that society should be ruled by the "innately superior."

4. Certain cultures and belief systems are considered superior to others. European cultures are held to be superior to non-European cultures, which are usually described as primitive and underdeveloped. Cultures which are not of Northern or Western European origin are believed to interfere with the psychological development and adjustment of their members. This "damaging culture" view has pervaded many theories and conceptual frameworks in the social sciences and mental health professions. The writings of both Piaget (1966) and Bruner and colleagues (1966) have implied that non-Western cultures interfere with intellectual development in children. McClelland (1961) concluded that certain characteristics of non-Western cultures interfere with intellectual development of need achievement, and Witkin and Berry (1975) viewed socialization practices of non-Western cultures as interfering with the development of psychological differentiation.

The Mestizo Worldview in the Social Sciences and Mental Health Professions

In contrast to the European worldview, the mestizo perspective reflected in the new social sciences emerging in the Americas had its origins in events and experiences unique to living and surviving in the New World. One of the most important of these was the challenge of survival in a new environment. The history of the Americas abounds with stories of people who went in search of new environments to effect new beginnings. From the legend of the Aztecs, describing their search for a new permanent home at a place where an eagle would be seen perched on a cactus eating a serpent, to the long voyages made by the European settlers to the new world, the lonely voyages of trappers in Canada and the traders in the Southwest and Northwest, and the long treks by wagon train that carried settlers from East to West, the story of the Americas is one of struggling to conquer a new environment. There were many instances in which early settlements in America did not survive. The key to survival was cooperation—collaboration among peoples of different backgrounds in order to learn skills and lifestyles that ensured success in the new environment. This cooperative experience eventually provided the impetus for mestizoization (multicultural/multiracial development).

Another factor that shaped the mestizo worldview was the common practice of intermarriage between the European settlers and the native peoples of North and South America as well as the Caribbean. This resulted in the development of a new race and a new culture representing combinations of New World and Western traditions, an amalgamation of two different worldviews and orientations to life. This cultural synthesis ensured that most people in the Americas would come to view themselves as "psychological mestizos"; that is, they felt that their lifestyles were the products of merging different cultures and ways of life. For most people in the Americas, even for those who were not genetic mestizos, involvement in a mestizo way of life was an inescapable reality that led them to the conclusion that multicultural/multiracial orientations to life were both possible and desirable.

A third set of sociopolitical events that contributed to the development of the mestizo worldview were those related to the amalgamation of Native American and European religious practices and ideologies. Some of the cultural products of the synthesis of Native American and European religions are the Native American Church and the Catholic religion of Mexicans and Mexican Americans. (Both of these mestizo religions are discussed in more detail in other chapters of this book.)

A fourth cluster of sociopolitical experiences that helped to stimulate the development of the Americas' worldview were the revolution against European domination and subsequent struggles to prevent European nations from establishing their influence in the hemisphere. These sets of experiences led to strong feelings among the peoples of the Americas of independence from European ideologies and life styles. They also created a strong feeling of "Americanness," making people in the Americas conscious of their differences from Europeans. Finally, the struggles for independence encouraged tenacity in holding onto one's heritage. While Americans were proud of their independence from Europe, they also believed that some of their old value systems and life ways should be preserved in their new environment. Thus, they made an attempt to hold onto some of the old while adopting the new. This orientation, this consciousness about group and individual identity, eventually encouraged development of the melting pot and *la raza cosmica* (the cosmic race) ideologies; and these, in turn, influenced pluralistic conceptualizations of the identity development process.

The following tenets of the mestizo worldview are influencing the development of the social sciences and mental health professions in the Americas and the world:

1. Knowledge obtained from living and surviving the challenges of life makes every individual's philosophy of life valuable and makes every person a potential teacher. History, heroes, heroines, legends, individual psychohistories, and family and community psychohistories are all important to a psychology of the Americas. Every person, every family, and every community can offer valuable lessons about survival and adjustment. Perhaps the most distinctive feature of the Americas is that everyone has a right to tell his/her story because every individual is considered to be a unique observer of life. Every person is believed to have attained a unique understanding of life from learning to confront certain challenges in life, from overcoming personal adversities, and from learning to adapt to certain life circumstances. It is also interesting to note that one of the most salient observations made by Tocqueville in *Democracy in America* (1835), and one that he felt was in direct contrast to what he had observed in Europe, was the genuine concern that people had for one another in the United States. In fact, he equated this interest in others with freedom. He believed that love of

freedom by Americans was related to the sincere interest they had in each other and their willingness to learn from one another. He observed (Stone and Mennell 1980), "indeed, it is no exaggeration to say that a man's admiration of absolute government is proportionate to the contempt he feels for those around him." He also noted: "In the United States the more opulent citizens take great care not to stand aloof from the people; on the contrary, they constantly keep on easy terms with the lower classes: they listen to them, they speak to them every day" (p. 297).

2. The second tenet of the mestizo worldview that had a major influence on the mental health professions and the social sciences in the Americas stresses the importance of ecology in personality development and functioning. Community psychology, which had its origins in the Americas, has evolved out of an ecological perspective in the social sciences. This perspective is represented in the philosophies and religions of the native peoples of the Americas (Lee 1976, Trimble 1981). The Indian cultures view the person as an open system that both affects and is affected by his/her surroundings. Harmony with the environment, both physical and social, is thus of primary concern in psychological adjustment.

3. The third tenet of the mestizo worldview speaks to the importance of openness to diversity; the ultimate criterion for achieving knowledge and sophistication in life is acceptance and respect for the beliefs of all cultures and religions. Rappaport (1977) referred to respect for diversity and the right to be different as the new paradigm in psychology. Accordingly, the person considers that all cultures and religions represent potentially important sources of knowledge about life that can be helpful to his/her own development. It is this acceptance of diversity that facilitated the development of the mestizoization process and that, in turn, resulted in the development of multicultural/multiracial identities and ways of life by many people in the Americas.

4. The fourth tenet of the mestizo worldview as reflected in the social sciences and helping professions concerns the advantages of pluralistic socialization: the more a person is willing to learn from the knowledge, life experiences, and life meanings of other

peoples' religion and cultures, the more opportunity he/she has to incorporate these into his/her own personality and, in turn, to make use of these additional resources to become more flexible and adaptable in meeting the diverse demands of life. The melting pot ideology that emerged in the United States in the late eighteenth and early nineteenth centuries was reflective of this belief (Crevecoeur 1904). This tenet also mirrors the views of two Mexican scholars, José Vasconcellos and Leopoldo Zea. In his two major works, La Raza Cosmica (1925) and Indologia (1927), Vasconcellos extolled the advantages of diversity reflected in the mestizo race and observed that in the mestizo race lies the greatest hope for the future of the Americas:

Our major hope for salvation is found in the fact that we are not a pure race, but an aggregation of races in formation, an aggregation that can produce a race more powerful than those who are products of only one race. [1927, p. 1202]

Vasconcellos predicted that a race composed of synthesis, a "cosmic race," would emerge to fulfill "the divine mission of America." This new race would represent the "synthesis of the four races now existing—the black, the brown, the yellow, and the white" (1925, pp. 52–53). Each member of the new race, he predicted, would be a "whole human." Furthermore, he concluded that the mestizos were the beginning of this new cosmic race. Like Vasconcellos, the social historian Leopoldo Zea (1945, 1974) described the advantages of synthesis, referring to a synthesis of worldviews and lifestyles rather than to one of races.

TWO PHILOSOPHIES OF
MENTAL HEALTH AND PERSONALITY

I began this chapter by proposing that the European and Americas worldviews influenced the development of opposing theories and orientations to personality and mental health. What follows is a detailed description of those differences.

General Characteristics of the Fields of Study and of the People Who Work in Them

The European worldview encourages the development of orientations to personality and mental health that are characterized largely by specialization, compartmentalization, and intellectualization. Social scientists and mental health professionals are trained to become specialists. They are trained in child or adolescent or adult psychology, in research or in practice, in mood or personality disorders. Differences among the various areas of specialization are usually highly intellectualized, and minor distinctions are viewed as major differences between the specialty areas. Intellectual isolation fostered by each specialty area leads to each having its own terminology, research, and intervention approaches and methodologies, and there is little cooperation between specialists in the different areas.

Within the context of the European worldview, researchers and mental health practitioners are selected for training primarily on the basis of their ability to think analytically, and they are trained to use inductive thinking approaches to theory construction. Training is based on the scientific model employed by physics and chemistry with considerable attention focused on the reductionistic approach, that is, to analyzing complex behaviors by breaking them down into their component parts.

The mestizo worldview encourages the development of a psychology that is interdisciplinary, synergistic, and unified. From the mestizo multicultural/multiracial perspective, the person is viewed as intimately linked to the sociocultural and physical environments in which he/she interacts. The mestizo orientation is, therefore, interdisciplinary, bringing together such diverse fields as biology, medicine, economics, political science, history, folklore, sociology, anthropology, literature, and the arts. The generalist scholar/practitioner modeled after the Latin American *pensador* is seen as the ideal psychologist and social scientist. The approaches to personality study and to community and individual intervention are global and holistic; there is no separation made between mind and body or between the intellectual and affective domains of behavior.

The Role of the Researcher and Practitioner

In the context of the European worldviews, social science researchers and mental health practitioners are encouraged to be objective and nonpolitical. Personal values and belief systems are kept separate from the problems being studied or the client/patient being treated. In fact, the values and belief systems of researchers and practitioners rarely become a source of focus in training unless the candidate is experiencing difficulty in the training program.

Ideally, it is also expected that the roles of interventionist and researcher will be kept separate, since it is believed that a person who is involved in intervention is likely to "lose his/her scientific objectivity." Much of the role of researchers and practitioners is also determined by the fact that the professional is expected to be responsible primarily to him/herself (that is, to his/her own goals and objectives in life) and to the academic or professional communities to which he/she belongs.

The mestizo worldview encourages social scientists and practitioners to adopt an advocate/conceptualizer role. For a proper understanding of the problems and/or the people with whom the professional is working, the belief is that it is necessary for him/her to share a worldview with the client or participant. It is also believed that the researcher/practitioner is primarily responsible to the community and/or to the people with whom he/she is working. The foremost goal in the professional's role is the well-being and betterment of those being studied or helped and to humanity as a whole.

Approaches to Research and Interpretation of Data

The European worldview approaches to social science and mental health research emulate methods used by the natural sciences. The assumption is that psychological reality is fixed in time and place, and methodology is characterized by maximum control and manipulation of variables. Tests and other techniques for data collection are held to be equally valid for all peoples regardless of race, gender, personal background, and culture. Data interpretation is made by using existing personality theories and concepts with minimal concern for the values, lifestyles, and belief systems of the people from whom the data were collected. Interpretation of data and of assessment information are usually done in the abstract, that is, independent of the sociocultural, economic, political, historical, and ecological variables in which the participants or clients are embedded. (See Segall's [1996] critique of the Triandis conceptual framework of individualism and collectivism.)

The mestizo worldview encourages research that is historical, contextual, and ecological in its orientation. Research in naturalistic settings and the use of assessment techniques that are observational and unobtrusive as well as holistic and historical are thought to be ideal. Life, family, and community histories are used to understand the complex dynamics of individuals and groups. The person-environment and person-historical interaction are considered to be of central importance. In choosing assessment methods and instruments, the values, lifestyles, and belief systems of the participants are given primary consideration. Data are interpreted by making use of conceptual frameworks and theories that are reflective of the reality of the persons being studied.

Goals of Applications and Interventions

In the context of the European worldview, clients/patients and research participants are generally considered to be responsible for their problems and the circumstances of life in which they exist. Consequently, most intervention approaches based on the European worldview are likely to focus on changing the client/patient or the participant rather than the institutions and the society in which he or she lives. Ryan (1971) referred to this orientation as "blaming the victim" and describes its application in intervention programs as follows:

> The formula for action becomes extraordinarily simple: change the victim. All of this happens so smoothly that it seems downright rational. First, identify a social problem. Second, study those affected by the problem and discover in what ways they are different from the rest of us as a consequence of deprivation and injustice. Third, define the differences as the cause of the social problem itself. Finally, of course,

assign a government bureaucrat to invent a humanitarian action program to correct the difference. [p. 8]

The basic assumption behind the blaming the victim philosophy is that mainstream society is preferred because it reflects the "superior" European value system and lifestyle—shades of the enculturation programs of the colonization period. Theories, concepts, and techniques for assessment and intervention are viewed as reflections of a superior culture that can help inferior and "culturally deprived" people to change for the better. It is thus not necessary to get to know the patients or participants well, for according to the blaming-the-victim line of reasoning, what they have to offer is not worth knowing. The interventionist is the expert, because he/she knows the superior culture, has the credentials to prove it, and, as a member of that culture, can become a model for the "disadvantaged" persons being studied and for whom intervention is intended. This leads us to still another characteristic of intervention according to the European worldview: only those with the proper credentials can serve as models in intervention.

The mestizo, multicultural/multiracial worldview encourages development of change in both the participant/client and in society and its institutions. As Ryan has observed, the client/participant needs to be helped to a higher level of morale and to develop more skills and knowledge to deal effectively with institutions and the society. These are the main goals of intervention done in the context of the mestizo worldview. In turn, society and its institutions must be changed to become more responsive to diversity and to provide equality of opportunity for those whose lifestyles and value systems differ from the majority. Intervention techniques are tailored to reflect the value systems and lifestyles of the participant/client. In the mestizo context, the most important criterion for determining intervention expertise is first-hand knowledge by the researcher or practitioner of the group he/she is working with and the degree to which he/she is accepted by that group. In this perspective indigenous healers such as *curanderos* and medicine men are placed in the category of expert, and the intervention approaches used must, at the very least, emerge partially from the cultures, lifestyles, and belief systems of the people with whom the interventions are being carried out.

Table 1–1. Major Differences between European and Mestizo Approaches to the Social Sciences and Helping Professions

Characteristics of Theories

European	Mestizo
Focus is specialized and compartmentalized. There is separation of cognitive and affective development, of nature and nurture, and of effects of sociocultural and biological-genetic influences on personality development and adjustment.	Focus is interdisciplinary. Personality is viewed as holistic and interwoven with physical, social, political, and spiritual enivornments.
Theories contain cultural, genetic, gender, and sexual orientation superiority notions that lead to the conclusion that certain groups are genetically superior to others (Herstein and Murray 1994, Jensen 1969) and that certain cultures and societies are superior to others (McClelland 1961).	Theories and conceptual frameworks are devoid of notions of cultural, genetic, gender, or sexual orientation superiority.
Isolation and separation are fostered by development of specialized terminology and methodology with little intercommunication and coopertion with researchers outside the discipline.	Emphasis is on communication and cooperation not only with other social scientists and practitioners, but with representatives of other disciplines as well (Iscoe 1982).

Characteristics of Researchers and Practitioners

European	Mestizo
Minimizes the importance of values, belief systems, and worldviews vis-à-vis personality and mental health, and of understanding relationship of own values/belief systems to personal research interests and to preference for certain theories, systems of psychotherapy, and research methodologies (Gergin 1976).	Aware of the relationship of own values and belief systems to personal interests in research and intervention; values ability to synthesize and to integrate different disciplines, approaches, and worldviews.
Analytical thinking is emphasized. The ideal is the "scientist" who is totally objective and removed from social, economic, and political realities of the people she/he works with.	The ideal is the generalist, the Latin American *pensador* (thinker-doer), who is knowledgeable about history, politics, economics, religion, art, and philosophy. It is preferable that practi-

Table 1–1. (*continued*)

Characteristics of Researchers and Practitioners

European	*Mestizo*
	tioner has lived through some of the same life experiences as the client or participant. Views self as a partner and equal to the client or participant.

Role of Researchers and Practitioners

European	*Mestizo*
Objective and nonpolitical; personal values and belief systems kept separate from research and intervention activities (at least as an ideal). The researcher or interventionist is the expert and the participant or patient is viewed as being sick, uninformed, underdeveloped, unfortunate, or uncivilized and in need of education, enlightenment, enculturation, and more sophisticated adjustment and development.	Participant/conceptualizer and change agent; deep personal commitment to solving social problems. The principal role is to create societal change that can promote fairness, justice, empowerment, and equality of opportunity.
Primary responsibility in research is to self and to academic community.	Primarily responsible to the client and to the members of the groups and communities with which the research or interventionist is working. Places the needs of the participants, clients, and communities above those of academia and science.
Being considered by peers to be a "true scientist and scholar" is a primary goal.	Being considered a change agent for her/his "people" is the primary goal; does not compromise the goals of total equality and social justice.

Approaches to Research and Interpretation Data

European	*Mestizo*
Laboratory-setting research, which maximizes control and manipulation of variables, is the ideal; the assumption that psychological reality is fixed in time (Cronbach 1975); instruments, research	Naturalist setting with nonobtrusive approaches for data collection is preferred; use of observational and life history approaches with person-environment and person-socio-

Table 1–1. (*continued*)

Approaches to Research and Interpretation Data

European	*Mestizo*
methods, and intervention approaches are considered to be valid for all peoples; data are interpreted using theories with no modifications or allowances made for differing views of patients/clients and participants; emphasis is on universalism (an etic perspective in cross-cultural research).	historical-political interactions given great importance; data are interpreted in the context of social, physical, and spiritual environments of the participants with the use of theoretical orientations and concepts that are consonant with the worldviews of participants and clients; emphasis is placed on individual and cultural differences (an emic perspective in cross-cultural research).

Approaches to Intervention

European	*Mestizo*
Patients (the designation for persons seeking mental health services) and participants are believed to be, for the most part, responsible for their problems (Ryan's [1971] blame-the-victim concept).	Society, and particularly oppression, racism, and inequality of opportunity (Sen 1995), are viewed as primarily responsible for the adjustment problems of patients/clients and participants.
The primary goal of intervention is to change the patient so that she/he conforms to the values and norms of the majority society (enculturation); interventionists see themselves as representatives of a "superior" culture and society that has all the answers for the patient.	The primary goal of intervention is to change both society and the client. Clients are helped to interact with institutions more effectively and are empowered to change society so that it becomes more responsible to diversity and more equitable in its treatment of citizens. Intervention techniques, research instruments, theories, and methodologies reflect the values and lifestyle of the client. Interventionist and researcher share the worldview of clients and participants and view them as important decision makers and partners in the change process.

Table 1–1. (*continued*)

Models of Identity Development and Culture Change

European	Mestizo
Two or more cultures cannot coexist in harmony, so there is conflict and confusion for the bicultural/multi-cultural person (identity crisis); models of acculturation are influenced by conflict-replacement and assimilationist notions. Instruments used to assess acculturation are unidirectional (assimilationist in orientation) and unidimensional (focus extensively on language use, and food and music preferences, ignoring other important variables); they ignore multicultural realities and assume that increments of involvement in mainstream American culture are accompanied by decrements of involvement in original culture (Rogler et al. 1991).	Two or more cultures can coexist without conflict (Valentine 1972) and they can merge to create new and more flexible orientations to life (Hall 1992, Ramirez 1978); persons are able to identify with two or more cultures simultaneously without experiencing conflict or confusion. Models of acculturation focus on flexibility, synthesis, and unity. Instruments for assessing acculturation focus on simultaneous participation in two or more cultures (McFee 1968) and on values, activities, friendship, and intimacy patterns (Rodriguez and Ramirez, in press).

Models of Culture Change and Identity Development

The most important differences between European and mestizo worldviews are embodied in the conceptualizations that each encouraged, vis-a-vis culture change and identity development. Within the European worldview perspective, diversity is perceived as potentially negative and as interfering with psychological development and adjustment. In the European view, two or more cultures cannot coexist in harmony and thus they create conflicts for the individual that lead to an identity crisis. In this context, the only alternative is abandonment of minority identities and cultures and complete and total acceptance of identities and cultures associated with the European worldview. The European-based cultures and lifestyles are viewed as being superior to others, thus all change is conceptualized as greater movement in the direction of accepting the European-based culture and lifestyle with simultaneous abandonment of minority cultures and lifestyles. This view of acculturation and identity development could be properly entitled conflict replacement/assimilation. The conflict replacement/assimilation models consider that synthesis of different cultures and lifestyles is impossible.

On the other hand, mestizo perspectives on culture change and diversity are characterized by a positive view of diversity and pluralism. Culture change is viewed as adoption of values, lifestyles, and perspectives of both European and non-European cultures. It is also believed that the characteristics of several cultures can merge together through synthesis. A pluralistic identity is viewed as ideal, representing a commitment to the person's original culture as well as to other cultures and lifestyles. The pluralistic identity represents a synthesis of different lifestyles, values, perceptual and thinking styles, and coping techniques. (An example of a pluralistic model of identity and culture change is presented in Chapter 4.) Table 1–1 summarizes the principal differences between European and mestizo social science and mental health as discussed in this chapter.

SUMMARY

Different socio-historico-political events in the histories of Europe and the Americas have influenced the development of two different worldviews about personality, adjustment, and mental health. These worldviews, in turn, have shaped widely divergent development of theories and research and intervention approaches in the social sciences and mental health professions. Differences in European and mestizo worldview can be observed in several domains: (1) general characteristics of fields of knowledge and of the persons who work in them, (2) roles of researchers and practitioners, (3) approaches to research and interpretation of data, (4) application and interventions, and (5) types of models, concepts, and instruments used to conceptualize and assess culture change and multicultural/multiracial identity development.

❖ 2 ❖

Cultural and Philosophical Foundations of a Mestizo Multicultural/Multiracial Psychology

The Sun Dancer believes that each person is a unique Living Medicine Wheel, powerful beyond imagination, that has been limited and placed upon the earth to Touch, Experience and Learn. . . . All the things of the Universe Wheel have spirit and life, including the rivers, rocks, earth, sky, plants and animals. But it is only man of all the Beings in the Wheel, who is a determiner. Our determining spirit can be made whole only through the learning of our harmony with all our brothers and sisters, and with all the other Spirits of the Universe. To do this we must learn to seek and to perceive.

—*Hyemeyohsts Storm (1972)*

The most consistent theme in the descriptions penned about the New World was amazement at the Indians' personal liberty, in particular their freedom from rulers and from social classes based on ownership of property. For the first time the French and British became aware of the possibility of living in social harmony and prosperity without the rule of a king.

—*Jack Weatherford (1988)*

The wise men were firmly convinced of the importance of finding "true roots" for man in this life. This was not an easy task, for as one Nahuatl poet remarked:

> What does your mind seek?
> Where is your heart?
> If you give your heart to everything,
> You lead it nowhere; you destroy your heart.
> Can anything be found on earth?

—*Miguel Leon-Portilla (1963)*

This chapter focuses on the concepts and principles of psychology, the social sciences in general, and the helping professions that are reflected in the cultures of the indigenous peoples of North and South America, as well as the Caribbean. These concepts are providing the basis for the framework on which mestizo multicultural/ multiracial psychology is being established, and they have also played an important role in the amalgamation of Native American, Asian, African, and European cultures, lifestyles, and worldviews. Also described is the role that the syncretic process of mestizoization has played in the development of mestizo multicultural/multiracial psychology. Finally, the chapter presents a short review of Mexican philosophy, a product of the mestizoization process in the Americas as well as the intellectual wellspring from which mestizo multicultural/multiracial psychology is emerging.

PSYCHOLOGY IN THE CULTURES OF THE INDIGENOUS PEOPLE OF NORTH AMERICA

From the varied beliefs of the Indian nations of North America, certain common psychological concepts have emerged to influence the development of mestizo multicultural/multiracial psychology. The Native American psychological concepts that have had the greatest impact on mestizo psychology are the following:

The person is an open system. The individual is viewed as an integral part of the environment and the universe and as being completely open to experience. What is learned from interactions with others and with the environment and the universe (both the natural and the supernatural) helps the person to achieve harmony with his/her surroundings and to arrive at understanding of the meaning of life. This concept is reflected in a passage from *Seven Arrows* (Storm 1972): "The Universe is the Mirror of the People and each person is a Mirror to every other person. . . . Any idea, person or object can be a Medicine Wheel, a Mirror for man. The tiniest flower can be such a Mirror, as can a wolf, a story, a touch, a religion or a mountain top" (p. 5).

Much of the education of children is based on the notion of the person as an open system and focuses on the teaching of sensitivity and openness to the environment. Lee (1976) observed:

> The mother initiated her unborn baby into relatedness with nature and continued to do so in various ways through infancy. She took the very tiny baby out and merely pointed to natural manifestations without labeling. Only after the baby experienced directly, only later, did she offer him concepts. She sang songs referring to the animals as his brothers, his cousins, his grandparents. Early in life he was also helped to develop a sensitivity toward nature, so that he might be enabled to relate openly. [p. 9]

In his autobiography, Russell Means (1995) describes how a person can learn from nature:

> That summer, I discovered an unhurried life that all indigenous people once shared. Without telephones or clocks, we learned that when you are free, there is no time. I sat endlessly among the trees, watching and contemplating, trying to understand the messages of life by observing it. I began to grasp the beauty and grace of being in the present, of living in harmony with everything in the natural world. . . . I discovered that I had enrolled in the university of the universe. Our relatives, the wild creatures who share this earth with us, never stop teaching if we are prepared to learn from them. [p. 413]

LaFramboise (1983) observed that protection of the environment is a central value of Native American cultures, and Means (1995) emphasized the respect that Indians have for "grandmother earth." He contrasts the respect for the environment in Native American nations with the values and belief systems of White society: "I said our culture is about having patience and building relationships with life itself, it is about becoming part of life, which allows us to live with nature rather than conquer nature" (p. 178).

The notion of interpenetration is an integral part of the view of the person as an open system. Specifically, information and knowledge coming from others and from the environment are seen as modifying, incorporating, and influencing the psychodynamics of the person. The individual modifies and affects others and the environment as he/she interacts with these. Lee (1976) explained this phenomenon:

> In such societies, though the self and the other are differentiated, they are not mutually exclusive. The self contains some of the other, participates in the other and is in part contained within the other. By this I do not mean what usually goes in the name of empathy. I mean rather that where such a concept of the self is operative, self-interest and other-interest are not clearly distinguished. [p. 112]
>
> It enables him to value himself as well as the other, to develop himself while developing the other and to relate himself in a transaction which enhances the value of both self and other. [p. 114]

The spiritual world holds the key to destiny, personal identity, and life mission. The spiritual world is perceived to be a great source of power and knowledge. By achieving communication with the spiritual world,

Native Americans believe that a person can have a vision or a dream that can provide him/her with an adult identity, a life mission, and a spirit-helper to facilitate the attainment of life goals. Communication with the spiritual world is encouraged both through individual contact with the supernatural in visions and group contact in organized ritual. Most of the Native American cultures of North America make use of the vision quest for making contact with the spiritual world. Driver (1969) provided the following description of the vision quest:

> A youth would travel to an isolated spot with a reputation as an abode of spirits, usually a mountain or a lake or an uninhabited wood. Here he remained for several days and nights, fasting from both food and water, naked in the cold, mutilating his body, and otherwise denying the desires of the flesh to the point that an hallucination was likely to occur. He prayed by asking a spirit to take pity on him in his condition of deprivation and want, the idea being that the more miserable his condition, the more likely was a spirit to come to his aid. Such "visions" usually took the form of both visual and auditory hallucinations. The neophyte would frequently see an animal spirit, which would speak to him, teach him a song or show him designs to paint on his body, clothing or weapons for protection against the enemy. On returning home, the youth would eventually describe his experience to his family or camp mates, sing the songs he had acquired, and paint the designs on his possessions. If his demonstration was convincing, he might later acquire a following on a future hunting or warring expedition. If the knowledge he acquired in the vision was efficacious in curing the sick, he could set himself up as a medicine man. [p. 391]

It is also believed that the power and knowledge of the spiritual world can be accessed by employing the help of a shaman or medicine man—someone who is seen as the mediator between the individual and the supernatural.

Community identity and responsibility to the group are of central importance. The individual is socialized to develop a strong sense of responsibility to the group. The person then comes to feel that at all times he or she is the representative of the group. "I am the people" is a statement often made by members of North American Indian groups.

Lee (1976) attested to the importance of community identity among the North American Indians. The individual was considered a representative of his camp circle; "what he asked of Waken Tanka, the Great Spirit, was: 'Help me that my people may live'" (p. 12). Lee continued:

> Concern and care for the community had to manifest themselves in behavior; a feeling of responsibility is not enough and this behavior predisposed development of all aspects of the self. So, the strengthening of character, of courage, of the capacity to endure; the development of powers of observation, of the ability to concentrate; the stretching of the span of attention; and everything we subsume under the name of education; all this the individual undertook as part of his responsibility to the community. [p. 34]

LaFramboise (1983) observed that a central value of Native American cultures is the importance of close ties to the homeland and extended family. She reported that this value is inculcated in children by having the entire community participate in the socialization process. She indicated that community socialization of children is embodied in the role of the "whipper man" of the Plateau tribes, as described by Shore and Nicholls (1975):

> The whipper man functioned in the role of disciplinarian. He was a tribal member, respected by elders and young alike and selected for that role by tribal leaders and relatives on the basis of personal integrity. His function was to punish children who displayed disrespect to elders. Today his role of regulator has been assigned to the tribe in the increased community control over the development and placement of Indian children. [p. 10]

Identification with family and community, LaFramboise commented, is also encouraged through extended family involvement in modeling and instruction in cultural traditions. This mode of socialization is most evident in the powwows (Parfit and Harvey 1994), which are held regularly by the Indian nations of North America. One of the functions served by powwows, or celebrations as they are referred to by Native Americans, is to maintain a sense of community by teaching traditions and values to the young.

Emphasis is on liberty, freedom, and respectful individualism in social institutions. Native American societies are free of rulers, of slavery, and of social classes based on land ownership, unlike many European societies. Most of the early European ethnographers and philosophers who described American Indian societies described them as just and equitable compared to the societies they had known in Europe (Weatherford 1988). For example, Thomas Paine criticized the British for the abusive treatment of Native Americans and was the first American to call for the abolition of slavery and the first to propose the name *United States of America* for the new country. Paine learned about democracy by living among the Iroquois. He wrote: "The fact is, that the condition of millions in every country in Europe is far worse than if they had been born before civilization began, or had been born among the Indians of North America at the present day" (1944, p. 338). Weatherford observed, "[T]he Hurons lived without social classes, without a government separate from their kinship system, and without private property" (1988, p. 123). Alexis de Tocqueville, writing in the first volume of *Democracy in America*, repeatedly used phrases such as "equal and free" to describe American Indian societies he had observed in the new world. He said that the European republics never showed more love of independence than did the Indians of North America.

The liberty and freedom in Indian nations encouraged development of the respectful individualism that characterized group activities such as powwows in Native American societies. Weatherford (1988) described these activities:

> This seems to be typical of Indian community events: no one is in control. . . . The event flows in an orderly fashion like hundreds of powwows before it, but leaders can only lead by example, by pleas or by exhortations. Everyone shows great respect for the elders and for warriors, who are repeatedly singled out for recognition, but at the same time children receive great respect for dancing and even the audience receives praise for watching. . . . The event unfolds as a collective activity of all participants, not as one mandated and controlled from the top. Each participant responds to the collective mentality and mood of the whole group, but not to a single, directing voice. [pp. 120–121]

Generosity is emphasized in interpersonal relationships. Going hand in hand with the de-emphasis on individual property ownership is the spirit of generosity that characterized interpersonal relationships in Native American communities. Parfit and Harvey (1994) described one of the most important activities of the powwow:

People mark their most important transitions here. They come to the powwow to honor their athletes, their retirees, their dead. Contests are regularly interrupted by Specials or Giveaways, 20- or 30-minute events. During a Special, Old Horn gives the cordless mike to another speaker, who describes the person being honored. Then a drum group sings, a crowd of aunts, uncles, grandparents, brothers, sisters, parents and children dance in a circle; people come out of the crowd to shake hands and dance with them, and then the family gives away blankets and cottonwood branches with dollar bills taped to the twigs. [p. 104]

Full development of abilities and skills is achieved through self-challenge. Self-challenge and endurance of pain, hardship, hunger, and frustration were used to encourage the development of the individual's full potential. Children were encouraged to seek out competitive situations, and the goal of education was the full development of capacity. Lee (1976) has observed: "They were taught to engage themselves in the elements—to meet them with an answering strength. If a torrential rain fell, they learned to strip and run out in it, however cool the weather. Little boys were trained to walk with men for miles through heavy snow drifts in the face of biting winds, and to take pride in the hardship endured" (p. 53).

One of the principal goals of self-challenge was to learn restraint and self-control. LaFramboise (1983) reported that respect is accorded to individuals who exhibit self-discipline.

Russell Means (1995) described his vision quest: "Naked and alone, with only a buffalo robe to sit on inside an altar bound with color tobacco ties, I faced the east. While crying for a vision, we neither eat nor drink" (p. 405).

PSYCHOLOGY IN THE CULTURES OF THE INDIGENOUS PEOPLE OF CENTRAL AND SOUTH AMERICA AND THE CARIBBEAN

Natives of North America are not alone in influencing mestizo, multicultural/multiracial thought. Psychological concepts that emerged from the cultures of Indian nations of Central and South America and the Caribbean have also influenced the development of this new psychology. These include the following:

The search for self-knowledge, individual identity, and life meaning is a primary life goal. Both the Mayas and the Nahuatl-speaking peoples of the Valley of Mexico believed that an individual comes to earth without a face, without an identity. An identity was achieved through socialization and education. In order to develop identity, it was believed, a person had to learn self-control. Achievement of identity through self-control and personal strength was believed to lead to development of free will. Much of education had as its major goal what the Nahuas referred to as self-admonishment, which meant to know for oneself what one should be. Leon-Portilla (1963) observed that the Nahuas, even more than the Greeks, had arrived at the relationship between identity and change of self-image; they conceived of the self as being in constant motion and change.

The individual is embedded in history and time. Knowledge of the history of one's group and accurate measurement of time were used to predict the destiny of both the individual and the group. The Nahuas had a book that they used to make calendaric diagnoses at the time of the infant's birth. To predict the destiny of a child, the Nahuas used the *Tonalamatl* (Book of Fortunes) in conjunction with the *Tonalpohualli* or "Count of Days" (the divine calendar of 20 groups of 13 days). Leon-Portilla (1963) described this process:

> First you had to attend to the character of the year in question (whose function depended on the particular century and spatial region of orientation). Also, the character of each Trecena of both years and days, then the twenty signs of Tonalamatl, and lastly the day, all had to be coordinated sign with number in order to show the various influences in the "Calendaric diagnosis." [p. 116]

A birth under a bad sign could be overcome both by baptizing the child on a day of a favorable sign and by ensuring that through education and socialization a child would develop a free will. Thus, knowledge was seen as the key to destiny and to control over one's life.

For the Mayas, time was even more important than for the Nahuas; the accurate measurement of time and the association of time with important events in the history of the group resulted in the development of an elaborate psychological system for prediction of the individual's future. As with the Nahuas, the Mayas sought favorable signs to overcome a bad fate. Leon-Portilla (1963) described this complex psychological time theory as follows:

The ancient concern in finding through the calendar the norms of the agricultural cycles and the moments to propitiate the gods, thus attains a fuller meaning. To ascertain the units of measurement of kinh, to know the order of its alternations, to investigate its past burdens, leads to the prediction of its future recurrences. Thus, religious thought, supported by observations and calculations, unites its peculiar form of cosmic history with an astrological knowledge so vitally important throughout the life of the Maya. [p. 104]

Those who recognized the presence of the different moment-deities, would find "remedies for their ills." They would be able to seek, thanks to the rites and sacrifices, and with the aid of computations, the favorable deities, those which confronted with adverse fates, would neutralize contrary influences. *In this way it was possible to escape absolute fatalism and open the door to knowledge leading man to better acting and thinking at prescribed moments.* [Emphasis added, p. 106]

There is a duality of origin and life in the universe. Polar opposites— male and female, religion and war, poetry and math—were often fused in the cultures of the Nahuas and the Mayas. In the religion of the Nahuas, the god Ometeotl represents the dual nature of the culture. Ometeotl is androgynous—both masculine and feminine, both father and mother of the gods. The duality for the culture is also reflected in the many male/female deities contained in the religion of the Nahuas. Duality was further present in other aspects of the Nahua and Mayan cultures, for example, the association of science with mysticism reflected in the time theory of the Mayas and the calendaric diagnoses of the Nahuas.

Education plays a central role in personality development. It is impossible to exaggerate the magnitude of the role that education played in the Mayan and Nahuatl cultures. It was seen as the key to the proper development of the personality and of a free will. Education was believed to be the responsibility of both the parents and the philosophers (*tlamatinime*). The parents educated the child up to about age 15, at which time he or she entered a school to be taught by the *tlamatinime*. Education was formalized and mandatory.

One of the rituals following the birth of a child was initiation of the infant into the school he or she would attend at adolescence. There were also specific scripts which parents had to follow in giving their children advice when they reached a certain prescribed age. For example, the script used by a father counseling his son on greed and vanity was as follows:

> Receive this word, listen to this word.
> I hope that for a little time you will live with Our Lord,
> He who is Master of the Close Vicinity.
> Live on earth;
> I hope you will last for a little time.
> Do you know much?
> With good judgment, look at things, observe them wisely.
> It is said that this is a place of hardship, of filth, of troubles.
> It is a place without pleasure, dreadful, which brings desolation.
> There is nothing true here . . .
> Here is how you must work and act;
> Safely kept, in a locked place,
> The elders left us these words
> At the time of their departure.
> Those of the white hair and the wrinkled faces, our ancestors. . . .
> [Leon-Portilla 1963, p. 149]

At a certain age, the child would attend a formal school. With respect to the education given at these schools, Duran (1964) wrote: "They had masters and teachers who would teach and instruct them in all kinds of art—military, ecclesiastical, and mechanical—and in astrology based on the knowledge of the stars. About all these things they had large and lovely books of paintings and characters" (p. 140).

The schools taught the culture and history of the group and sought to identify the proper life mission that each individual should adopt. Instruction consisted primarily of history, poetry, and mathematics. The goal of education was to humanize the passions, to make the students wise, and to give them a firmness of purpose. The ultimate goal was to develop a free will that was not subject to the passions of the individual, but that could serve the individual and his/her people. With a free will, the person could overcome a negative fate or keep from straying from the path of a positive fate.

The most important personality characteristics in Nahuatl culture are reflected in the following passage, contained in one of the codices: "The mature man is a heart solid as a rock, is a wise face. Possessor of a face, possessor of a heart, he is able and understanding" (quoted in Leon-Portilla 1963, p. 141).

MESTIZOIZATION OF PEOPLES
AND CULTURES IN THE AMERICAS

The psychological concepts discussed above have played a central role in encouraging the development of the synergistic process that evolved in the Americas. Mestizoization involved the confluence and amalgamation of peoples and cultures from two continents as well as the bringing together of religions, lifestyles, and worldviews based on European and New World thought.

Of all the psychological/philosophical concepts that emerged from the cultures of the native peoples of the Americas, the individual as an open system was probably most influential in encouraging the mestizoization process. Their openness to experience and diversity, and sensitivity to the environment and the universe, made the indigenous Americans receptive to other ways of life and other philosophies. The concept of duality, combining opposites, also encouraged the incorporation of other peoples and ways of life in the cultures of the native peoples of the Americas. But it was the perpetual search for self-knowledge and for life mission that was most influential in stimulating the development of the mestizoization process in the Americas. Every person, every culture, every worldview was believed to reflect knowledge necessary to understand the mysteries of life and the self. Diversity was accepted and incorporated into the self through both genetic and cultural amalgamation.

The Emergence of Genetic Mestizos

Genetic mestizos were a necessary precursor to the development of mestizo, multicultural/multiracial cultures and lifestyles. Persons who were the genetic products of European and Native American peoples facilitated the integration of European and Native American cultures and ideologies. These mestizos could play the roles of cultural "ambassadors" and "brokers" because they spoke two or more languages, and they were familiar with the sociocultural systems that were being amalgamated.

Genetic mestizoization was more common in some areas of the Americas than in others. Because of this unevenness, cultural and religious mestizoization would be more evident in some regions of the hemisphere than in others. For example, genetic mestizoization was less common in those areas settled by the English on the East Coast of North America, because these areas were settled mainly by families. Single men settled many parts of Canada, the southwestern United States, Central and South America, and the Caribbean and looked to native populations for wives and companions. The religious philosophies of the European settlers also played a major role in the development of the mestizoization process. Driver (1969) noted:

> The presence of English women in the colonies and the strict Protestant moral codes prevented the creation of a mestizo class from large numbers of mixed concubinages and marriages, [and] the Puritans were too narrow-minded on the whole to have devoted much effort to Christianizing the Indians who they regarded as agents of Satan. [p. 480]

The situation on the East Coast of the United States thus contrasts with that in Canada, the southwestern region of North America, Latin America, and the Caribbean. In these latter regions, genetic mestizoization was more common and, with it, cultural mestizoization flourished.

Cultural Mestizoization

In North America, religion among African Americans, Latinos, and Native Americans is a product of the cultural mestizoization process. In all areas of the hemisphere, cultural mestizoization has influenced the social sciences and mental health practices through healing and religion. Driver (1969) offered the following description of the Native American Church:

> The doctrine includes the belief in supernatural power, in spirits, and in incarnation of power in human beings. Spirits consist of the Christian Trinity (the Father, the Son and the Holy Ghost); other Christian spirits such as the devil and the angels; and still other spirits derived exclusively from Indian religion. The Christian spirits tend to be equated with comparable Indian spirits: God is the Great Spirit, Jesus is the culture hero; the devil is the evil spirit. [p. 524]

Driver described the rituals of the religion:

Peyote ritual is heavily weighted in favor of Indian elements, such as the eagle-bone whistle, cedar incense, the fan of bird tail feathers, the bundle of sage sprigs, the gourd rattle, and the water drum. Eating peyote induces rapport with the supernatural and brings various spirits of departed ones, sometimes with aid in solving personal problems and with warning to abandon evil thoughts and deeds. [p. 525]

One of the best examples of cultural mestizoization in Latin America and in the Caribbean is folk healing. *Curanderos(as)* (folkhealers) and *espiritistas* (spiritists) use a combination of rituals and paraphernalia common to both Indian and European religions. In the case of Puerto Rican *espiritistas*, African beliefs and practices are also combined with the Indian and European (see Chapter 7 for a more extensive description of folk medicine).

From the point of view of mestizo social sciences and mental health practices, the most important product of the mestizoization process is Mexican philosophy. The writings of Mexican philosophers have provided most of the philosophical base upon which mestizo social science and mental health practices and approaches are being developed. Mexican philosophy succeeded in integrating the psychological concepts of the Native American cultures with important contributions by European philosophers. What follows is a short history of the development of those aspects of Mexican philosophy that have had the greatest influence on the development of mestizo philosophy and psychiatry.

PHILOSOPHICAL ROOTS OF MESTIZO SOCIAL SCIENCE AND MENTAL HEALTH

The young philosophers who were active in the period of Mexican history which preceded the Revolution of 1910 were described by Romanell (1971) as the "intellectual forerunners of the Mexican revolution." These scholars were members of a group which became known as the *Ateneo de la Juventud* or the "Athenaeum of Youth." Romanell observed:

The Ateneo de la Juventud was founded in Mexico City on October 28, 1909. Its first president was Antonio Caso. The membership came to fifty or so, a few of whom lived in the provinces, like Diego Rivera, the famous mural painter. The members came from all walks of life and the majority of them were lawyers by profession. Though the group was heterogeneous in composition, the members had a common goal: to contribute to the spiritualization of a demoralized country. [p. 57]

In 1910 the Ateneo organized a series of lectures on the personality and work of Spanish-American thinkers and artisans. The focus on Spanish-American culture was a reflection of the interest of the group in expressing themselves and not merely in imitating European thought. The Ateneo was also a reaction against the positivistic school that had been dominant in Mexican philosophy during the presidency of Porfirio Diaz. The positivists had adapted concepts from European science and philosophy and applied them to Mexico. They were organized into a political party known as the Party of Scientists, and they used Darwinian arguments to justify the dishonest and oppressive government of Diaz. Romanell (1971) observed:

They had the audacity to affirm that the very survival of the powers that be signified that they were the fittest to govern the country. Along with the doctrine of "honest tyranny" for home consumption, they urged Saxonization of the Latin soul to compete with the "great nation" growing by leaps and bounds across the border. [p. 53]

The focus of philosophy that the members of the Ateneo adopted could be identified as perspectivistic, and it was based on the writings of Jose Ortega y Gasset (1946). According to this perspectivistic view, philosophy is not a quest for certainty but the search for *a point of view on human life*. This was, in every sense, a cross-cultural philosophy since every point of view on human life reflects a particular sociocultural system.

Romanell (1971) observed that the contributions made by the members of the Ateneo succeed in "initiating the rehabilitation of thought of a mestizo peoples." Thus, it provided the initial philosophical base on which mestizo multicultural/multiracial social science could be established. In fact, the writings of the Ateneo members were based on a concept of central importance to cross-cultural psychology in general and to a mestizo philosophy in particular—the emic point of view, that is, the belief that peoples and cultures must be studied and understood on their own terms.

The adoption of the emic perspective was initiated by the writings and works of José Vasconcellos, of the Ateneo, who became known as the intellectual of the Mexican Revolution. The two works by Vasconcellos that have the greatest implications for a mestizo aproach to the social sciences and mental health professions are *La Raza Cosmica* (1925) and *Indologia* (1927).

Although Vasconcellos engaged in much speculation in these two books and also contradicted himself on various points, he nevertheless consistently argued for the synthesis of diversity through the process of mestizoization. He asserted his belief that genetic and cultural amalgamation of different races and cultures could contribute to greater knowledge of life for all. Vasconcellos saw the mestizo race as the greatest hope for the future of Latin America. He stated: "Our major hope for salvation is found in the fact that we are not a pure race, but an aggregation of races in formation, an aggregation that can produce a race more powerful than those which are the products of only one race" (1927, p. 1202).

Although Vasconcellos argued for the development of a new Latin race, his was, above all, a philosophy of synthesis, that is, it was not exclusivistic. He specifically stated that the new race should not exclude white peoples. Latin America, he observed, owed much of what it was to the European whites and to North Americans.

A general theme that ran through much of Vasconcellos's writings was his strong conviction regarding the value of indigenous culture in the Americas. This argument was prevalent in the writings of another famous Mexican philosopher, the first president of the Ateneo, Antonio Caso. Caso (1943a,b) emphasized the importance of understanding Mexico's roots in order to properly understand Mexico. He felt that the most serious and immediate problem facing Mexico was the establishment of a Mexican collective consciousness. Caso's philosophy was instrumental in the rejection of the ideology of European science in Mexico and also in the rejection of Nietzsche's ideal of the "superman." He accepted the premises of traditional Darwinism as true in biology but false in ethics. Romanell (1971) observed:

For Caso science is only a part of the truth, the rest must be found in metaphysics; because man is more than reason, he is sentiment and will. Science cannot penetrate to the depths of life. This world is only accessible to intuition. Intuition unites the metaphysics of the mystic and the laws of the scientist by obtaining concrete reality, like the mystic wanted and the universal knowledge, like the intellectualists demanded. [p. 91]

Caso emphasized the importance of personalism—the fact that the person is a unique element in the universe and thus the most essential part of reality (Klor de Alva 1972). Caso's writings provided two critical concepts for the philosophical base on which the mestizo social sciences and helping professions are being established: (1) a methodology that is an amalgamation of phenomenology and the best of the European scientific approach, and (2) the uniqueness of the individual. Thus, Caso provided an important concept for the philosophical base on which the mestizo multicultural/multiracial outlook was to be founded: a mestizo multicultural/multiracial methodology.

The work of Vasconcellos and Caso was continued by Samuel Ramos, who had studied under Caso and worked with Vasconcellos at the Secretariat of Public Instruction. Ramos, like Caso, believed that Mexico needed to develop a national consciousness. To help in the achievement of this goal, he applied historicism and perspectivism. These two approaches were evident in his major work, *Profile of Man and Culture in Mexico*, published in 1934. His principal argument in this work was that Mexican intellectuals and political leaders were suffering from an inferiority complex that had its origins in the Spanish Conquest, and that had been reinforced by the Spanish colonization period as well as by the interventions of France and the United States. He argued that this inferiority complex had forced Mexicans to look to Europe for guidance and direction. Ramos (1975) wrote:

> Throughout its history Mexico has fed on European traditions and expressed much interest and appreciation for their value. . . . No one can deny that interest in foreign culture has signified for many Mexicans a spiritual flight from their own land. In this case, "culture" is a cloister in which men who disdain native realities take refuge in order to ignore them. From this erroneous attitude Mexican "self-denigration" was born more than a century ago, and its effects have been crucial in our historical orientation. [p. 17]

He concluded his analysis by providing an antidote to the poison of self-denigration and inferiority feeling—an education that was established on the Mexican experience. The basis of all educational reform in the country, he argued, should be the study of the culture and the people of Mexico. He called for the establishment of a new philosophical anthropology that could free the people of Mexico from their psychological maladjustment:

> When these depressive complexes vanish, our false character will automatically disappear. Like a disguise it has covered the Mexican's authentic way of being as a compensation for painful feelings of inferiority. That day will be the beginning of our second War of Independence, which may turn out to be more transcendental than the first, because it will free the spirit for the fulfillment of its own destiny. [pp. 114–115]
>
> The concepts of Mexico that appear in the textbooks must be revised, for they have been distorted by self-denegration and an inferiority complex. There must be enthusiasm and respect for Mexican things. Observing our circumstances objectively, one discovers surprising values, the knowledge of which will undoubtedly contribute to uplifting the Mexican spirit. [pp. 131–132]

Ramos's principal contributions to the mestizo view in the social sciences and mental health professions were his focus on the psychodynamics of self-rejection characteristic of Mexicans who were denying their original culture and his arguments that Mexico, a nation that is a product of the mestizo experience, should evolve a philosophy based on its mestizo culture. It is unfortunate that Ramos employed a European theory of personality, that of Alfred Adler, to explain some of the observations he made of Mexican psychodynamics. The use of Adlerian theory forced him into conclusions that were extremely pessimistic and negative. (A more detailed discussion is presented in Chapter 3.)

Ramos's detailed descriptions of the psychodynamics of self-denial did, nevertheless, lay the groundwork for mestizo multicultural/multiracial psychology vis-à-vis a focus on identity development in multicultural/multiracial settings. However, his most important contribution regarding the philosophical base of a mestizo worldview was his insistence that Mexico develop a culture and a consciousness based on its mestizo experience. It was this idea that influenced the work of the Mexican philosopher/social historian Leopoldo Zea.

Zea focused on the experience of the individual in the Americas, indicating that his/her feelings of inferiority and anomie were the result of not having a native philosophy—a philosophy of the Americas—for guidance. Zea (1945) thus argued for an American philosophy, a framework for an American culture that could help people in the nations of the hemisphere to solve the major problems that they face and to avoid the failures of Europe. Zea pointed out that if we are to succeed in creating an American philosophy and culture, we need to accept the diversity that is evident in all areas of the hemisphere. In addition, he emphasized that the nations and peoples of the Americas need to put notions of cultural and individual superiority aside. He stated that a necessary prerequisite to the development of an American culture and philosophy is the meeting of the peoples of North and South America on an equal basis, recognizing the value of the unique experience that each individual, each nation, and each continent has to offer. In the following passage, he provided the basic tenets of the philosophical base on which mestizo social sciences are being developed:

> The objective should be to incorporate the culture of the white man, the European culture, Western culture, the same holds for all cultural expression from all human beings, without having to sacrifice who we are as blacks and Latin Americans. Being black or Latin American should be enriched, expanded, but not negated or rejected. In turn, the white man, the Western man, all men can enrich their cultural expressions by incorporating the culture of the black and Latin American. What blacks and Latin Americans have to offer is cultural experience in other life circumstances, other settings, in another context of life challenges. These experiences need to be known by other human beings in other parts of the world so that the diversity of the human race will be more familiar to all of its members. [1945, p. 71]

SUMMARY

The cultures and philosophies of the indigenous people of North and South America form basic components of the philosophical framework for the mestizo, multicultural/multiracial theory of personality psychology, social sciences, and mental health professions and serve as the primary impetus for the mestizoization of peoples and culture. The most important contributions to the philosophical base of a mestizo multicultural/multiracial worldview have been made by Mexican philosophy, which is a product of the mestizoization process. Contributions of Mexican philosophers such as Vasconcellos, Caso, Ramos, and Zea, along with the ideas of the melting pot ideology of the United States, set the stage for contributions by mestizo social scientists and mental health practitioners.

❖ **3** ❖

Social Science Foundations of a Multicultural/Multiracial Theory of Personality

The notion of diversity promotes an inclusive exploration of people in context and mitigates against developing a psychology that marginalizes nonprivileged groups as special interests. In the human diversity paradigm "all" populations and worldviews are subject to inquiry.

—*Trickett, Watts, and Birman (1994)*

The discovery of America meant not only the geographical exploration of new lands, but also the unveiling of a spiritual world. . . . [T]he life cycle of Spanish America gravitates around behavioral patterns indelibly established in pre-Columbian times, some of which are still alien to traditional European standards.

—*Francisco Guerra (1971)*

Contemporary man has rationalized the myths, but he has not been able to destroy them. Many of our scientific truths, like the majority of our moral, political, and philosophical conceptions, are only new ways of expressing tendencies that were embodied earlier in mythical forms.

—*Octavio Paz (1961)*

The social science knowledge base upon which a mestizo multicultural/multiracial psychology of personality is being established has emerged primarily from research with mestizo peoples in Latin America. Most of the work has been done in Mexico and with Latinos and other people of mixed ethnic heritage in the United States, but in the last two decades data important to the development of mestizo, multicultural/multiracial psychology have also emerged from research done in other countries of Central and South America and in the Caribbean.

This chapter does not attempt to provide a comprehensive review of the social science literature on Latinos and other multicultural/multiracial people; rather, it is an effort to examine the research that has had the greatest impact, by either negative or positive influence, on the development of a mestizo perspective in the social sciences

and helping professions. Discussion begins with the early anthropological and psychological research in Latin America; it proceeds to a
review of the philosophical works of the Mexican national character; it continues with the psychoanalytically oriented psychological
research conducted in Mexico. The chapter concludes with a review
of research done on multicultural/multiracial people in the Americas,
which resulted in a drive for the development of a psychology of individual and cultural differences and of liberation and empowerment.

EARLY CULTURE-PERSONALITY RESEARCH

Although the earliest research on culture and personality in Mexico
had been done by Gamio (1922), it was the research by Redfield
(1930), Lewis (1951), and Foster (1952) in Mexico and that of La
Farge (1947) and Gillin (1952) in Guatemala that attracted the attention of most social scientists in the Americas. Most of these studies focused on the effects of cultural change and, in particular, on
the effects of modernization on the life and psychological adjustments
of the person and his/her community. In general, these early researchers adopted one of two perspectives: they either idealized the life of
Latino peasants (happy, noble savages à la Rousseau) or they presented
a negative picture of their psychodynamics and their lifestyles. The
perspective of these early researchers was heavily influenced by the
European worldview. The following description of the behavior of
Guatemalan peasants, which was provided by La Farge (1947), gives
a good example of the European worldview-based approach of interpreting behavior independent of the historical, political, social,
economic, and ecological context in which it occurs: "Like the Hopis,
these Indians are at once peaceful and quarrelsome; dreading open
warfare and overt action, they bicker endlessly. One feels that living
too close together, plus the effects of a religion of fear and much belief
in black magic, has produced a condition of exasperation expressed
in gossip, fear and ill-will" (p.305).

Foster (1948) described Mexican peasants in a similar negative vein:
"Self-criticism is an unknown virture—if such it is—and failure is
always due to elements beyond one's control: the weather, bad luck
and the unscrupulousness of other persons, but never is it the fault
of the individual himself" (p. 305).

Gillin (1952) also provided a pathological picture of his *Ladino* (mestizo) participants in Guatemala. The following conclusions were drawn from observations and data he collected with the Rorschach Inkblot Test:

> In contrast to the manifested personality characteristics of Indians, the Ladinos show much more emotionalism; not only are likes and dislikes more demonstratively expressed, but the average Ladino is characterized by mood swings which range from depression and helplessness to feelings of high euphoria. He has no feeling of certainty that any of his available culture patterns will produce satisfactions which he expects and he is uncertain about their effectiveness when practiced outside the community. The result is that many Ladinos tend to withdraw from or be hesitant about interaction in the larger world outside, but since they wish to adjust to the larger world, this produces feelings of frustration and inadequacy. Ladinos are much more aggressive, at least on the overt level, both toward themselves and toward members of the other caste. This aggressiveness can be interpreted in the light of frustration which Ladinos face. Furthermore, the Ladinos show a higher percentage of hypochondriasis, psychosomatic ailments, neurotic twitches, and the like. [p. 209]

Redfield's writings present a positive view of the Latino peasant, but his use of simple dichotomies to explain complex processes resulted in a misleading picture of the people and their culture. Redfield's (1930) conceptual framework categorized societies as either folk or urban. Members of folk societies were described in idyllic terms. For example, he described the people of Tepoztlan, Mexico, as a relatively homogeneous, isolated, smoothly functioning, and well-integrated society made up of a contented and well-adjusted people. However, he also saw these people as vulnerable to the evils of modernization. Because of his fears of the destructive influences of modernization, Redfield (1950) predicted a sad destiny for the people of Chan Kom, another community he studied:

> The people of Chan Kom are then a people who have no choice, but to go forward with technology, with a declining religious faith and moral conviction, into a dangerous world. They are a people who must and will come to identify their interests with those people far away, outside the traditional circle of loyalties and political responsibilities.

As such they should have the sympathies of readers of these pages. [p. 178]

Using a perspective reflective of the mestizo worldview, Herskovitz (1947) criticized Redfield's folk/urban model. He based his criticisms on observations he had made in Africa regarding the bicultural nature (a combination of urban and folk characteristics) of villages there:

> In West Africa, however, many urban communities are to be found that range from one hundred thousand inhabitants [the approximate size of Merida, Redfield's Yucatan city] to over three hundred and fifty thousand. These populations have complex specialized economies exhibiting, as we have seen, the use of money and presence of profit motivation. Yet in these cities relationships are as personal as in any "folk society" and religion is the focal aspect of the culture. In short here we have an anomaly, that is, in terms of the concept of the folk society—of urban sacred communities. [p. 606]

This is an important observation because it provides an analogy for conceptualizing the pluralistic or multicultural/multiracial identity of individuals—one of the most important differences between mestizo and European worldview–based psychologies.

The writings of another anthropologist, Oscar Lewis (1951, 1961, 1965), have had considerable influence on the development of a mestizo, multicultural/multiracial psychology of personality. On the negative side, Lewis (like Redfield, Foster, and La Farge) made extensive use of European worldview–based perspectives; he also introduced the notion of the culture of poverty, which is closely tied to a European worldview ideology. More positively, Lewis introduced a research methodology that is consonant with mestizo values and lifestyles and, more importantly, a methodology that has produced data that clearly contradicted the negative, simplistic picture of mestizos presented by previous research. Unfortunately, Lewis himself largely ignored the complex and positive picture of psychodynamics reflected in the verbalizations of his subjects, relying too heavily on data from the Rorschach Inkblot Test to draw conclusions about personality and about psychological development in general. It was his reliance on psychoanalytic theory and its techniques for personality assessment that led him to make statements such as, "The Rios family is closer to the expression of the unbridled id than any other people I have studied" (1965, p. xxvi).

Despite the questionable nature of his psychoanalytic interpretations of Latino behavior and culture, Lewis made a significant positive contribution to the development of mestizo psychology through the introduction of the technique that he referred to as the "multiple autobiography of the family." This approach involved the use of the life history interview with different members of a single family; it presents the life history of the family as seen through the eyes of each of its members. This approach to data collection is consonant with the worldview and value system of mestizo populations and also represents a significant departure from approaches that had been used by social scientists in the past, projective tests and participant observation. The method afforded an opportunity to examine how the subjects viewed themselves and their environment. The most important advantage of this approach is that the material does not have to pass through the researcher's interpretive filters. Thus, in the words of Lewis's subjects, we can see the complex interrelationships that exist between the person, family, and society in the world of the Latino. Many of his subjects emerge as articulate, introspective, and historically and politically sophisticated people who are struggling with enormous challenges and demands in life. The following excerpts from *Pedro Martinez, The Children of Sanchez*, and *La Vida* reflect the psychological sophistication of the Mexican and Puerto Rican who is poor and who has had little or no formal education. The picture given to the reader by the words of Lewis's subjects contrasts sharply with the psychoanalytic interpretations he made and with views reflected in his culture of poverty model.

In the prologue to *Pedro Martinez* Oscar Lewis quotes Martinez as saying:

> Anyone who is a man of ideas is that way from birth. Such a man is aware of what goes on. Others die just as they are born, still children. Some study, yet they are nothing—no better than the rest. At dawn, when God awakes, off they go to the fields, and from the fields, back home to supper, and from supper to bed . . . and that is all. These men are like dead ideas. . . .

I always want to be poor. My thought has been to improve the village not myself. No! The Lord came to struggle for the people, not for Himself! I fought with Zapata in the Revolution and since then I have been struggling for justice. That's why I have nothing and my family has suffered. To be a hero, a man cannot think of how his home or his children or parents will suffer. They must suffer! There is no other way. A man who thinks first of his family is not a hero or a patriot. He is nothing. [1964, p. 3]

Consuelo, in *The Children of Sanchez*, said of her brother Roberto:

Even though Roberto was a man, he walked along the highway of life like a child of eight or nine, in knee pants, short-sleeved shirt and heavy boots. He was a frightened child whose intelligence had been sidetracked by the broken road. His way was full of accidents and he had fallen countless times, leaving him deeply scarred. He walked with his right hand stretched out trying to reach something. . . . In contrast to Manuel, Roberto had a fixed goal—to find the security he needed. When he has finally found it, the sobbing will end and he will smile as he looks back over the whole course he covered. [1961, p. 273]

Lewis quoted Cruz in *La Vida*:

I don't ever want to live in New York again. I'm better off in my own country because I went to the States twice and suffered a lot. I have suffered in Puerto Rico, but not as much. To me La Esmeralda is wonderful, better than New York or any other place. For me it's home. When I arrived here from New York, I felt happiness rise up in me again. I kept telling everybody that La Esmeralda was like a magnet who drew me back. [1965, p. 653]

These excerpts stand in sharp contrast with some of the characteristics of the "culture of poverty" as described by Lewis (1965):

- a lack of effective participation of the poor in the major institutions of the larger society (feelings of powerlessness);
- a minimum of organization beyond the level of the nuclear and extended families;
- an absence of childhood as a specially prolonged and protected stage in the life cycle;
- female- or mother-centered families;

- a feeling of *marginality, helplessness, of dependence and inferiority* [emphasis added].

These characteristics, according to Lewis (1965), were the result of "maternal deprivation of orality, weak ego structures, lack of impulse control, present-time orientation, and a sense of resignation and fatalism" (p. xlvii). The influence of the European worldview on Lewis's thinking is obvious. He took a "blaming the victim" perspective. Because people were poor and powerless, he assumed that they had a non-culture or, worse yet, a negative culture that interfered with their psychological development (the "damaging culture" view).

The culture of poverty and the European worldview were also very evident in much of the early social science research done with Mexican Americans in the southwestern United States. The writings of Ruth Tuck (1946), Lyle Saunders (1954), Celia Heller (1968), and William Madsen (1964) present a uniform picture of a passive people held back because of the limitations of their culture. Mexican Americans were viewed as a people with a way of life that interfered with their assimilation into mainstream American culture, thus preventing them from reaping the educational and economic opportunities offered by mainstream American society. The anthropologist Octavio Romano (1973) criticized the "culture is damaging" perspective used by William Madsen (1964) in his research with Mexican Americans of South Texas and equated this model with that used by Oscar Lewis:

> To summarize Madsen's views, due to their own culture, Mexican Americans are the generators of their own problems. This impedes their material advancement. Therefore, today they are just as they have always been, and they will not progress until they change completely. Thus, Madsen has equated economic determinism with cultural determinism, just as Oscar Lewis has done. Finally, Madsen has made Mexican-American culture the final cause of all of the problems that Mexican Americans have encountered throughout history. [p. 50]

PHILOSOPHICAL-PSYCHOLOGICAL WORKS

The influence of the European worldview is also reflected in the writings of the philosophers-psychologists in Mexico and in the early psychological research done by Mexican social scientists. One of the most influential of the early works was Ramos's *Profile of Man and Culture in Mexico* (1934). As stated in Chapter 2, Ramos argued that excessive reliance on European culture and ideology has interfered with the development of a true Mexican culture and consciousness. The following excerpts from his book reflect his arguments:

> Whoever aspires to a serious study of "Mexican culture" will find himself in a realm of vagueness. He will be struck by an abundance of Mexican works lacking qualities that could be said to proclaim the existence of an original vernacular style. But the existence of unoriginal works does not mean that the nation in which they appear lacks a culture of her own. . . . So it is that in the absence of objectivity, culture may still exist in another form; in subjectivity. . . . [pp. 15–16]

Unfortunately, Ramos used a European worldview–based theory of personality psychology—that of Alfred Adler—to explain the psychodynamics of the Mexican people. Ramos explained that the Mexicans' tendency to rely on European culture was based on unconscious feelings of inferiority resulting from historical events such as the Spanish conquest, the reign of Maximillian, and the various invasions by France and the United States. Thus, we have an example of the persuasiveness of the European worldview; even in the process of making the argument that Mexico should develop its own culture independent of European influences, Ramos used a European worldview–based theory of personality to explain Mexican behavior.

The observations of still another Mexican psychologist-philosopher, Octavio Paz, also reflect the belief that Mexicans have an inferiority complex that is linked to their history. Paz used this argument to explain the behavior of Mexicans who had migrated to the United States, concluding that an inferiority complex was interfering with the assimilation of Mexican Americans into mainstream American culture. In one of the chapters ("The Pachuco and Other Extremes") in his book *The Labyrinth of Solitude* (1961), he employed the European-based conflict/replacement model of identity and acculturation to describe the behavior of the Mexican-American zoot suiters in the 1940s. He faulted these young adults for not identifying completely with mainstream American culture, picturing them as people in identity crisis. Paz failed to recognize that the zoot suiters' unique lifestyle and dress may have represented an attempt to develop new coping styles in a hostile environment. He failed to take into account the fact that the urban Mexican-American male of the 1940s was straddling two cultures and evolving new lifestyles and coping patterns by integrating aspects of the two sociocultural systems—a multicultural/multiracial identity. Thus, in adopting the European worldview, Paz ignored the possibility that these young people may have been developing pluralistic orientations to life.

PSYCHOANALYTICALLY ORIENTED WORKS

Although Ramos and Paz have both been influenced substantially by psychoanalytic theories, the best examples of the use of these theories to explain Mexican behavior and culture can be found in the works of Rogelio Diaz-Guerrero (1955) and Aniceto Aramoni (1972). Diaz-Guerrero was trained as both a psychologist and a psychiatrist, and he has been doing research in Mexico since the 1940s. Although his most recent work (1992), which will be discussed later in this chapter, is partially supportive of the mestizo worldview, his earlier writings were greatly influenced by European worldview–based theories and perspectives in psychology and psychiatry. In an article entitled "Neurosis and the Mexican Family Structure," Diaz-Guerrero (1955) concluded that there is a disproportionately high incidence of neurosis among Mexicans because they suffer from conflicts fostered by the dynamics of the family and the separation of sex roles in the culture.

At a more specific level we can easily deduce that in the male there should be: (1) problems of submission, conflict, and rebellion in the area of authority; (2) preoccupation and anxiety regarding sexual potency; (3) conflict and ambivalence regarding his double role. He must at times love and act maternally and tenderly, and at other times sexually and virilely; (4) difficulties in superseding the maternal stage: dependent-feminine individuals; (5) problems before and during marriage: mother's love interferes with the love to another woman (Here one should expect an important area of stress where the husband, the wife, and the husband's mother play the dynamics of jealousy); (6) *the Oedipus complex, as Freud describes it: almost every aspect of the ideal setting for its development is provided by the premises of the culture and the role playing.* [Emphasis added, p. 415]

Aniceto Aramoni (1972) also relied extensively on psychoanalytic theory to explain the behavior of adult males in Mexico. For example, in an attempt to explain the phenomenon of machismo, that is, the belief in super masculinity that is often attributed to Mexican males, Aramoni used a psychoanalytic perspective. The following excerpts from his writings represent his attempt to explain what he considered to be the disordered development of the male role in the Mexican family and culture:

> From the outsider's perspective, machismo represents an essentially pointless and destructive struggle by the man to overcome the humiliation of being an ineffectual little boy, especially in his mother's eyes. It is an ill-fated drama wherein the man, painfully attached to his mother, his sisters, and the Virgin, seeks their exclusive admiration and worship [p. 69]. . . . Further, there is reason to assume that the man unconsciously hates and fears the woman. This is why she must be disarmed, subdued, made impotent and harmless. But the woman subjugated and regarded as an object then resorts to her children to justify her existence, reflecting in them all of her hopes and frustrations, hatred and vindictiveness. [p. 72]

In the works reviewed above, both Aramoni and Diaz-Guerrero used the European worldview-based approach of taking observations and data out of the context of culture, history, politics, and economics. The writings of both men also present an incomplete definition of machismo, ignoring that the concept is also used to refer to persons who live up to their social commitments and who are true to their word, who manifest courage, dignity, and respect for others and love and affection for family (Carrasco et al. 1996). The works by Diaz-Guerrero and Aramoni also seem to imply that machismo is unique to Mexican culture, ignoring the fact that similar behavior was also characteristic of the knights of medieval Europe and Anglo cultural image of the cowboy (Paredes 1978).

Other examples of the misapplication of the European-based personality theories and research methodologies to Mexican people can be found in the work of Fromm and Maccoby (1970). These researchers made use of psychoanalytic theory to interpret data they had collected on social character types in a Mexican village. Using a questionnaire, the Rorschach Inkblot Test, the Thematic Apperception Test, and the Children's Apperception Test, they identified three main types of social characters: the productive-hoarding, the unproductive-receptive, and the productive-exploitative. The authors concluded that these three character types represented adaptations to distinct socioeconomic conditions in the country. Although the majority of the correlation's reported were in the .2 to .4 range, the authors nevertheless concluded that the productive-hoarding type was the most adaptable and psychologically sophisticated of the three. As could be expected, it was the characteristics of people in this productive-exploitative type that were those most valued by the European Protestant ethic, and those that were characteristic of the "new merchant" class that evolved in Europe and America in the seventeenth and eighteenth centuries. The traits were those of being practical, economical, patient, orderly, devoted, optimistic, and so forth. The authors employed a social Darwinistic perspective to explain how this entrepreneurial type had developed in the village they studied. The productive-hoarding type evolved and flourished, they argued, because of the socioeconomic conditions that were evident in Mexico at that time. They argued that in a climate of developing capitalism the obsessional, hoarding type of person was the most successful—shades of Darwinian natural selection.

RECENT PSYCHOLOGICAL RESEARCH IN LATIN AMERICA

The influence of the European worldview is still pervasive in psychology as it is being taught and practiced in Mexico and other countries in Latin America. In an article in the *American Psychologist*, Ardila (1982) observed that psychology in Latin America had been heavily influenced by psychology in the United States. What Ardila failed to point out, however, was that in the areas of personality, developmental, and clinical psychology, European worldview masquerades as American ideology. The continuing dominance of the Eurocentric perspective in the social sciences and helping professions in Latin America is evident in many of the articles published in the *Revista InterAmericana de Psicologia*, the *Revista Latino Americana de Psicologia*, and the *International Journal of Psychology*. The persuasiveness of the European worldview is also evident in keynote addresses, workshops, and presentations in international congresses. In a recent meeting sponsored by the International Union of Psychologists and the Mexican Society of Social Psychology, held in Merida, Mexico, Ramirez (1994a) observed:

> North American and Western European psychology should be viewed as it really is, a psychology of superiority and colonialism, so it should be used with great caution in Latin America. Like the warning provided in cigarette packages, North American/ Western European psychology should be introduced to the people of Latin America with the following words of caution, "Warning, this psychology could be harmful to your self esteem and to the well-being of all culturally/racially different people." [p. 3]

Ramirez went on to observe that in spite of the continuing dominance of a European perspective in Latin American social sciences and the helping professions, there were some rays of hope evident in recent works by Latin American psychologists. For example, Diaz-Guerrero (1992), in a publication entitled *The Need for an Ethnopsychology of Cognition and Personality*, argued for the importance of a multicultural/multiracial worldview in cross-cultural psychology, particularly with respect to the study of flexibility in personality. Eduardo Almeida Acosta and his colleagues (1985, 1996), who have been the true pioneers of an applied mestizo multicultural/multiracial heritage social science in Mexico, continue their important community psychology work in mestizo communities in the state of Puebla and also provide a much-needed caution. Researchers, they warn, need to be cognizant of the possibility that when they are doing research on cultural values, the belief systems they attribute to a culture could reflect cultural expectations and not the true belief systems of the people being studied. Almeida presented the basic tenets of the mestizo community social psychology—a conception of social psychology as a scientific social model and a conception of the community as a set of economic, political, ethnic-cultural and technological/ecological forces, and social justice. Pick de Weiss and Diaz-Loving (1986), in a review of applied psychology in Mexico, concluded that psychologists in Mexico are increasingly becoming focused on social problems important to many Mexican communities; this orientation was also described by Martiza Montero (1979) and Jose Miguel Salazar (1981) as being typical of Venezuelan psychology. Reid and Aguilar (1991) also reviewed developments in community psychology in Mexico, and they emphasized that Mexican psychology needs a strong community emphasis. In spite of the gains reviewed above, there are some recent disturbing trends such as the application of Triandis's individualism and collectivism and other European conceptual frameworks to Mexican culture (Diaz-Loving et al. 1995). This trend is reminiscent of the inferiority complex in Mexican scholarship that Ramos had cautioned about as early as 1934.

Although for the most part the developments in Latin American psychology reviewed here indicate that some strides are being made in the development of a mestizo worldview in Latin America, the majority of the impetus for mestizo orientations in the social sciences and helping professions is coming from the work of mestizo social scientists and providers of mental health services in the United States. Ardila (1982) and M. Ramirez (1983) noted this well over a decade ago.

It seems incongruous that while the philosophical base for a mestizo worldview has been provided by Latin American scholarship, most of the social science research base has emerged from work by social scientists in the United States. Perhaps this is testament to the fact that although some domains of United States society have been described as racist (United States Kerner Commission 1968), the sociopolitical-intellectual climate unique to the United States has provided the necessary atmosphere for development of multicultural/multiracial orientations to life.

THE CALL FOR A MESTIZO PSYCHOLOGY

A history of Chicano psychology authored by Padilla (1995) contained a decidedly Eurocentric bias and thus provided a distorted picture of the development of a mestizo multicultural/multiracial psychology. The origins of the mestizo worldview in the social sciences and helping professions do not lie in Spain, as Padilla mistakenly asserted. Rather they are rooted in Native American philosophy and belief systems (Ardila 1986) and in the writings of the first North American ethnic minority social scientist of mixed ethnic heritage: W. E. B. DuBois. The true origins of the mestizo worldview are also based on the civil rights movement in the United States, which was as much a struggle for cultural democracy (the right to maintain and to continue to develop the language and culture of origin as the person participates in mainstream culture and learns the dominant language) as it was a struggle for political empowerment. The civil rights movement and the bilingual/multicultural education movement that it spawned produced important multicultural/multiracial models such as Dr. Martin Luther King, Jr., Rosa Parks, Malcolm X, Ralph Abernathy, Cesar Chavez, Dolores Huerta, Russell Means, Dennis Banks, Dr. George I. Sanchez, and Drs. Mami and Kenneth Clark. In the history he authored, Padilla (1995) rightly recognized the critical role played by Dr. George I. Sanchez, who published articles as early as 1934 in which he criticized the use of Eurocentric intelligence tests with Latino children. In other publications Sanchez referred to Native Americans and Latinos in the United States as "forgotten Americans" (1948, 1967). He identified one of the critical tenets of the European worldview in the intelligence testing movement: he posited that the facts of genetics and heredity were being "garbled" in order to champion the superiority of one race over another. In many of his writings, Sanchez lamented the belief that the schools were not responsive to the cultures of Latino and Native American children and thus failed to serve them adequately. He continued to be a strong advocate for diversity in American society all his life. In testimony he gave before a congressional committee during the hearings held prior to the passage of the Bilingual Education Act in 1968, he likened the preservation of native languages in the United States to the preservation of natural resources. This testimony reiterated a view he had expressed in 1934: "The progress of our country is dependent on the most efficient utilization of the heterogeneous masses which constitute its population" (p. 13).

A major contribution to research methodology of mestizo psychology was made by a Mexican anthropologist doing research with Mexican immigrants and with second-generation Mexican Americans in the United States. Manuel Gamio (1931) employed an open-ended life history interview to study the adjustment process of Mexicans and Mexican Americans in the United States. Gamio's data (like those of Oscar Lewis, which were to follow years later) showed that the poor mestizos with little formal education were articulate, introspective, perceptive, philosophical, and cognizant of historical, social, economic, and political factors affecting their lives.

Another major contribution to mestizo research methodology was the study done by the anthropologist Octavio Romano (1964) concerning the life and works of the famous Mexican-American *curandero* (folkhealer) Don Pedrito Jaramillo. Romano's study succeeded in placing his subject in cultural, social, and historical context, thereby allowing social scientists to better understand the relationship of folk medicine to Latino culture in South Texas.

Some of the first psychologically oriented studies with Mexican Americans in the United States focused on adolescents living in urban centers in the states of California and Texas (Ramirez 1967, 1969). The first of these studies named family values with which Mexican-American adolescents and young adults were identified. The second study identified adolescent patterns of adjustment to acculturation stress. The focus of this latter study was on the stress experienced by students as a consequence of conflicts between the values of Mexican-American culture and those represented by the schools they attended. The findings of a subsequent study (Ramirez and Castañeda 1974) indicated that children and adolescents who had developed bicultural orientations to life were the most successful in academic and social activities and were less likely to drop out of school even when they encountered severe frustration.

THE BILINGUAL/BICULTURAL MOVEMENT

With the passage of the Bilingual Education Act in 1968, researchers began to focus more intensively on the development of bilingualism and multiculturalism in Mexican-American, Cuban-American, Puerto Rican, African-American, Asian-American, and Native American children and adolescents. Specifically, these studies sought to identify any advantages or disadvantages related to the learning of two languages and simultaneous participation in more than one culture. Early work on bilingualism was done by Amado Padilla (1977) and his colleagues at the University of California at Los Angeles and by Eugene Garcia (1977) and his students at the University of Utah. In general, the results of both these research programs concluded that learning two languages did not have an adverse effect on the intellectual development of Mexican-American children and that little interference between English and Spanish was experienced by children who were being exposed to both languages simultaneously. Research at the University of Texas on bilingual memory (Lopez et al. 1974) also served to dispel some of the myths concerning language switching by bilingual children. Thus the findings on bilingualism with Mexican Americans seemed to support the observations made by Sanchez in the 1930s and also tended to corroborate the findings of Lambert and his colleagues with French-English bilinguals in Canada (Peal and Lambert 1962).

The findings of research on dual culture participation were heavily weighted on the side of advantages accruing to simultaneous participation in more than one culture (Buriel 1993a, Ramirez 1969, Ramirez et al. 1971). Ramirez and Castañeda (1974) conceptualized biculturalism/multiculturalism in Mexican Americans in terms of a culture/cognitive styles conceptual framework. They postulated that traditional Mexican-American culture primarily (but not exclusively) encouraged development of a personality style characterized by global-deductive thinking, a personal style of relating to others, an orientation toward social rewards, and a cooperative orientation to achievement—a field-sensitive cognitive style; whereas mainstream American culture primarily, but not exclusively, encouraged the development of a personality style characterized by analytical thinking, an impersonal style of relating to others, an orientation toward non-social rewards, and a competitive orientation to achievement—a field-independent cognitive style. Through their observations of children (both Mexican-American and non-Mexican-American) in schools, Ramirez and Castañeda identified subjects who could use both cognitive styles interchangeably and who could combine elements of both styles to arrive at new coping and problem-solving behaviors. Additionally, the investigators noted that those children who were cognitively flexible or bicognitive were also bicultural, that is, they had been socialized in both Mexican-American and Anglo cultures, and they participated actively in both.

Ramirez and Castañeda (1974) also discovered that the tests of cognitive style used by Witkin and colleagues (1962) had a definite field-independent and European worldview bias. That is, these tests valued behavior associated with the European worldview: analytical thinking, individual identity, and individual competition. As an alternative to the Rod and Frame and Embedded Figures Tests, Ramirez and Castañeda (1974) introduced two behavior observation instruments: one to assess cognitive styles in children and the other to assess cognitive styles of teachers. Basing their procedures on a mestizo worldview in psychology, they arrived at the following conclusions:

- the behavior of teachers and children must be observed in the context in which it occurs;
- cognitive styles must be viewed as multidimensional and not unidimensional variables;
- cultural and cognitive style changes in individuals can occur in both the directions of Anglo and Mexican-American cultures as well as in the directions of field sensitive or field-independent behavior;
- it is possible for children and adults to be bicognitive and multicultural; and
- to encourage development of greater flexibility (greater bicognition and multiculturalism), children, teachers, and schools must change to reflect pluralistic perspectives.

In addition, Ramirez and Castañeda (1974) presented the framework for an instructional program that could encourage the development of cognitive flexibility in children and teachers in the context of bicognitive/multicultural education. Cox and colleagues (1982) developed a multidisciplinary instructional program for encouraging bicognitive and multicultural development in preschool and elementary school children. The effectiveness of this bicognitive program has been documented by other researchers (Kagan and Buriel 1977). These approaches have now been recognized as essential to multicultural education (Darder 1991, Gollnick and Chinn 1990). Part and parcel of the bilingual/multicultural educational movement was the focus on ethnic identity development that is such an important part of the history of the multicultural/multiracial heritage worldview in the social sciences and helping professions.

Research on dual and multiple cultural participation (Ramirez 1969, 1977, Ramirez et al. 1980) by adolescent and young adult Mexican Americans has shown that active involvement in two or more cultures (biculturalism/multiculturalism) does not result in severe value conflicts or in identity crises; rather, such involvement tends to foster flexibility of personality functioning and development of skills as cultural facilitators and leaders in mixed ethnic group situations. Thus, active involvement in different cultures seems to make the person more adaptable by virtue of introducing him/her to different coping techniques, different problem-solving strategies, and different ways of perceiving life problems and challenges.

Research with Cuban-American adolescents (Szapocznik et al. 1978) showed that those adolescents who were bicultural tended to be better adjusted psychologically than those who participated in either Cuban or Anglo culture exclusively. As is the case with Mexican Americans, identification with two cultures in Cuban Americans leads to a healthier adjustment than does a monocultural orientation to life. The authors concluded:

> The mounting evidence concerning the nature of the acculturation process and its implications for adjustment . . . suggests that in bicultural communities such as Dade County, exaggerated acculturation or exaggerated maintenance of ethnic identity, one to the exclusion of the other, is detrimental to the mental health of immigrant groups. [p. 24]

Upon reviewing much of the social science research with mestizos in the Americas, Ramirez called for the development of a mestizo psychology that could guide research, intervention, and theoretical development in all the Americas (1967, 1977, 1983). He observed that theories of personality based on the European worldview are misleading when applied to mestizos. Particularly misleading are those models of acculturation and culture change derived from European perspectives. Ramirez argued that findings of research throughout the Americas show that multicultural/multiracial development and functioning are a reality—a reality which must be reflected in theories of personality and approaches to intervention and research.

SUMMARY

A review of the social science research done with people of mixed heritage/mestizos in the Americas showed that the European worldview contributed to the perspective of these people as pathological and psychologically underdeveloped. In the past two decades research and theoretical development in Latin America as well as the United States has produced a definite shift toward a multicultural/multiracial mestizo worldview. Research findings showing the positive effects of bilingualism and multicultural orientations to life have resulted in a call for the development of a multicultural/multiracial psychology that reflects the experience of the Americas.

❖ **4** ❖

A Multicultural/Multiracial Theory for the Social Sciences and Helping Professions

Any conception of African Americans that fails to see them as engaged in exercising their human agency—sometimes successfully, sometimes not—cannot hope to grasp what they are all about.

—*Adelbert H. Jenkins (1995)*

The choice of identifying with both cultures was positive for some in the respect that it helped the individuals realize that they did not have to try to fit into a single racial mold.

—*C. C. I. Hall (1992)*

Man is always situated in a circumstance which offers its own solutions to the problems it creates. (The history of culture is the history of man struggling with his circumstances.) Every man has his own point of view, circumstances, and personality from which he must solve his own problems of life.

—*Leopoldo Zea (1945)*

This chapter presents the framework for a theory of personality based on the mestizo multicultural/multiracial worldview. The intention is not to present a complete, polished theory but, rather, to outline the major assumptions and some of the components of such a theory. This chapter also introduces a model that has been derived from the mestizo multicultural/multiracial theory of personality for understanding the development of pluralistic identities and orientation to life—a model that is based on research data obtained from members of several the mestizo groups of the Americas.

GENERAL DESCRIPTION OF THE THEORY

In 1972 the Mexican psychologist and psychiatrist Rogelio Diaz-Guerrero published a book entitled *Toward a Historico-Bio-Psycho-Socio-Cultural Theory of Human Behavior*. The complexity of the title of this book reflects the interdisciplinary nature of the mestizo worldview vis-à-vis personality psychology and the helping professions. In fact, the title of Diaz-Guerrero's book falls somewhat short of representing the global nature of the mestizo worldview. A multicultural/multiracial theory of personality should include knowledge from psychology, physiology, anthropology, sociology, and history, but, in addition, it should also include genetics, philosophy, folklore, economics, and politics. Finally, a mestizo multicultural/multiracial theory of personality should reflect ecological and survivalist perspectives of adjustment.

PRINCIPAL ASSUMPTIONS OF THE THEORY

Ecology shapes personality, affecting development and functioning through both the physical and social environments. The person is an open system, inseparable from the physical and social environments in which he/she lives. Traits, characteristics, skills, perceptions of the world, and philosophies of life evolve by meeting the environmental challenges the person encounters. In this ecological context, person-environment fit is the primary criterion for determining the quality of human adaptation. Also important is the concept of circumstantialism as described in the philosophy of the Americas proposed by Leopoldo Zea (1945): each set of life circumstances represents certain problems and challenges of life through which each individual finds solutions and adaptations, thus developing his/her unique personality and philosophy of life. From the circumstantialist point of view, diversity is important because it reflects the different adaptations that individuals and groups have made to the various physical, social, and political environments in the Americas; each pattern of adaptation represents a lesson on overcoming the challenges of life, from which everyone can learn.

The ecological psychology of Barker (1968) and the social ecology approach (Kelly 1971), both important developments in community psychology, provide conceptual frameworks and research and intervention methodologies that are consonant with the mestizo theory of personality psychology. Garza and Lipton (1982) also proposed a social-ecological model for understanding the behavior of mestizos.

Personality is shaped by history and culture. The history and culture of the group or groups to which a person belongs are major determinants of that individual's personality. This assumption is the cornerstone of culture-and-personality psychology, a branch of psychology that had its origins in the Americas. The influence of the culture-personality perspective has been felt very strongly in both North and South America, as well as in the Caribbean. The approach had its birth at the Institute of Human Relations at Yale in the 1930s where an interdisciplinary group of anthropologists, sociologists, and psychologists approached the study of human behavior from a global perspective. Psychologists concentrated on how an organism interacts with the environment; anthropologists and sociologists contributed information about the nature of those environments. An important product of the work at the Institute of Human Relations was the establishment of the Human Relations Area Files, a compilation of ethnographic reports arranged in such a manner that quantitative cross-cultural testing of hypotheses became a real possibility. Prior to the establishment of the Institute of Human Relations at Yale, several Mexican philosophers (see Chapter 2) emphasized the important role that history and culture play in personality development. Vasconcellos (1927) argued for the identification of the unique Mexican culture and personality—the mestizo—that had evolved as a result of the amalgamation of the Hispanic-European and Native American cultures. Ramos (1975) showed how culture and history affected the development of personality in Mexico and urged his countrymen to adopt a "living culture." The philosopher Paz (1961, 1972) and Rogelio Diaz-Guerrero (1972b) followed along the path pioneered by Vasconcellos and Ramos. The influence of history and culture on personality development is prominently represented in the theory of personality that has been proposed by Diaz-Guerrero (1972b), mentioned at the beginning of this chapter. Ramirez (1978) also emphasized the important role of history and culture in the development of pluralistic identities in the United States, that is, for individuals being socialized in a multicultural environment, the history and culture of the different sociocultural groups in which he/she is participating must be taken into consideration in explaining and predicting behavior.

Genetics and physiology figure importantly in personality development and functioning. Mind and body function in an integrated manner; they are inseparable. To achieve healthy adjustment, synchrony between mind and body is essential. Approaches to treatment of adjustment disorders are holistic and synergistic. The predisposition to adjust effectively to certain life circumstances and environments can be inherited. Certain personality traits, skills, and characteristics are linked to specific ecologies, geographic regions, communities, and families.

In the context of the mestizo worldview, adaptive traits, coping techniques, and skills that have been developed by individuals can be transmitted to offspring: certain traits, coping styles, and skills have been developed by individuals in specific geographic regions, communities, and families to solve the specific problems of human experience associated with their life circumstances and these are heritable. But in the mestizo perspective, there is more to genetic transmission of personality than is reflected in the German notion of *Volksgeist* (Herbart 1897), which was based on the assumption that the characteristic traits of a people are biologically transmitted. Mestizo psychology views inheritance of traits in much the same way as the American sociologist William Graham Sumner (1906). Sumner's position was that folkways are habits of the individual and customs of the society that arise from efforts to satisfy certain needs. They become regulating for succeeding generations and take on the character of a social force. In the mestizo view, then, what is inherited is the predisposition to develop certain traits, skills, and characteristics in specific cultural, social, and geographic settings. From this perspective, Sumner described the initial development of the mestizoization process in North America: "In the early days of the settlement of North America many whites Indianized; they took to the mode of life of Indians" (p. 84).

Furthermore, herbs and plants are believed to play an important role in healing, self-understanding, and achieving unity with the supernatural. Lopez-Austin (1975) and Guerra (1971) documented the extensive use of herbs and plants in the medicine practiced by both the Nahuas and the Mayas in Mexico. Benitez (1975), Crow Dog and Erodes (1990), and Spindler (1952) also described the use of peyote in the religious practices of contemporary native peoples in the Americas.

Spiritualism, with its specific focus on identity development, plays a major role in personality development. In the context of multicultural/ multiracial worldview of the social sciences, spiritualism is of central importance in the individual's search for identity and life mission. As discussed in Chapter 2, spiritualism serves to link the individual with supernatural forces in the cosmos and can influence individual and group destiny. The emphasis on development is both on achieving control over the supernatural by attaining self-control and self-knowledge and also on enlisting the help of a person or spirit who can mediate between the supernatural and the individual. A strong identity with the group to whom the individual belongs is also important, because the group can provide access to knowledge concerning the maintenance of a proper balance between the individual and the supernatural. A good example of this is the astro-magical predictive models that both the Nahuas and the Mayas developed to achieve control over the destiny of their group as well as that of their individual members (see Chapter 2).

Those persons who are believed to have special knowledge—access to supernatural powers or possession of such powers—play an important role in personality development and functioning. *Curanderos*, *espiritistas*, *shamans*, and the clergy all help individuals in their search for self-knowledge and identity and also treat and advise those who are experiencing problems of adjustment. (The specific roles played by *curanderos*, *espiritistas*, and *shamans* will be discussed in greater detail in Chapter 7.)

Religion is also perceived as playing an important role in achieving harmony with and protection from negative supernatural forces. Not only does religion provide models with which to identify and codes of conduct that facilitate the achievement of meaning of life and death, but it also provides confession as a means of achieving reconciliation with the self and the supernatural. With respect to this latter point, Guerra (1971) observed:

> The distress of the pre-Columbian mind at not being at one with one-self was resolved by the mechanism of confession and the individual reached internal harmony at the moment of the interplay of time, place, attitude, and the sanctioned ritual converged. The patient at the moment of the pre-Columbia confession was also demanding immediate answers to questions and problems that had been taking shape for the better part of his lifetime within the pattern of behavior of the American civilizations. [pp. 280–281]

The pervasive presence of spiritualism and religion in psychological adjustment and in the development of attitudes toward mental health services was documented in a recent study by Castro (1996). This investigator found that the values of spiritualism and religion accounted for major differences in attitudes toward white middle-class approaches to mental health services. He not only found that Latinos are more likely than Anglos to seek mental health care from priests and other religious, but also that a major role is attributed to God and the Catholic religion in mental health. He concluded, "Primarily, those who were interviewed spontaneously compared the confidence they have in a mental health care practitioner to the confidence they have in God" (p. 94) and also, "Mexican Americans suggested that Mexican-American Catholicism provides a different ways of perceiving mental illness." Typical responses from Mexican Americans included: "The Church provides you a different perspective on mental health"; "It is God's view and you learn that God has an idea of what kind of person you should be"; and "There is a spiritual solution to everything" (p. 95).

Personality is shaped by family and community. A multicultural/multiracial heritage psychology is, first and foremost, a psychology of family and community. Individual identity is considered to be secondary to family identity, and individual needs are subordinated to those of the family. From the perspective of the mestizo worldview, the individual is seen as embedded in the context of the family group. Recognition of the important role of family identity or familism in the social sciences and helping professions has been one of the major contributions of the native cultures of the Americas and the world.

The earliest research done with families of mixed heritage was conducted by W. E. B. DuBois (1898, 1903). His first major research project was a study of families in the Seventh Ward in Philadelphia (DuBois 1967). In his biography of DuBois, D. L. Lewis (1993) described the scope and importance of the Philadelphia study: "Historian Herbert Aptheker has calculated that DuBois spent some 835 hours interviewing approximately 2,500 households over the three month field research beginning in August of 1896. No representative sampling for DuBois. As he tabulated some 1,500 household schedules, he had before him life histories of the entire black population of the Seventh Ward—nearly 10,000 men, women and children" (pp. 190–191, 209).

A later study of families in the rural South was no less extensive. Lewis (1993) says of the resultant publication, entitled *The Negroes of Farmville, Virginia: A Social Study*: "[A]long with the moralizing came the first documented sociological insights into evolving Afro-America" (p. 195). Lewis went on to observe: "DuBois predicted the disintegrative pressure on the race as it became urbanized. The black family, he insisted, was still recovering from the ravages of slavery. Its fragility would place African Americans at high risk as they experienced the shock of modernization" (p. 196).

Oscar Lewis, an anthropologist, focused on mestizo families living in urban and rural areas in Mexico and Puerto Rico (1959, 1965). Lewis developed a research approach for studying families that is very compatible with a mestizo, multicultural/multiracial worldview. (This research methodology is described in more detail in Chapter 5.)

Rogelio Diaz-Guerrero (1972a) emphasized the importance of family values in personality development in Mexico. His theoretical model, based on sociocultural premises, gives a central role to family values.

Basing his work on the research of Diaz-Guerrero, Fernandez-Marina et al. (1958) assessed family values in research he did in Puerto Rico. Ramirez (1967), in turn, developed the Family Attitudes Scale, which reflected the values of Mexican-American families. The instrument was later modified (Ramirez and Carrasco, in press, Rodriguez et al., in press) to include items reflecting the values of mainstream American middle-class families so that it can be used to assess acculturation and multicultural identity development.

The pervasiveness of familism, in spite of acculturation, has been documented by Buriel (1987) and more recently by Castro (1996). Buriel studied the relationship between generational status and acculturation in Latino and white second- and third-grade students and found, "there was no support for the assumption that Mexican Americans discard their ancestral culture when acculturating to Anglo American society" (pp. 151–152). Castro (1996) studied Latino community college students living in three Texas communities located at varying distances from the Mexican border. The participants were classified on the basis of scores on a scale of acculturation. Follow-up interviews indicated that many Mexican Americans did not separate Mexican-American Catholicism from familism. As one Mexican American from Austin observed about the priest from his hometown on the border, "We called him 'Father' for a reason. He was part of the family and you could go to him on anything." Another Mexican American from San Antonio said virtually the some thing: "It's almost like the church is an extended part of the family. When we were talking about the family thing, the priest is part of the family" (p. 74).

The central role played by the family in acculturation has been documented by Rogler and Cooney (1984) in intergenerational studies done with Puerto Rican families living in New York City. The important influence of the family in intervention work has also been recognized in the concept of "retribalization" employed by Attneave (1969) and Speck and Attneave (1974) in their therapy with people who suffer from schizophrenia. This model was based on the ongoing reciprocal support of extended Native American families and was entitled "network therapy." (This approach is described in more detail in Chapter 7.) A model for family therapy based on mestizo family values was also developed by Szapocznik and colleagues (1978a) as an outgrowth of their work with Cuban-American adolescents who were experiencing problems with adjustment and with their families.

The community, through participation in socialization of children, also plays a central role in the personality development of people of mixed heritage. It is expected that the extended family and other members of the community will participate in child socialization. Witness the example of the Plateau tribe "whipper man," described in Chapter 2, who was selected by the tribe to function as community disciplinarian (Shore and Nicholls 1975). Mary Crow Dog (1990) described the role of the *tiyospaye*, the extended family group in child rearing in Sioux society. The use of the Kiva to socialize children in the Hopi nation also reflected the belief in the involvement of the community in child socialization and in passing on the history of the group through the oral tradition. Among peoples of African descent, the role of the community in child socialization is reflected in the belief that it is communities and not just parents who socialize children.

Economic and political variables affect personality development and functioning. The history of the cultures of mixed ethnic peoples is one of struggle against political and economic repression, and the stories surrounding these struggles are important in the education and socialization of children. The heroes of these struggles are held up as models for young children and adolescents. In Mexico countless novels, movies, radio and television programs, and schoolbooks have been written about the war of independence from Spain, the overthrow of the reign of Maximilllian by Benito Juarez, and the revolution of 1930. Similarly, in the United States, holidays, school curricula, and the media have emphasized the War of Independence; the freeing of the slaves; the Civil Rights Movement spearheaded by Martin Luther King, Jr., Rosa Parks, and Malcolm X; and the struggle of the farm workers, with an emphasis on the efforts of Dolores Huerta and Cesar Chavez.

Poverty, human misery, racism, and repression of individual rights and equality of opportunity are all visible realities for people of mixed heritage. These realities also affect the socialization of individuals, and they are the principal reason for the pragmatic orientation of a mestizo, multicultural/multiracial psychology.

The impact of economic pressures has been pervasive in Mexican and Mexican-American families because of the economic crises in Mexico. For Native Americans, African Americans, Asian Americans, and white mestizos, it has been the change from a production to an information economy that has been most devastating. To study the impact of economic pressures stemming from the Mexican economic crisis and the reduction of social programs during the Reagan era, Ramirez (1987) studied mestizo families in San Antonio, Texas, and Monterrey, Mexico. Data were collected from three types of families: 1) first-generation Mexican-American families (both parents were born in Mexico and all the children were born in the United States), 2) second- or third-generation Mexican-American families (mother and all the children were born in the United States), and 3) Mexican families. All families were from the working class. The author concluded:

> The findings seem to indicate that stress resulting from economic and/ or culture change is related to different problems reported by families of the three cultural groups studied. In Mexican families economic and cultural changes seem to be having a negative impact on husband–wife relationships. In addition stress also appears to be related to physical and mental health problems in mothers and young adults of the Mexican group. [p. 193]

In first-generation Mexican-American families, stress seemed to have encouraged the development of close ties among members of the entire family. However, the negative effects of economic and culture change stress were being experienced in terms of limited opportunities in higher education for young adults. For second- and third-generation Mexican-American families, stress seemed to be related to extremes in harmony in husband–wife relationships, from the highly positive (initiation of wife–husband joint ventures in business) to the extremely negative (a high divorce rate). In second- and third-generation families, economic stress had a decidedly negative effect on quality of parent–child relationships. Economic pressures seemed to be having more impact in second- and third-generation families because of decreased future expectations.

Political variables have figured importantly in the personality development of people of mixed heritage. In particular two youth organizations—the Student Nonviolent Coordinating Committee (SNCC) and Mexican-American Youth Organization (MAYO)—played central roles in identity development. An outgrowth of the lunch counter sit-in movement, SNCC was established in 1958 (Branch 1988) and later played a significant role in voter registration efforts across the South. MAYO was made up primarily of Latino college students, high school students, and barrio youth who were not in school. Organized in Texas in 1967, it was successful in promoting election of Mexican-American candidates in several communities in South Texas and became the forerunner of the Raza Unida Party, which nominated a candidate to run for governor of Texas in 1972 (Navarro 1995).

Thus, student political action groups have played a major role in the socialization of mixed-heritage youth. Some of the spirit of unity and community empowerment that was so much a part of SNCC and MAYO can still be seen today in youth programs such as CLARO, which is described in more detail in Chapter 7.

The process of confronting life's problems and challenges and, in particular, the process of coping with change lead to development of a unique individual identity and determine the person's orientation toward diversity. In the mestizo view, personality is the sum total of the experiences of coping with life's challenges and problems. In addition, personality is also reflective of the changes—environmental and social as well as personal—that have been encountered in life. The life history of every person is a series of lessons resulting from successes and failures in meeting the diverse challenges in life. The nature and quality of experiences with life challenges and change determine the degree to which the person is open to and accepting of pluralism and diversity in his/her environment. The person is either open to and accepting of diversity, viewing it as the key to surviving rapid and radical change, or he/she is protective, self-centered, and easily threatened by diversity and change.

For example, the process of coming to terms with a mixed heritage encourages development of multicultural orientations to life and acceptance of diversity. As Root (1992) observed, children and adolescents of mixed heritage usually encounter stress and ambivalence as they are confronted with questions such as "What are you?" "Which one are you?" "What group do you identify with the most?" Jacobs (1992) studied the process of biracial development in children and documented the experience of racial ambivalence and the process by which this transitory state eventually leads to establishment of a comfortable biracial and bicultural identity. Kitahara Kich (1992) and Hall (1992) reported the feelings of differentness and dissonance described by the participants of mixed ethnic heritage in their research. Both of those researchers also found that the participants in their studies eventually established a good adjustment and a tolerance for accepting diversity in others as a consequence of their period of trial.

The general conclusion reached by researchers studying identity development in children, adolescents, and adults of mixed ethnic heritage is that feelings of differentness and racial ambivalence provide the crucible for the development of multicultural orientations to life and of multicultural identities.

In summary, the mestizo theory of personality is circumstantialistic, holistic, synergistic, and unified. It focuses on person-environment fit and places the person in the context of cultural, familial, social, political, historical, and economic forces. The theory views openness to diversity and flexibility of functioning as the principal goals of development.

The thread common to most of the assumptions of mestizo psychology is identity development. It is in the identity development process that the principal drama of personality development of people of mixed heritage unfolds. Thus, the mestizo theory of personality focuses on identity development.

STAGES OF IDENTITY DEVELOPMENT
IN TRADITIONAL MESTIZO CULTURES

Early Childhood Years

In the earliest years of development, the child reared in traditional mestizo multicultural/multiracial cultures is encouraged to develop strong family ties and a strong sense of family identity. Family history is discussed frequently by parents, grandparents, and other relatives. Family members (both living and deceased) who are admired for their accomplishments are discussed often and held up as models for young children and adolescents.

Children are expected to inherit talents, abilities, character flaws, personality traits, and characteristics from both the mother's and the father's families. Through their personalities and life histories, children are expected to recapitulate part of the history of the families of both their parents.

Development of a gender-appropriate identity is emphasized during the early childhood years. Traditionally, in many mestizo families, there is considerable separation of sex roles, and young children are frequently discouraged from engaging in play activities or from participating in family roles that are considered to be inappropriate to their gender. In recent years, there have been major changes in definition of gender roles in the family, with the most extensive changes taking place in families residing in urban areas.

For bi- or multiracial children this may be a time of racial ambivalence as they try to assimilate racial and ethnic labels that are more complex and less readily available than those used by their parents. Children may need help from their parents to verbalize racial thoughts and feelings. Jacobs (1992) observed, "It is important for parents of biracial children to realize that their children's racial ambivalence is a developmental attainment that allows the continued exploration of racial identity. Supportive interest rather than alarm at the child's ambivalence will facilitate identity development" (p. 205).

Identification with ethnic or national culture is given great importance by both the family and the community. National and ethnic cultural heroines and heroes are held up as models, and celebrations of national holidays are taken as opportunities to teach history and cultural and national pride. Very early in development, the child is given the clear picture that rejection of national and cultural identities is tantamount to rejecting the self.

Middle Years of Childhood

Continued exploration of racial/ethnic identity in children of mixed heritage usually occurs about the age of 6 or 7, and the peer group plays an important role in this process. The peer group in neighborhoods and communities becomes the extension of the family. In some cases peer groups represent coalitions of families who reside in certain neighborhoods or sections of the city.

Acceptance by the peer group becomes of critical importance during this stage of development. Research by Kitahara Kich (1992) has shown, "In reaching out of the parental and extended family orbit, children become more aware of how others see them and their families. . . . Experiences of differentness are heightened and intensified by school attendance" (p. 312). Regarding the quest for the acceptance, Kitahara Kich (1992) goes on to observe:

> [B]ecause of their prior attempts at acceptance within many different groups, biracial people often can recognize the parameters of group roles, rules, and characteristics. As a result, their ability to gain some acceptance by many different groups potentially is expanded. . . . Many actively seek out involvement of other biracial and bicultural people, as well as those of other ethnic and racial groups. [p. 316]

Competition between peer groups of different neighborhoods in the same city or between those of different cities or towns encourages and reinforces group and community identity. In most cases the competition is in sports, such as soccer or baseball, but in some cases peer group competition takes the form of gang conflict. Gangs have been depicted in a negative light by the media, law enforcement agencies, and social scientists who have adopted a European worldview. What is lost in this restricted view is that most gangs have some positive effects on identity development and self-esteem and that some gangs are not involved in drugs and violence. Older peers and relatives often become role models and mentors who teach preadolescents about street habits and customs (street socialization). As Diego Vigil (1983) observed, "Enculturation to street values and customs proceeds apace with youth social interactions and networks" (p. 102) and "Much of the socializing of toughness occurs in the context of emotional support (e.g., befriending an unprotected individual) and camaraderie (e.g., joint efforts to deter aggressions) which the gang furnishes" (p. 108).

Adulthood

The influence of the peer group often continues into adulthood and even into late adulthood if the person settles in the community in which she/he lived during preadolescence and adolescence.

In general, peer group relationships tend to move into the background once the young adult enters into marriage or other serious intimate commitment. At this stage in life, identification with the family assumes a prominent role once again. Having children and forming an alliance with another family through marriage renews the person's ties to the nuclear and extended family. The focus on family identity is also renewed through the socialization of children and the practice of encouraging children to identify with the family. Grandparents, aunts, uncles, cousins, and siblings play important roles in encouraging the young child to feel closely identified with the nuclear and extended family. This effort also serves to renew the parent's relationship with family and community, as well as with the national and ethnic group to which he/she belongs.

Adulthood can be a trying time for the person of mixed heritage, because of problems of acceptance in intimate relationships. The choice of a partner may be difficult, particularly in environments in which the politics of conflict between value systems (Castañeda 1984) is such that it discourages interracial/interethnic relationships.

There is also a high incidence of single-parent families in the urban areas in which many mestizos live. This presents a different set of stressors for the person of mixed heritage, particularly when she/he has to confront expectations of traditional family values from grandparents and extended family members of the absent parent's family. For biracial children the absence of a parent who represents one of the ethnic/racial groups makes it difficult to have the lifestyle of that group represented and thus makes development of a comfortable bicultural/biracial identity more challenging.

Maturity

As a person moves into late middle age, he/she usually assumes the role of historian, mentor, and advisor. As historian, the person plays an important part in encouraging children and adolescents, and in some cases other adults as well, to identify with family, community, and/or cultural and national group(s). The older person may also play the role of counselor or folk healer, because adults often develop strong spiritualistic orientations in the later stages of life.

Monte (1994) summarized the findings of Erikson in describing this phase of life: "The strength of care develops in the seventh stage of development. Erikson described this as the stage in which a person plays the nurturing role of the older generation toward the younger generation—for example, as teachers, parents and mentors" (p. 133). This is best exemplified in the following excerpt (Ramirez and Castañeda 1974) from a life history interview in which a Mexican-American college student describes his grandparents:

Our grandparents' home, which was within walking distance from our own home, was the focal point in the community for our family. We grandchildren frequently stayed at our grandmother's for the weekends. My cousins and I all used to look forward to this because at night my grandmother would sit on the floor with us and tell many different *cuentos*, or stories, about persons and places in Mexico. The stories I remember most are the ones about *La Llorona*, the *Virgen de Guadalupe*, and about the Indians of Mexico and all the knowledge that they had, especially about medicine and plants. I also remember her telling stories about how in Mexico a man's arm had withered away because he rose it against his father, and also of other people who were swallowed up by the earth for lying to their parents.

My grandmother, in her tales about Mexico, talked very much about religious things, especially the *Virgen de Guadalupe* and *El Santo Nino de Atocha*. She also spoke about how villages in Mexico named after some saint would have large fiestas lasting a week or longer in commemoration of their patron saint.

My grandmother used to tell us the story of how in 1907 my grandfather and her and three of my grandfather's cousins and their families all left their small village in Mexico and set out for the United States. [pp. 49–50]

PROBLEMS OF IDENTITY

Most problems of identity development in people of mixed heritage communities and cultures are related to the rapid and extensive changes that are taking place in the countries of Latin America, the Caribbean, and North America. Industrialization, urbanization, and economic and political problems in rural communities are causing severe tensions in families and neighborhoods. In many rural regions, people are having to leave their extended families (and in some cases their nuclear ones) to look for better opportunities in urban areas of their own country or in other countries in the Americas. In urban areas, extensive changes are taking place in family roles and structures as divorce and re-marriage occur. Patterns of family structure and gender- and age-related roles are changing rapidly. Parents also find it more difficult to pass on family and community histories to their children, because it is not uncommon for the nuclear family to live at a considerable distance from the extended family and the community of origin.

Other major sources of identity problems in mestizo communities are the generational disparities in lifestyle, values, and worldview that are developing between parents and children in many families. The effects of multicultural/multiracial stress are being experienced by both parents and children. They experience the marginalization effects of having to participate in several cultures and choose between traditionalistic and modernistic belief systems (Castañeda 1984, Nisbet 1970). Although these problems are common to most mestizo cultures in the Americas, they are more in evidence in the United States, where generational differences may be linguistic as well as cultural and generational. Most of the research on multicultural/multiracial stress in the Americas has been focused on Mexican Americans, African Americans, Asian Americans, Cuban Americans, and Native Americans. Several researchers (Atkinson et al. 1989, Cross 1971, Madsen 1964, Padilla and Ruiz 1973, M. Ramirez 1969, Sommers 1964) have documented the particular types of identity conflicts exhibited by Mexican-American adolescents and other multicultural/multiracial young adults who are experiencing multiculturation stress. Ramirez (1969) identified two patterns of negative adjustment: the first displayed a rejection of mainstream American culture; adolescents who exhibited this pattern rejected American culture and expressed bitterness and resentment toward its belief system and institutions. These adolescents were often alienated from school personnel and from peers who were members of the mainstream American culture. They experienced frequent difficulties with police, truant officers, and teachers. The second pattern involved rejection of Mexican and Mexican-American culture with accompanying efforts to become totally assimilated into Anglo society. Adolescents and young adults who had adopted this pattern of adjustment became alienated from their parents, their Mexican-American peers, and from Mexican-American authority figures. They functioned effectively within mainstream culture, but they seemed somewhat confused and ambivalent about their feelings toward Mexican and Mexican-American culture. Madsen (1964) found that young adults who exhibited this latter pattern of behavior experienced severe feelings of guilt and often turned to alcohol for relief. He labeled these individuals "alcoholic agringados."

More recently researchers (Jacobs 1992, Kitahara Kich 1992) identified problems of biracial stress and racial ambivalence in children and adolescents of mixed heritage. Kitahara Kich identified the following stages of biracial/bicultural identity development:

1. An initial awareness of differentness and dissonance between self-perceptions and other perceptions (3–10 years of age),
2. A struggle for acceptance from others (age 8 through late adolescence and young adulthood), and
3. Self-acceptance as people with biracial and bicultural identity (late adolescence through adulthood). [cited in Root 1992, p. 305]

Two other patterns of adjustment to biculturation stress have been described more recently. One of these patterns has been identified among adolescents from families who have recently moved to the United States from Mexico. The behavior of these adolescents is characterized by confusion. They are closely identified with Mexican rural culture, and they have a tendency to reject both principal groups and to interact exclusively with other individuals like themselves. A fourth type of adjustment pattern is evident in the behavior of those adolescents and young adults who were born in the United States, but who tend to participate minimally in both the Mexican-

American and mainstream cultures of their communities. These young people maintain a marginal existence with respect to both cultures. They are minimally fluent in either English or Spanish; they know little about the history of either cultural group; and they have little or no commitment to the goals of either group. The individuals characterized by this pattern of adjustment also tend to isolate themselves from members of other groups in their communities.

Multicultural/multiracial stress is also experienced by parents. The most common reaction experienced by parents is the feeling that their children are becoming alienated from them. They fear that their children will reject the cultural and familial patterns and roles with which they themselves feel most comfortable. These concerns and fears are exacerbated by the fact that the children's dominant language may be English, whereas their own may be Spanish, Chinese, Vietnamese, or Hindi. The inability to communicate effectively is in itself a major problem and contributes to greater distance between children and parents and between children and grandparents. Parents also express concern over the fact that in many urban areas of the United States, middle-class mainstream culture encourages adolescents to develop values and lifestyles that differ from those of adults. Parents become especially defensive when it appears that their children are losing respect for them and for other adults. It is not uncommon, then, for parents to become repressive in their socialization and to use techniques of behavioral control that lead to increased conflict and distance between themselves and their children.

The atmosphere of acceptance of diversity in a community plays an important role in identity conflicts in persons of mixed heritage. The role of the community was conceptualized by Castañeda (1984) as the "politics of conflict" between modern and traditional value systems. Albert Ramirez (1988) highlighted the central role of prejudice, discrimination, and racism in a culturally monolithic society that limits opportunities for development of pluralistic identities. The important role of the community has also been emphasized by Johnson (1992). She states, "The racial climate of a community or school may be related to its racial composition, class structure, region of the country or population density, to name a few. A final element is that of available supports for the child in the community" (p. 48).

OPPORTUNITIES FOR MULTICULTURAL DEVELOPMENT

Growing up in mestizo, multicultural/multiracial communities and cultures of the Americas and the world poses some dangers and difficulties in identity development. It also affords important opportunities for development of flexibility and diversity in orientations to life and for development of pluralistic identities. Many mestizo communities emphasize the advantages of being open to heterogeneity and of accepting different values and ways of life. The mestizo perspective views survival of life challenges and acceptance of change as important to adjustment, so adaptability and flexibility of coping are seen as the most important criteria of psychological health and competent functioning. The ability to relate to people who are of different origins and backgrounds—the rich and the poor, the rural and the urban, the young and the old—is considered to be one of the person's most important assets. The individual is expected to be able to empathize, to step into the other person's shoes, and to look at life through his/her eyes. The person is also encouraged to draw from other cultures and peoples in order to learn how to better the condition of his/her own people, community, and family. Multicultural/multiracial cultures and communities thus value multicultural/multiracial identities that facilitate the development of pluralistic/transcendent lifestyles. Peter Adler (1974) of the East-West Center at the University of Hawaii has provided one of the most thorough descriptions of multicultural personality:

> What is considered uniquely new about this emerging human being is a psychocultural style of self process that transcends the structured images a given culture may impress upon the individual in his or her youth. The navigating image at the core of the multicultural images is premised upon the assumption of many cultural realities. The multicultural person, therefore, is not simply the person who is sensitive to many different cultures. Rather, he is a person who is always in the process of becoming *a part of* and *apart from* a given cultural context. He is very much a formative being, resilient, changing and evolutionary. He has no permanent cultural character but neither is he free from the influences of culture. In the shifts and movements of his identity process, multicultural man is constantly recreating the symbols of himself. [p. 31]

Our research (Ramirez et al. 1978) with adults who are multicultural led us to certain conclusions regarding the process by which individuals develop multicultural orientations to life and pluralistic-transcedent identities. Data from intensive life histories we have done with multicultural people of different ethnic backgrounds in the Americas led to the identification of several socialization-life experiences that were common to most of these people:

1. Exposure to socialization practices that provided positive attitudes toward diversity and also positive experiences with diverse peoples and cultures: parents and significant others served as models and provided opportunities for positive experiences with diversity.
2. Positive experiences with diversity in the school and neighborhood: beginning in early childhood, the person has opportunities to participate in several sociocultural environments and to shuttle back and forth between different sociocultural environments.
3. Experiences with situations in which previous patterns of behavior and problem-solving styles did not work (learning dilemmas): in pre-adolescence, adolescence, and early adulthood, the person was challenged to develop the multicultural coping skills, perceptual styles, attitudes, values, and worldviews needed to function effectively in multicultural settings (see leadership study in Chapter 6). To cope with multicultural settings, the person combined personality resources acquired from experience with two or more sociocultural systems. This new combination of resources provided the building blocks for development of a multicultural orientation to life.
4. Experience with continual reformulation of identity and self-image: beginning in adolescence and early adulthood, the person made frequent and extensive changes in identity and self-image as he/she participated in different sociocultural and multicultural contexts (see Figure 4–1).

These data led us to specific conclusions concerning the dynamics that are characteristic of the development of multicultural/multiracial orientations to life and pluralistic-transcendent identities: socialization and life experiences that reflect the tenets of the mestizo worldview tend to encourage an interest in diversity and a desire to

Figure 4–1. Steps in Multicultural Development

Socialization and life experience that promote the
development of receptiveness to diversity

Parents have negative attitudes
toward diversity and express racist,
sexist attitudes as well as
intolerance toward "the different" in
general; no opportunities to
experience diversity in home,
neighborhood, and community and/or
negative politics of ethnic/racial
group conflict in the community

Parents have positive attitudes
toward diversity; they either make
experiences with diversity available
in the home and/or live in
neighborhoods that are diverse
and encourage interethnic/
interracial cooperation

Degrees of openness to diversity and of willingness to
experience diversity in life

Degree of heterogeneity of pool of personality resources

Low

High

Personality resources are learned
from one culture, one group of people,
and from only one set of sociocultural
and physical environments

Personality resources are learned
from many different cultures and
people and also from different
sociocultural and physical
environments

Monocultural orientation to life; can
function in only one culture and is
identified with one culture

Multicultural orientation to life; can
function effectively in more than one
culture, but exhibits a monocultural
identity

Multicultural learning dilemmas

Combining personality resources and
elements from more than one culture

Can function effectively in
multicultural settings and develops a
pluralistic-transcendent identity and
philosophy of life

participate in multicultural activities. This interest and desire are reflected in the philosophy that there is a potential lesson in living in every person, culture, and environmental setting. Socialization that is reflective of the mestizo worldview also encourages development of respect for different lifestyles, philosophies of life, cultures, values, and belief systems. Thus, through socialization and life experiences, the mestizo worldview encourages the individual to be open to and receptive of diversity. The individual is willing to learn from others and from experiences with diverse physical and social environments. What is learned from experience with diversity is stored in a reservoir of personality-building resources or elements. The more learning experiences the individual has had with diversity, the more heterogeneous is this pool, and thus the more he/she can participate effectively in different sociocultural systems and environments. Also, there is more likelihood that he/she will achieve a pluralistic-transcendent identity.

In the early phases of development, personality-building elements and resources in the individual's repertoire are exclusively linked to the cultural, socioeconomic, sexual, racial, religious, political, and geographic contexts in which they were learned; therefore, challenges to adapt to multicultural/multiracial environments and situations are an important precursor to development of multicultural/multiracial lifestyles and pluralistic-transcendent identities. These challenges encourage the individual to reorganize and synthesize the resources and elements in his/her repertoire so that efforts to adapt involve forming combinations of resources and elements learned from different cultures, environments, and peoples. The resultant coping techniques and orientations toward life are pluralistic. For example, in order to achieve consensus in a group in which members are diverse, the leader must arrive at a pluralistic leadership style and pluralistic perspectives on problems which are representative of the diversity that exists in the group he/she is leading. (This is explained in greater detail in Chapter 6.)

Also important to the development of multiculturalism/multiracialism are continual reformulations of self-picture and philosophy of life throughout the life span of the individual. As the person is exposed to more diversity and to more challenges for multicultural/multiracial adaptations, he/she continually modifies his/her self-picture and philosophy of life. Eventually, the person makes a definite commitment to growth by continually seeking diversity challenges. It is at this point that the person begins to develop a pluralistic-transcendent identity. That is, the person no longer comes to see him/herself as a product of any one particular culture or group but instead expresses a strong life-long commitment to the well-being of all peoples, cultures, and groups. She/he is especially well-suited to work in multicultural/multiracial settings because of an ability to evaluate every culture and group objectively (including his/her group or culture of origin), becoming cognizant of their strengths and weaknesses. In this way, the multicultural/multiracial person is able to arrive at innovative solutions to social problems.

Some researchers (Atkinson et al. 1989, Cross 1971, Hall 1992, Parham 1989) have described the development of multicultural/multiracial orientations to life in different peoples of mixed heritage. Some of these conceptualizations of multicultural/multiracial identity development are stage theories that imply that individuals who are engaged in working through identity issues proceed through the various phases in a stagewise, linear fashion ranging from rejection of the group or origin and total acceptance of Anglo culture to development of identity with the group of origin to the exclusion of other groups, and finally progressing to a pluralistic stage. Parham introduced the concept of "recycling" to account for the fact that mixed heritage individuals often show behavioral characteristics and attitudes that are characteristic of an earlier stage of development even though they have supposedly already reached a pluralistic stage. Parham (1989) explained:

> Recycling is defined as the reinitiation of the racial identity struggle and resolution process after having gone through the identity development process at an earlier stage in one's life. In essence, a person could theoretically achieve identity resolution by completing one cycle through the Nigrescence process (Internationalization) and, as a result of some new experiences that stimulate identity confusion, recycle through the stages. [p. 213]

Helms (1994) recently introduced the idea of ego statuses as a way to conceptualize the recycling process. Regardless of whether conceptualization of multicultural identity development is a stage or process model, all researchers recognize the importance of the development of pluralistic orientations to life and of feelings of altruism that transcend group lines and monocultural/monoracial world views.

SUMMARY

Theories of personality development and functioning based on the mestizo multicultural/multiracial worldview should be multidisciplinary. Included in a diversity theory of personality is knowledge contributed by the fields of psychology, physiology, anthropology, sociology, natural science, and history. Additionally, knowledge from genetics, philosophy, folklore, and economics contributes to a multicultural/multiracial theory of personality. The principal focus of the mestizo theory is on identity development and on pluralistic and altruistic orientations to life. The mestizo theory reflects the fact that there is an increasing trend toward mestizoization (both genetic and cultural) in the world. A multicultural/multiracial theory of identity development helps us to understand ourselves and others so that we can live in peace and harmony in a diverse world that is shrinking rapidly and in which racial and ethnic lines are becoming increasingly blurred.

❖ 5 ❖

Research Methods and the Multicultural/Multiracial Worldview

I was very dissatisfied with Oscar Lewis' portrayal of the people of Tepoztlan (Lewis 1959) and first depressed and then angry with the application of Frommian characterology to Mexican villagers.

—*Rogelio Diaz-Guerrero (1977)*

One of our main tasks is to recover our history and to once again give proper recognition to the knowledge of the past and of the indigenous cultures which can be even more important than Aristotelian philosophy.

—*Orlando Fals Borda (1987)*

Virtually ignored in this book [Triandis's *Individualism, Collectivism*] are the powerful potential of economic forces, political ideologies, and religious and ethnic fundamentalisms to influence behavior patterns in most societies. For some societies we can all name, such forces are so strong that the societies' location on the individualism-collectivism cultural syndrome map seem trivial. Has Triandis the psychologist overpsychologized complex social, political and economic phenomena? I fear so.

—*Marshal H. Segall (1996)*

The future of mestizo multicultural/multiracial psychology is closely linked to the research methodologies and the instruments for data collection that are used with mixed heritage populations and communities. As we have seen from the brief review of the social science literature on mestizos presented in Chapter 3, the use of research methodologies and instruments that are reflective of the European worldview have, for the most part, resulted in a distorted picture of the psychodynamics of multicultural/multiracial people, their communities, and their cultures. This chapter takes a closer look at the European worldview–based research methodologies and instruments that have been used with multicultural/multiracial participants; it then identifies new instruments and intervention approaches based on specific components of the psychodynamics of mestizo participants. The chapter concludes with the presentation of a procedure that can be used to assess the degree to which research and intervention projects are consonant with the tenets of the mestizo worldview in the social sciences and helping professions.

METHODOLOGIES AND INSTRUMENTS REFLECTING THE EUROPEAN WORLDVIEW

Some of the distorted perceptions that social scientists and mental health professionals have developed of mestizo participants and their cultures have emerged from research based on instruments and methodologies dependent on psychoanalytic theory. The notion of culture of poverty introduced by Oscar Lewis (1965) is an example of the erroneous picture created by reliance on psychoanalytic methodologies and concepts. In his research in Tepoztlan, Mexico, as well as his studies in New York and Puerto Rico, Lewis used the Rorschach, the Thematic Apperception, and Sentence Completion tests—all instruments based on the tenets of psychoanalytic theory—to collect data. The influences of psychoanalytic theory are apparent in his description of how the culture of poverty affects the behavior of individuals. Lewis (1965) concluded:

> On the level of the individual the major characteristics are a strong feeling of marginality, of helplessness, of dependence and of inferiority. . . . Other traits include a high incidence of maternal deprivation, of orality, of weak ego structure, confusion of sexual identification, a lack of impulse control, a strong present time orientation with relatively little ability to defer gratification and to plan for the future, a sense of resignation and fatalism, a widespread belief in male superiority and a high tolerance for psychological pathology of all sorts. [pp. xlvii–xlviii]

The concept of a culture of poverty led social scientists and psychiatrists to conclude that mestizos did not possess an authentic culture, a worldview that was legitimately different from the European perspective. Furthermore, it led to the conclusion that the only culture people of mixed heritage possessed was negative—one that interfered with psychological development and mental health. It was no accident, then, that the "war on poverty" of the late 1960s and the early 1970s in the United States was based on some of the assumptions of the culture of poverty. As a consequence of the influence of culture of poverty ideology, one of the principal goals of that effort was to encourage mestizos to assimilate to values and lifestyles that were reflective of the European worldview. Ramirez and Castañeda (1974), writing about Mexican Americans, observed that the concept of culture of poverty was supportive of a damaging-culture perspective that had been evident in the social sciences since the 1920s:

> The theory that the culture and values of Mexican Americans are the ultimate and final cause of their low economic status and low academic achievement—the damaging-culture view—has been almost exclusively the framework within which social scientists have written about Mexican Americans. [p. 14]

The link between culture of poverty and damaging-culture is also evident in Fromm and Maccoby's work in Mexico (1970). These researchers also relied on a psychoanalytic methodology to collect their data. While Oscar Lewis relied only partially on psychoanalytic techniques, Fromm and Maccoby relied exclusively on these methods. They studied a small village of 800 inhabitants in the state of Morelos, located about fifty miles from Mexico City. To collect their data, they used questionnaires, the Rorschach, the Thematic Apperception Test, and the Children's Apperception Test. The questionnaire they developed for the study—the "interpretative questionnaire"—was clearly psychoanalytically based. The authors observed that the most important element of the interpretative questionnaire was the "interpretation of the answers with regard to their unconscious or unintended meaning." They continued:

> The task of interpretation is, like any other psychoanalytic interpretation, difficult and takes a great deal of time. It requires knowledge of psychoanalytic theory and therapy (including the experience of one's own analysis), a clinical psychoanalytic experience, and, as in everything else, skill and talent. Psychoanalytic interpretation—of associations and dreams as well as of answers to a questionnaire—is an art like the practice of medicine, in which certain theoretical principles are applied to empirical data. [p. 26]

Fromm and Maccoby's methodological orientation also led to a negative picture of mestizos and of their traditional culture. Their conclusion was that the passive-receptive character type—the pathological type prone to alcoholism and the tendency to avoid change—was the type most closely associated with the traditional culture of the village. The productive-hoarding type—that most closely associated with European values and beliefs—was seen as the most sophisticated in terms of psychological development. With respect to this latter type, they observed:

> The adventurous, individualistic entrepreneur has become a symbol of progress, of the better and glamorous life which the villager sees only on the screen. But the entrepreneurs are by no means only symbols. They take the lead in promoting those changes in village life and its institutions which destroy traditional culture and replace it by the modern principle of rational purposefulness. [p. 231]

Culture of poverty and the theory of "social selection" of character types are both products of the European worldview as reflected in psychoanalytic theory, and both contribute to unfavorable assumptions regarding multicultural/multiracial people and their cultures. From these assumptions, social scientists concluded that to better the lot of mestizos it was necessary to modernize, or rather Westernize, their cultures and lifestyles. The Fromm and Maccoby study also supported the damaging-culture perspective among social scientists and reinforced the beliefs that only those mestizos who exhibited European characteristics in their behavior and psychodynamics were achievement oriented and well adjusted psychologically.

While psychoanalytically based methodologies have contributed to a negative picture of mestizo adults, those methodologies based on the conceptual framework of psychological differentiation (Witkin et al. 1962) have contributed to a negative picture of mestizo children and adolescents. Psychological differentiation is based on the ideas of the British philosopher Herbert Spencer. Spencer (1897) proposed that as something develops, it becomes increasingly differentiated in parts and function, better integrated in the way the parts work together, and more segregated. By segregation, Spencer meant that each part attained more individualized qualities that distinguished it from other parts as time passed. The differentiation concept was applied to psychological development by Witkin and his colleagues (1962). Cognitive styles were defined as the characteristic self-consistent modes of functioning found pervasively throughout an individual's perceptual and intellectual activities. These modes of functioning are believed to lie along a dimension from global to articulated or from undifferentiated to differentiated. It is believed that at birth and in the early stages of development, the individual exhibits a global mode or is undifferentiated (field dependent cognitive style), but, if proper socialization experiences are provided in the home and society in general, then the child becomes gradually more differentiated with age (more field-independent in cognitive style).

To assess degree of field independence in children and adults, Witkin and his colleagues used several "cognitive" tests such as the Embedded Figures Test, the Portable Rod and Frame Test, and the Draw-a-Person Test. Culture and cognitive styles were believed to be linked through the socialization practices characteristic of certain sociocultural groups. For example, Dershowitz (1971) tested three groups (two Jewish and one Anglo) of 10–year-old boys in New York City. His findings showed that the Anglo group had achieved the highest scores on the tests (more field independent); they were followed by the more assimilated Jewish group and then by the Orthodox Jews. Dershowitz concluded that the values and patterns of traditional living characteristic of the Orthodox Jewish group inhibited the development of a sense of separate identity, thereby resulting in less psychological differentiation.

This same belief that traditional values inhibit the development of a sense of separate identity in children was used to interpret the findings of a study (Holtzman et al. 1975) that compared Anglo children in Austin, Texas, with children in Mexico City. The two groups of children were compared using several instruments and tests including the Embedded Figures Test, the Wechsler Intelligence Scale for Children (WISC), and the Holtzman Inkblot Technique (research instruments having questionable validity for use in cross-cultural research since they were developed with whites). The findings showed that the Mexican children had scored lower (in a more field-dependent direction) on the Embedded Figures Test than did the Anglo children although, interestingly enough, the first-grade group of Mexican children performed better than their Anglo counterparts on the arithmetic and block design subtests of the Weschsler—two tasks that are usually correlated with field independence. Nevertheless, a European worldview perspective was used in interpreting those findings (Holtzman 1979), which indicated that there were differences between the two cultures:

From differences noted in the two cultures, *one would expect that in the traditional, passive, affiliative hierarchy of Mexico, there would be more value placed on affective rather than cognitive aspects of life, coupled with a preference for a static rather than a dynamic approach.* The Mexican should be family-centered rather than individual-centered; should prefer external controls to self-directed impulsiveness. At the same time the Mexican should be more pessimistic about the hardships of life and passive-obedient rather than active-rebelling in style of coping with stresses in the environment. For the U.S., on the other hand, the opposite of each of these statements should tend to be true. The many significant differences found between Mexican and North American children led to the above generalizations (emphasis added). [pp. 40–41]

In considering the results of the Austin–Mexico City study, together with those of other investigators who had worked with Mexican and U.S. populations, Holtzman (1979) proposed six major hypotheses concerning personality differences between Mexicans and white Americans. Again, the influences of the European worldview are obvious:

1. White Americans tend to be more active than Mexicans in their style of coping with life's problems and challenges;
2. White Americans tend to be more technological, dynamic, and external than Mexicans in the meaning of activity within subjective culture;
3. White Americans tend to be more complex and differentiated in cognitive structure than Mexicans;
4. Mexicans tend to be more family-centered, while white Americans are more individual-centered;
5. Mexicans tend to be more cooperative in interpersonal activities, while white Americans are more competitive; and
6. Mexicans tend to be more fatalistic and pessimistic in outlook on life than white Americans. [pp. 41–43]

The general conclusion reached by Holtzman and colleagues (1975) was that Anglo-American children are more field independent because American culture places a greater emphasis on autonomy in child rearing and because American society is more loosely structured.

Mexican children, on the other hand, are more field dependent because of the emphasis Mexican culture places on conformity to adult authority and because Mexican society is characterized by a strict hierarchical social organization. However, no explanation was given for the fact that in the first grade (an age when children are most influenced by their families) Mexican children performed better than Anglo children on the math and block design subtests of the WISC, two indicators of field independence.

Research with Anglo-American and Mexican-American children in Houston, Texas, (Ramirez and Price-Williams 1974b) showed that Anglos had scored in a more field-independent direction than did Mexican Americans. However, when a research methodology was employed that is more consonant with the mestizo world-emic view in subsequent studies with children of the same two cultural groups, the findings were different (Ramirez and Castañeda 1974). In the latter study, the researchers administered the Portable Rod and Frame and the Children's Embedded Figures Tests to Anglo and Mexican-American elementary school children and did intensive observations of the behavior of their participants in school settings. The results obtained indicated that Witkin's cognitive tests did not do justice to the richness of behavior exhibited by the children. Both the Embedded Figures and Portable Rod and Frame Tests were measures of field independence and did not reflect the flexibility of behavior which was being observed. The flexibility of behavior observed by Ramirez and Castañeda explains the contradictory findings obtained by Holtzman and colleagues (1975) discussed above. More intensive studies of these children and their families in both the Anglo and the Latinos groups revealed that most of them could shift between field-independent and field-dependent behaviors.

It was also observed that the field-dependent behaviors, which Ramirez and Castañeda labeled "field sensitive," were not as negative and unadaptive as Witkin and his colleagues had assumed them to be. That is, when performing in a field-sensitive mode, children tended to be more cooperative, more attentive to the global features of a task, and more motivated to work for social rewards. Most important, however, was the observation that the most flexible children tended to have been socialized in bilingual/bicultural families. That is, both Anglo and Mexican-American children who had been socialized in mainstream American middle-class and Mexican-American and/or Mexican culture, and who had learned both English and Spanish demonstrated that they were the most bicognitive. They could function in both the field-sensitive and field-independent cognitive styles, and they could use elements of both styles to arrive at new problem solving and coping styles. Figure 5–1 describes the relationship between culture, language, and cognitive style.

From the perspective of the bicognitive model proposed by Ramirez and Casteñeda (1974) and by Ramirez (1994b), European worldview–based research methodologies and instruments produce a fragmented and incomplete picture of individual psychodynamics. If exposure to pluralistic values and lifestyles and to different languages encourages bicognitive development, then use of cognitive tests will, at best, provide researchers with only half the picture of the individual's psychodynamics. This distorted picture can lead social scientists and mental health professionals to arrive at inaccurate and unfavorable conclusions regarding the psychodynamics of mestizo subjects and the value systems and lifestyles of their cultures.

INTELLIGENCE AND PEOPLE OF MIXED HERITAGE

Recent examples of the distorted perception of the psychodynamics and cultures of people of mixed heritage have been made in *The Bell Curve* (1994). Using a European perspective and citing research employing European methodology and instruments, Herstein and

Figure 5.1. Relationship between Culture, Language, and Cognitive Styles*

Traditional value/belief systems ⟶ Predominant field
of a culture, community, or home; sensitive cognitive style
Spanish language dominance

Bicultural/multicultural, bilingual ⟶ Bicognitive

Modernistic values/belief systems ⟶ Predominant field
of a culture, community, or home; independent cognitive style
English language dominance

*Reprinted from Ramirez 1994b by permission of Allyn & Bacon.

Murray (1994) conclude that, "Latino and black immigrants are, at least in the short run, putting some downward pressure on the distribution of intelligence" (pp. 360–361).

Basing their conclusions on many biased sources take from white supremacist publications such as *The Mankind Quarterly* (Lane 1994), Herstein and Murray ignore the research of the Latino scholar George Sanchez (1932, 1934) and the African-American psychologist Horace Mann Bond (1927), which showed that differences between scores on intelligence tests of whites and people of mixed heritage are primarily due to lack of fluency in the English language, unfamiliarity with mainstream American middle-class culture, and socioeconomic class. They also ignored work showing that most intelligence tests reflect learning/problem-solving style(s) that are more characteristic of European cultures (Ramirez and Gonzales 1973). The authors of *The Bell Curve* overlooked evidence that there are differences in the achievement motivation of whites and people of mixed heritage (Ramirez and Price-Williams 1974). Furthermore, recent research (Franco 1996) has found that cultural variables such as language, acculturation, and family values are related to differences in the performance of Latino and white high school students on tests of intelligence and neuropsychological assessment instruments.

EUROPEAN VS. MULTICULTURAL/MULTIRACIAL WORLDVIEWS IN CROSS-CULTURAL PSYCHOLOGY

The European worldview/mestizo worldview controversy in mental health and social science research is analogous to the emic-etic controversy in cross-cultural psychology. The emic-etic distinction was first employed in anthropology by Pike (1954), who made an analogy with the usage of the term's components in linguistics. Phonetics involves application of a universal coding system for sounds employed in any language, and phonemics involves study of meaning-bearing units in a particular language. Pike argued that social scientists should try to enter a culture and to see it as its own members do. Thus, the emic approach that he suggested was designed to show how a particular people classify their experiences in life. One of the best arguments for the use of the emic approach in cross-cultural research can be found in the book by Cole and Scribner entitled *Culture and*

Thought (1974). However, most cross-cultural psychologists have been reluctant to reject universalistic perspectives. Even Cole and Scribner refused to take a definite position on this issue:

> The key problem . . . is that any fact, or small set of facts, is open to a wide variety of interpretations. So long as we are only concerned with demonstrating that human cultural groups differ enormously in their beliefs and theories about the world and in their art products and tech-nological accomplishments, there can be no question: there are marked and multitudinous cultural differences. But are these differences the result of differences in basic cognitive processes, or are they merely the expressions of the many products that a universal human mind can manufacture, given wide variations of conditions of life and culturally valued activities? Our review has not answered this question. [p. 172]

Nevertheless, Cole and Scribner issued a stern warning against the use of influential psychological theories (such as Piaget's theory) in other cultures:

> But carrying such theories overseas without some awareness of their cultural roots and their real limitations, even in cultures in which they arose, carries with it the risk of experimental egocentrism—mistaking as universals the particular organizations of cognitive skills that have arisen in the historical circumstances of our own society, and interpret-ing their absence in other cultures as "deficiency." [p. 200]

Although Price-Williams (1975) has taken a strong stand in sup-port of the emic point of view, other influential cross-cultural psy-chologists have proposed combining the etic and emic perspectives. Koivukari (1977) criticized these proposals:

> From my most critical viewpoint, all strategies that take an "assumed etic" or "what appears to be a universal construct" as a starting point latently involve a flaw in two respects: 1) The "assumed etic" is, at any rate in several cases and at least partly, Euroamerican emic. How shall we obliterate the cultural bias of our concepts *before* entering the field of observations? 2) The correctional method, while striving at mini-mizing bias, still entails a danger, common to any deductive strategy. When we approach a field of observations with preformed concep-tualizations, we run the risk of selecting what we observe and of cate-gorizing and interpreting what we have observed as a function of those

preformed concepts, thus losing and distorting the information we would otherwise obtain. Our best intentions of testing the constructs against our observations will not ensure that such bias will be eliminated. The "emic" measurements may have construct validity because the construct directed our choice of the operationalizations to be measured and the "emic definitions" of "etic constructs" are influenced by the fact that we had the construct in mind when we started exploring the field of possible emic operationalizations. [p. 27]

Koivukari is right in asserting that as long as European worldview-based methodologies and constructs are used in cross-cultural research, it will be impossible to obtain an unbiased view of the subjects and cultures being studied. For example, research by Garza (1977) showed that the items of internal-external locus of control instruments have different meanings for Mexican Americans than they do for Anglos. Garza administered Rotter's Internal-External scale to 203 Anglo and 244 Mexican-American university undergraduates. The data from both groups of subjects were factor analyzed separately. The findings showed that out of five conceptually based factors that emerged from the data, the cultural equivalence of three of these factors was questionable. The content of the items that loaded on some of the factors for Anglos and Mexican Americans indicated that the concepts themselves did not appear to carry the same meanings for the members of the two groups. Garza concluded:

> The problem of cultural equivalence is extremely complex and entails more than merely controlling for such obvious factors as readability and language usage. As clearly indicated by the data presented in the present paper, even simple statements regarding beliefs in internal as opposed to external control may evoke totally different meanings for Chicanos in comparison with Anglos. It is conceivable that a great deal of research literature comparing Chicanos and Anglos may be based on equivocal measurements of given psychological constructs, casting serious doubt on the validity of the findings. [pp. 106–107]

The pervasiveness of the etic perspective has also resulted in administration of instruments and techniques to mestizo subjects that are no more than translations of instruments reflecting the European worldview. Researchers committed to the etic point of view have not been cognizant of the fact that translating an instrument into another language does not alter its culturally biased content and structure. That is, translating the semantic differential does not alter the fact that it encourages a segmented, fragmented view of psychodynamics not in keeping with the mestizo worldview.

One of the best examples of the fallacy of the etic-quasi-emic approach is Triandis and colleagues' (1972) model of subjective culture. Triandis defined subjective culture as a cultural group's characteristic way of perceiving the man-made part of its environment—the perception of the rules and the group's norms, roles, and values. Although the conceptualization of the subjective culture notion is reflective of both the emic and mestizo perspectives, the methodology that Triandis and his colleagues have used to collect most of their data is not—they rely heavily on the semantic differential technique.

A recent publication in the *American Psychologist* (Betancourt and Lopez 1993) offered some suggestions for doing appropriate research from the perspective of the mixed heritage–mestizo worldview. The authors observed that mainstream researchers usually do not consider culture in their research and theories, and that cross-cultural researchers who study cultural differences frequently fail to identify the specific aspects of culture and related variables that are thought to influence behavior. The authors asserted, "Consequently we learn that cultural group, race or ethnicity may be related to a given psychological phenomenon, but we learn little about the specific elements of these group variables that contribute to the proposed relationship" (p. 629).

To correct for these oversights the authors recommend two approaches—a bottom-up approach in which investigators begin with a phenomenon observed in the study of culture and then apply it cross-culturally to test theories of human behavior, and a top-down strategy in which the investigator begins with a theory that ignored culture and incorporates cultural elements to broaden the theoretical domains. Unfortunately, these recommendations seem to reflect the European perspective—the use of existing theories based on the European worldview is referred to as a top-down strategy while the use of native and culturally unique perspectives is labeled a bottom-up procedure.

Also, the bottom-up suggestion ignores the fact that many mixed heritage cultures have psychological-philosophical views that should be considered to be as epistomologically legitimate as European-based theories. In addition, the authors fail to emphasize that, regardless of which of the two recommended approaches is used, it is the perspective of the investigator(s) that is most important in determining whether culture is going to be accurately represented and emphasized to the degree it deserves in social science research and intervention. Some of the suggestions made by Betancourt and Lopez could be dangerous because, like the concept of subjective culture proposed by Triandis et al. and discussed above, they could lead to the use of an etic approach that is disguised as emic (pseudoemic). In fact a publication cited by the authors show the dangers involved. They laud a methodological approach in cross-cultural research used by Triandis and Marin (1983), who started with an instrument developed from an etic perspective (one used to study differences between mainstream Americans and Greeks) and then added items that are culture specific (in this case Hispanic) in order to compare Hispanics and mainstream Americans. Triandis and Marin refer to this approach as etic plus emic. However, a careful reading of the manuscript reveals that the authors engaged in some semantic gymnastics and incorrect assumptions reflective of a European worldview perspective. For example, the authors reported that a critic of their manuscript indicated that the original instrument used with Greeks and Americans was American-Greek etic. The authors countered by stating, "It seems reasonable, since one is dealing with U.S. Hispanics, that they are more similar to Americans than are Greeks" (p. 498).

How was it decided that U.S. Hispanics are more similar to mainstream Americans than are Greeks? Which U.S. Hispanics? Which mainstream Americans? And which Greeks? Is this not one of the major criticisms which Betancourt and Lopez make of cross-cultural research?

Thus, the aforementioned publications led to a reaffirmation of the conclusion about the general state of the art regarding research on mixed ethnic heritage populations that were made in the previous edition of this book published in 1983: priority must be given to the development of research methods and instruments that are consonant with the psychodynamics of mestizo. What follows is a review of methodologies, instruments, and intervention strategies whose development has been inspired by the specific characteristics of the psychodynamics and cultures of peoples of mixed heritage.

RESEARCH METHODOLOGIES AND INSTRUMENTS
INSPIRED BY A MESTIZO WORLDVIEW

Importance of Individual Uniqueness

"*Cada cabeza un mundo*" (Everyone is a world unto himself). This saying, used so often in Latino cultures, attests to the importance of the belief that every individual is unique because he/she has a perspective on life that no other person can duplicate. This assertion is reflected in the philosophy of the Americas proposed by Leopoldo Zea, which was discussed in Chapter 2: the unique life circumstances of the individual have shaped the person's lifestyle and his/her view of life.

The Life History. The life history approach can capture the essence of the individual and the nature of the life circumstances that shaped his/her personality. The most important work on the use of this approach in social science research was written by John Dollard, a sociologist and social psychologist, in 1935. In contrasting the perspective of the person that could be obtained through the life history with that afforded by the "conventional cultural view" used most often by social scientists studying other cultures, he identified the advantages of the life history method:

> In the long-section or life history view the individual remains organically present as an object of study; he must be accounted for in his full, immediate, personal reality. The eye remains on the details of his behavior and these we must research on and explain. Here culture is bedded down in a specific organic locus. The culture forms a continuous and connected wrap for the organic life. From the standpoint of the life history the person is viewed as an organic center of feeling moving through a culture and drawing magnetically to him the main strands of the culture. In the end the individual appears as a person, as a microcosm of the group features of his culture. It is possible that detailed studies of the lives of individuals will reveal new perspectives on the culture as a whole which are not accessible when one remains on the formal cross-sectional plane of observation. In pure cultural studies, on the other hand, the organic man has disappeared and only that abstracted portion of him remains that is isolated and identified by the culture pattern. If, in the "pure" cultural study, the organic reality

of the person is lost, then we should expect that cultural studies would tell us little about individual experience and meaning. [pp. 4–5]

This quotation not only reflects some of the major tenets of the mestizo worldview in psychology, but also provides guidelines for research that would have helped us to avoid many etic-emic methodological problems in cross-cultural research. If we were to substitute "European worldview" for "pure cultural studies" in the quotation, Dollard, almost fifty years ago, would have foreseen the methodological problems which we are currently experiencing in cross-cultural research.

Doing research with the life history approach, Ramirez and colleagues (Ramirez 1994b, Ramirez et al. 1977, 1978) developed a life history interview for college students with a special focus on development of pluralistic identities. The interview follows five different periods in the person's life: early childhood, elementary school, middle school, high school, and college. The length of the interview varies from an hour and fifteen minutes to an hour and thirty minutes. Questions asked included the following issues: language learning and usage; family and community life; school experiences; academic achievement; peer relations; relationships with authority figures; political activities; religious beliefs; life crises; identity crises; perceived advantages and disadvantages of mainstream American, Mexican, and Mexican-American cultures; degree of comfort and acceptance experienced while participating in different cultures; contemporary sociocultural identity; preference for ethnic background of marriage partners; philosophy of life; and career goals. Information obtained from the Psychohistory Schedule for Assessing Multiculturalism (PSAM) is scored on variables relating to four major areas of functioning: sociocultural competencies, multicultural participation, interethnic facilitation, and leadership experience in pluralistic situations. With respect to sociocultural competencies, the interviewee is assessed according to successful experiential history in three general domains or settings (the home, the community, and the school) in both Mexican-American and mainstream American cultures. Three areas of functioning are assessed in this manner: language, peer relations, and relations with authority figures. Scoring is done by using a five-point scale for each of these variables. Scores for interethnic facilitation, multicultural participation, and leadership experience in pluralistic situations are assigned on a three-point scale in each of the domains of school, home, and community. Use of the PSAM to study multicultural subjects is described in Chapter 6.

Individual Uniqueness in Learning Styles

Behavior observation instruments that focus on assessing the preferred learning and teaching behaviors of persons of mixed heritage have been shown to be important in research with mestizo children and adults. This is particularly the case because many multicultural/multiracial children and adults are misdiagnosed as suffering from learning and emotional disabilities. In an attempt to identify the learning and teaching styles of Latino cultures, Ramirez and his colleagues (Cox et al. 1982, Ramirez and Castañeda 1974) developed observation instruments for assessing learning styles and teaching styles that have their origins in mestizo cultures and that permit the development of learning environments that match the learning styles of children of mixed heritage. Table 5–1 presents guidelines for evaluating how well mestizo standards are being considered in studies or in instruments.

Importance of Family Identity

From the perspective of the mestizo worldview, the individual is seen as embedded in the context of the family group. Recognition of the important role played by the family in individual psychodynamics has been one of the major contributions of the cultures of the peoples of mixed heritage to the social sciences and helping professions.

The Multiple Autobiography in a Single Family. Oscar Lewis's multiple autobiography in a single family (1961) is a major contribution to mestizo research methodology, because it identifies the nature of the familial context in which the individual has been reared and in which he/she finds himself/herself. This technique is not only reflective of the important and central role that the family plays in the psychodynamics of the individual, but it also affords a view of the unique perception that each member has of the family. This latter point permits us to see that families can be viewed as both positive

Table 5–1. How Well Does the Study or Program Meet Multicultural/ Multiracial Standards?

Each of the following standards are evaluated on a scale of 1 (not at all characteristic) to 5 (very characteristic)

Theory or conceptual framework
1. Degree to which the theory or conceptual frame work is consistent with mestizo multicultural/multiracial worldview.

Participants
2. Degree to which participants reflect intracultural diversity of target group or groups.
3. Degree to which SES, linguistic, generational status, and acculturation/ multiculturation information were taken into consideration in selection of participants.
4. If two or more groups were compared, degree to which groups are comparable.

Instruments
5. Degree to which content of the instruments was reflective of the mestizo view.
6. Degree to which structure of the instruments was reflective of the mestizo view.
7. Degree to which demands that the instruments made on the participants were consistent with the mestizo view.

Data collection and interpretation
8. Degree to which data were collected in a historical, social, economic, political, cultural, and religious/spiritual context.
9. Degree to which data were interpreted in a historical, social, economic, political, cultural, and religious/spiritual context.

and negative by individuals in terms of different life events and stages of development. Another advantage of the technique is that it permits a view of the same family from the perspectives of different members. Thus, the multiple autobiography in a single family can assess the quality and the degree of the individual's identity with the family and the true nature of that identity, that is, what identification with the family really means to the individual. The advantages offered by the multiple autobiography in a single family are best described by Lewis himself:

Each member of the family tells his own life story in his own words. This approach gives us a cumulative, multifaceted, panoramic view of each individual, of the family as a whole, and of many aspects of lower-class Mexican life. The independent versions of the same incidents given by the various members provide a built-in check upon the reliability and validity of much of the data and thereby partially offset the subjectivity inherent in a single autobiography. At the same time it reveals the discrepancies in the way events are recalled by each member of the family. . . . The tape recorder used in taking down the life stories . . . has made possible the beginning of a new kind of literature of social realism. With the aid of the tape recorder, unskilled, uneducated, and even illiterate persons can talk about themselves and relate their observations and experiences in an uninhibited, spontaneous, and natural manner. . . . This method of multiple autobiographies also tends to reduce the element of investigator bias because the accounts are not put through the sieve of a middle-class North American mind but are given in the words of the subjects themselves. . . . While I use a directive approach in the interviews, I encouraged free association, and I was a good listener. I attempted to cover systematically a wide range of subjects: their earliest memories, their dreams, their hopes, fears, joys and sufferings; sex life, their concepts of justice, religion, and politics; their knowledge of geography and history; in short, their total view of the world. Many of my questions stimulated them to express themselves on subjects which they might otherwise never have thought of or volunteered information about. However, the answers were their own. [pp. xi, xii, xxi]

The Family History Questionnaire. As an outgrowth of his work with the Psychohistory Schedule for Assessing Multiculturalism, described above, Ramirez (1987) developed the Family History Questionnaire. The approach involves holding separate interviews with both husband and wife concerning the good and bad times experienced by the family. The interviewer also focuses on how individual and family problems were resolved and on the particular people, agencies, and institutions that husband and wife view as sources of support in times of crisis. Questions asked in the interview focus on the following topics: degree to which the husband's and wife's families approved of the marriage; recollection of the best times experienced by the family; recollection of the greatest family crisis endured and how the family coped with the situation; perceived sources of support in times of crisis (both hypothetical and actual); and the perceived ability of the family to confront a crisis in the past, in the present, and in the future. The results of a study (Ramirez 1987) in which the Family History Questionnaire was used with mothers in San Antonio, Texas, and Monterrey, Mexico, revealed that the technique was useful in assessing the degree of effectiveness with which families cope with life stress. In addition, data collected with the instrument indicated the degree to which families rely on members of the extended family and on institutions outside the family such as religion, churches, schools, hospitals, welfare agencies, and neighborhood organizations in coping with life crises.

A recent study (Gottman 1994) on variables that predict dissolution of marriage employed oral history (recasting the entire history of the marriage), a research technique similar to the Family History Questionnaire.

Importance of Cultural Identity, Acculturation, and Mestizo Orientations to Life

From the mestizo perspective, identification with the culture is a definite indicator of the person's stability and sense of meaning in life. However, the mestizo worldview also recognizes that cultural change is a reality that all individuals must face. Thus, the research methodologies and instruments to be used with people of mixed ethnic heritage should reflect not only the salience of cultural and individual identity but also the important role that cultural change plays in multicultural/multiracial identity development and personality dynamics in general.

Cultural Identity

Historical-Sociocultural Premises (HSCPs). Diaz-Guerrero (1992) has devoted much of his research career to the development of a Mexican ethnopsychology and of instruments for assessment of the traditional beliefs and modes of coping of traditional Mexican culture. Use of the HSCPs with different populations in Mexico has led to the identification of 13 scales. Diaz-Guerrero observes, "I theorized that an individual Mexican's score on these factorial scales represented his or her personal position in the culture/counterculture dialectic. In other words, how traditionally Mexican one is, or how much one has rebelled and therefore individualized oneself away from one's culture could be indicated by one's score" (p. 46).

Family Attitudes Scale (FAS). Influenced by the works of Diaz-Guerrero on Historic-Sociocultural Premises, Ramirez (1967, 1969) developed an inventory of Mexican-American family values in order to assess the degree to which Mexican-American adolescents and young adults were identified with the values of traditional Mexican-American culture. Ramirez and Carrasco (cited in Carrasco 1990) revised and expanded the FAS to tap eight dimensions of a traditional Mexican-American value orientation: loyalty to the family, strictness in child rearing, respect for adults, separation of sex roles, male superiority, time orientation, religious ideology, and socialization of competitiveness and cooperation. The new scale not only assesses identity with Mexican-American culture but also assesses degree of identity with the values of mainstream American white culture as well. Research (Rodriguez et al. in press) has demonstrated that the values of Mexican-American adolescents and their parents are significantly different from those of Mexican and of white (United States) families. The values of Mexican Americans were reflective of an amalgamation of Mexican and mainstream United States values— a bicultural value system. Research by Ramirez (1969) with middle school and high school Latino students in California identified three groups of Mexican-American adolescents based on their responses to the Family Attitudes Scale: Identifiers (most identified with traditional Mexican-American values), the Anglicized (who rejected the values of their group of origin), and the Biculturals (who identified with both Mexican-American and Anglo values).

Traditional-Modern Values

Castañeda (1984) conceptualized value differences between most mestizos and most Whites around the world in terms of traditionalism and modernism. As Castañeda observed, "Modern and traditional define a different perception of reality and may be thought of as the genesis of diametrically opposed sets of values and goals" (p. 356). Castañeda noted that the lifestyles of traditional societies are focused around the following beliefs: (1) the universe was created by a supernatural force or forces; (2) the individual should primarily be identified with his/her family, tribe, religious, and ethnic or racial group; and (3) institutions should be hierarchical in structure with the authority determined in terms of age and birth right or position in the family or group. Modern societies, Castañeda indicated, are based on a different set of beliefs: (1) the universe was created by natural forces that can be explained by a rational science; (2) individual identity (individualism) is more important than loyalty to family, community, group, or religion; and (3) institutions should be based on principles of democracy and egalitarianism.

To attempt to assess identity with the traditional and modern values as described by Castañeda, Ramirez and Doell (1982) developed an instrument, the Traditionalism-Modernism Inventory (TMI) that assessed gender role differences, attitudes toward ritual and tradition; attitudes toward religion, age status, and family responsibilities; respect for authority; and time orientation. The TMI was recently revised (Ramirez et al., in progress) to include items reflecting attitudes toward homosexuality, abortion, and the death penalty.

Bicultural Identity

Cultural flexibility as reflected in amalgamation of mainstream white and mestizo family values in particular, and traditional and modern values in general, was reported by Ramirez and Castañeda as early as 1974. Dual identity, or merging, had been proposed as an ultimate goal for African Americans by W. E. B. DuBois (1903). Gamio (1922) also identified synthesis of values and lifestyles among Mexican immigrants who came to the United States in search of employment.

McFee (1968) focused on bicultural behaviors (degree of functional participation in two cultures) in his research in bicultural communities on Native American reservations. Keefe and Padilla (1978) followed the earlier work of Ramirez and Castañeda (1974) and Ramirez and colleagues (1977) to develop an approach to assess ethnic identity, in which they administered questionnaires that included two types of items—cultural awareness (CA) and ethnic loyalty (EL).

After administering the questionnaire to 381 respondents in southern California and doing a factor analysis on the data, the investigators concluded that four factors were found to be related to the dimensions of CA: the respondent's cultural heritage, the spouse's cultural heritage and pride, the parents' cultural heritage and pride, and perceived discrimination. Similarly, four factors were found to be related to the dimensions of EL: language preference and use, cultural pride and affiliation, cultural identification, and social behavior orientation. From these data, Padilla (1980) constructed profiles of acculturation types. The following is an example of one of the profiles identified:

An individual with low CA (according to the model) has a cultural orientation that reflects the mainstream "American" culture (as do the parents and the individual's spouse, if married). This is manifested by knowledge of, identification with, and preference for the United States's "American" culture and for English as the language of preference. In all probability, this person will also score low on EL, which would indicate little pride in the culture of origin and little affiliation with more Mexican-oriented acquaintances. The person would also perceive little or no discrimination toward Mexicans at either the individual or group level. Finally, the social behavior of this particular individual would be non Mexican-oriented (p. 66).

The Racial Identity Attitude Scale. The Racial Identity Attitude Scale was developed by Parham and based on Cross's model of psychological nigrescence. The instrument assesses the degree to which a participant can be identified as falling into one of four stages of nigrescence or black self-actualization: pre-encounter, encounter, immersion/emersion, and internalization.

Asian Values Scale. Mar (1988) developed an instrument, the Asian Values Scale, to assess the extent to which respondents endorse values associated with traditional Asian cultures. Marcia (1980) has also developed an identity status interview that focuses on the racial group that the participant's parents identify with, as well as trying to identify situations in which the person feels ambivalent or marginal about being Asian.

Buriel (1981, 1993a,b) has made a significant contribution by highlighting the critical role played by generation level in bicultural development in Latino children. Buriel (1993a) collected data on first-, second-, and third-generation Mexican-American children. His findings indicated that although first-generation children are the most "Mexicanized" in terms of their cultural identities, they are also the most bicultural. The investigator concluded:

the significant positive correlation between the two sets of identity ratings for first and second generation children indicates that for these Mexican American students identity with Anglo American culture tends to be greatest among those individuals having the strongest identity with their ancestral culture. . . . At least for first and second generation children whose early socialization is heavily influenced by Mexican American culture, embeddedness in the ancestral culture may provide rewarding personal experiences and feelings of self-worth and security. This in turn may encourage and facilitate explorations of new cultural avenues and the formation of a bicultural identity. [pp. 10–11]

LaFramboise and colleagues (1993) and Birman (1994) have provided useful summaries of the different models that have been used to conceptualize biculturation processes.

Acculturation

The study of the amalgamation and synthesis of values and behaviors eventually led to a focus on acculturation process. This new direction for research has proved to be somewhat confusing, and the methodology used to collect data has been problematic. Some scholars have confused acculturation with enculturation, that is, culture change has been assumed to be unidirectional, from the original mestizo culture to the mainstream white culture. Ramirez (1978) attempted to reduce the confusion by presenting two models of acculturation: one that involved unidirectional change and eventual enculturation (the conflict replacement model) and another that involved continued identity with two or more groups with which the person is identified and the integration of values and behaviors to achieve multicultural orientations to life (synthesis, unity, and expansion model).

Early measures developed to assess acculturation reflected the conflict-replacement model. The Acculturation Rating Scale for Mexican Americans (ARSMA) is an example of this type of instrument. Cuellar and colleagues (1980) developed a unidirectional instrument that over-employed attitudes and preferences for language, music, and food and that seemed to imply that the only possible cultural change for Latinos was from identification with the original mestizo culture to identification with white culture. Rogler and colleagues (1991) rightly criticized the ARSMA as being unidirectional in its orientation. Another important criticism (Felix-Ortiz et al. 1994) directed at the ARSMA and other similar instruments of acculturation focused on the fact that these instruments do not reflect biculturality and the multidimensional and multifaceted aspects characteristic of the complex phenomenon of cultural identity.

As a result of those criticisms Cuellar and colleagues (1995) developed the ARSMA-II. While the ARSMA-II is an improvement over the previous version of the instrument, its primary focus is still on attitudes and preferences for language, food, and music, to the exclusion of behavior. To these authors' credit, they have incorporated some of the items reflecting actual behavior developed by Ramirez and colleagues (Ramirez 1983, Ramirez et al. 1978a) in the Multicultural Experience Inventory.

Multicultural/Multiracial Identity

In recent years research on identity and acculturation has begun to focus on the synthesis, unity, and expansion model that evolved from a philosophy of cultural democracy. The multicultural model was based on the research on multicultural processes by Ramirez and colleagues (1977, 1978a) and by Ramirez (1994b). The Multiculturalism Experience Inventory, described in Chapter 6 and included in the Appendix, has evolved from research on multicultural identity with college students of different ethnic groups and with adults who have been exposed to the multicultural model of psychotherapy and counseling (Ramirez 1994b). The research of Phinney and Alepurea (1996) also reflects the synthesis, unity, and expansion model. These researchers have developed a Multigroup Ethnic Identity Measure for assessing ethnic identity in African Americans and Latinos.

Multiracial Identity

The focus of identity of bicultural and multicultural peoples (Hall 1992, Root 1992, 1996) led to the development of instruments that can assess identity in mixed race individuals. Hall (1992) developed the Hall Ethnic Identity Questionnaire, which taps the following dimensions: ethnic identity choice, subjective and objective cultural knowledge, racial resemblance to particular ethnic groups, and acceptance of and by particular ethnic groups.

Negy (1993) used the Family Attitude Scale (1969 version) to assess acculturation in Latino college students. His concern, like that of Felix-Ortiz and his colleagues, is that acculturation scales like the ARSMA focus too much on language, food, music, and other cultural customs, and ignore values.

Rodriguez and Ramirez (in press) are doing research with Latino college students using the revised FAS (Carrasco 1990) and the Multicultural Experience Inventory to develop a new approach for assessing acculturation. It focuses on values and behaviors, is organic, and takes into account bicultural and multicultural processes that are characteristic of contemporary and very diverse cultural milieus.

Future research should focus on the integration of multicultural and multiracial assessment instruments that can accurately reflect the increasing trend toward genetic and cultural mestizoization taking place in all parts of the world.

Importance of Political, Economic, Spiritual, and Historical Variables

In the context of the mestizo worldview, the individual develops and functions in a political, historical, economic, and religious milieu from which he/she cannot be extricated. In other words, the individual cannot be understood separate and apart from those forces that have shaped his/her lifestyle and worldview and that influence his/her present behavior and philosophy of life. As noted in Chapter 2, the Mexican philosophers and social scientists and members of the helping professions in Latin America, Canada, and the United States have recognized the important role that historical, political, economic, and religious variables play in psychodynamics.

John Dollard (1935) was one of the first social scientists in the Americas to emphasize the important and extensive role culture plays in personality development and functioning. For Dollard, culture was an all-encompassing force in the life of the individual. Of all the culture and personality studies he reviewed, only one, Thomas and Znaniecki's *Polish Peasants in Europe and America* (1927), met his strict criteria for culture personality research. With respect to Dollard's praise for the work by Thomas and Znaniecki, Sarason (1974) observed:

> Even a cursory reading of the Thomas and Znaniecki volumes, or for that matter, any good anthropological account of particular people and locale, makes clear that a community is a highly differentiated and configurated set of relationships, things, functions, and symbols, grounded in implicit and explicit traditions which in turn reflect geographic, economic, religious, political, and educational factors. Dollard is quite correct in maintaining that when psychologists and psychiatrists use such words as "milieu" or "environment" or "social factors," they recognize the inextricable relationship between culture and personality at the same time that they expose their ignorance of the dimension by which the culture becomes comprehensible. [pp. 101–102]

Focus on Religious/Spiritual Variables. One aspect of culture that most social scientists and mental health professionals have ignored has been religion. Because of the separation that occurred between science and religion in Europe (as discussed in Chapter 1), most mental health professionals influenced by the European worldview have not only ignored religion in the study of personality, but, as Sarason has observed, they have even rejected those professionals who ventured to deal with it. Sarason (1974), for example, explained how Dewey was labeled a philosopher because he focused on the influence of religion on personality development:

> Dewey was, of course, a philosopher and proudly so, but one has only to sample the corpus of his later work to recognize how much of it is directly relevant to present-day psychology's problems as a social science—the nature of inquiry, the means and end of action, and the processes of social change. Dewey created his school at the University of Chicago in 1896, a time when psychology was winning its independence from philosophy and advancing into the laboratory to study the elements of human behavior, or that of some other animal, with the methodological trappings of science. The bold, freewheeling scientific spirit became a sacrifice to the worship of false gods. It is no wonder that for decades Dewey was viewed as an erstwhile psychologist who became an educator and philosopher. [pp. 47–48]

Sarason further observed that William James was also labeled a philosopher because of his interest in religious phenomena:

To a lesser extent William James suffered a fate similar to that of Dewey, as his interests and activities took him from the psychological laboratory to such areas as pragmatism and *religious phenomena*. From the standpoint of academic psychology, he too "became" a philosopher. What did pragmatism and religious phenomena have to with psychological science? [pp. 48–49]

Fortunately, some contemporary researchers have had the courage to include the role of religion in the study of personality. The American psychiatrist Robert Coles (1975), through the use of a modified life history approach combined with the use of photographs, not only demonstrated the important role of religion in personality, but also showed that economic, political, and historical values play a central role. In his book *The Old Ones of New Mexico* (1975), he described his approach to data collection:

I have been visiting certain families, talking with them, trying to find out how they live and what they believe in. I make weekly, sometimes twice-weekly, calls, but have no standard questions in mind, no methodology to implement. I simply talk with my hosts at their leisure. Whatever comes up I am grateful to hear about. The men and women have spoken to me in both Spanish and English, often in one language for a spell, then in the other. [p. xiv]

In addition to information obtained by way of his interviews, Coles also presented photographs (taken by colleague Alex Harris) of people from the mountains of northern New Mexico, the same area in which he conducted his interviews. The contribution made by these photographs in terms of placing his subjects in an economic, historical, and religious context is best described by Coles himself:

The people he [Harris] presents here are not the people whose words I present, but they might well have been, because they are very similar in appearance and life history, and in their faith. I cannot emphasize strongly enough my gratitude to this young and dedicated photographer-colleague of mine. If I have learned a lot from listening to the people about to have their say in this book's pages, I have also learned so very much from looking at Alex Harris's photographs and talking with him about what he had seen and heard. This book is our joint effort to set down some of our observations. [p. xv]

Coles' observations emphasized the important role that photo-graphs can play in placing subjects in the broad context of their socio-cultural environment. The following quotation from Coles' interviews serves to give a flavor for the historical, political, economic, and reli-gious context in which his subjects lived:

> Sometimes after church Domingo and I walk through the cemetery. It is a lovely place, small and familiar. We pay our respects to our par-ents, to our aunts and uncles, to our children. A family is a river; some of it has passed on and more is to come, and nothing is still, because we all move along, day by day, toward our destination. We both feel joy in our hearts when we kneel on the grass before the stones and say a prayer. At the edge of the cemetery near the gate is a statue of the Virgin Mary, larger than all the other stones. She is kneeling and on her shoulder is the Cross. She is carrying it—the burden of her Son's death. She is sad, but she has not given up. We know that she has never lost faith. It is a lesson to keep in mind. [p. 50]

The following quotation, also from Coles' interviews, exemplifies the strong identification with native culture and language:

> My great-uncle was very proud of our blood; he would argue with my grandfather right in front of us, and we would sit and watch them and forget everything else—and that does not happen often with young children! My grandfather would insist that we are American, even if we speak Spanish and came originally from Spain. My great-uncle would say that nations have empires, even when they lose the land that went to make up the empire: so long as the people are scattered all over, there is the empire. "We are the Spanish empire," he would say. [p. 60]

This next excerpt from Coles' interviews describes the powerful forces of acculturation faced by the people in the mountains of New Mexico.

> You bend with the wind. And Anglo people are a strong wind. They want their own way; they can be like a tornado, out to pass over every-one as they go somewhere. I don't mean to talk out of turn. There are Anglos who don't fit my words. But we are outsiders in a land that is ours. We are part of an Anglo country and that will not change. I had to teach the facts of life to my four sons, and in doing so I learned my own lesson well. [p. 22]

Culler and Diaz-Guerrero (1982) identified certain religious persons, symbols, and activities Mexican-American and Mexican mothers and adolescents had rated as supportive (both morally and emotionally) in overcoming life crises: Our Lady of Guadalupe, Jesus Christ, religion, special saints, prayer, receiving communion, going to church, attending mass, praying the rosary, the parish priest, religious festivals, confession, and medals and scapularies. Chavez (1985) used a semi-structured life history interview to study the religious call in the context of adult development in Mexican-American Roman Catholic nuns. This approach afforded a holistic, contextual view of the relationship of cultural values to the decision to heed the call to a religious life and to personality development in the context of religious communities. More recently Castro (1996) used the FAS to study the relationship of values of religion and spirituality to utilization of mental health services and attitudes toward mental illness and mental health.

Focus on Political Variables. Two researchers from Venezuela did pioneer work with mestizos regarding the effects of political factors on personality development. Montero (1980) constructed an instrument to assess degree of political socialization in Venezuelan adolescents. Salazar (1975) assessed attitudes concerning nationalism and patriotism in Venezuelan children and their parents.

In a study that focused on the effects of social power on the behavior of Mexican-American and Anglo schoolchildren, Albert Ramirez (1977) found that the social influence of an Anglo authority figure was greater than that of a Mexican-American authority figure. The investigator concluded that the results reflect the fact that both Mexican-American and Anglo students have little exposure to Mexican Americans occupying positions of power. Gurin and Epps (1975) used in-depth interviews and a longitudinal follow-up approach to study the relationship of civil rights activism to individual and collectivistic achievement orientations among African-American students in historically black colleges. Martin-Baro (1985) proposed a theoretical orientation and methodology for social scientists who are studying political oppression in Latin America. His pro-social action research focuses on examining behavior in context and consists of three perspectives: cooperation, solidarity, and altruism.

Navarro (1995) used four research methods—in-depth interviews, documentary content analysis, participant observation, and archival research—to examine the development of the Mexican-American Youth Organization (MAYO) in Texas and to assess the critical role that this organization played in the development of the Latino Civil Rights Movement.

Focus on Economic Variables. The impact of economic factors on personality development is strongly represented in the community psychology that is evolving in Latin America. Escovar (1980) described this developmental trend as follows:

> Community psychology constitutes the last trend of Latin American social psychology. It emerges directly from the previous trend and the efforts of social psychologists to develop a discipline more consonant with economic development effects. Within this trend there are two tendencies: one that can be called Community Social Psychology and the other Community Psychology. The former comes closer to being an applied social psychology in the "community"; whereas the latter focuses on the relationship between the individual and his environment and his control or lack over contingencies to that environment. Both the emphasis on economic and political variables are evident in the definition of Community Psychology given by Montero (1980), that brand of Psychology which has as the main objective the study of those psychosocial factors important in the development and maintenance of an individual's control and power over his personal and social environment. . . . [p. 15]

The Colombian sociologist Fals Borda (1987) presented the guidelines for the development of a unique mixed-heritage methodology for studying the impact of economic variables on the development of individuals and communities in rural areas of Latin America. Participative-action research requires the researcher to become intimately involved with the community and its members and focuses on using research findings to empower participants. The best example of the methodology that Fals Borda described is provided in a social transformation project that was conducted in a rural Indian community in the state of Puebla (Almeida and Sanchez 1985). The project began with an extended dialogue between researchers and community members and evolved into regular meetings between them in which several community development projects were initiated. Salazar (1985) also developed a native methodology used to assess the relationship of self-image in Venezuelans to their willingness to purchase clothing that is locally manufactured, view films produced in the country, and listen to Venezuelan folk music.

Focus on Historical Variables. The Mexican *pensador* Samuel Ramos (1934), who was discussed in Chapter 2, concluded that the psychodynamics of self-rejection characteristic of Mexican scholars who were denying their original culture had its origins in the history of the country: in the Spanish conquest and subsequent Spanish colonization as well as the interventions of France and the United States. His methodological contribution is that he demonstrates that social scientists should be cognizant of the history of the mixed-ethnic peoples they study. This emphasis on historical forces had first been emphasized by W. E. B. DuBois (1903), who had studied the relationship of the emancipation and the post-civil rights era to the psychodynamics of African American individuals, families, and communities. Franz Fanon (1967) also highlighted the importance of the history of colonization and oppression on the psychology of colonized peoples.

Focus on Racism, Prejudice, and Discrimination

Research by Albert Ramirez (1988) has documented the impact of socialization in a culturally monolithic system (in which the most powerful positions are occupied by members of one group) has on subservient behavior as well as attitudes and beliefs of adult African-American and Latino participants. Ainslie's study (1995) of a community in Texas demonstrated that as people who have been subservient in the past become more bicultural, they affect changes in their communities that eliminate racism and prejudice. Combining psychoanalytic methods with those used by Oscar Lewis and Robert Coles, his research methodology reflects a multicultural/multiracial perspective.

In conclusion, the new methodologies and intervention approaches being developed in work with people of mixed heritage are making it possible for social scientists and members of the helping professions to be less dependent on European worldview theories, conceptual frameworks, and methodologies. Furthermore, these innovative development efforts are helping researchers to see the advantages of being multicultural and multiracial in contemporary society. Finally we are getting away from unidirectional and pathological models that force adherence to one group or to one set of values or coping techniques.

But often researchers are forced by funding agencies, colleagues who evaluate them for employment and promotion, and journal reviewers and editors to use European theories and approaches to research for studying people of mixed heritage. This is also the case when graduate students are discouraged by professors from being innovative.

ARE RESEARCH AND INTERVENTION PROJECTS CONSONANT WITH THE MULTICULTURAL/MULTIRACIAL WORLDVIEW?

Warning: This psychology could be damaging to your self-esteem and to the well-being of all culturally/racially different peoples. At present, European-influenced psychology, with its emphasis on the laboratory method, and control and manipulation of variables, and its beliefs in universal concepts, theories, and instruments for collecting data, has a powerful hold on training programs in the helping professions and the social sciences in general. In addition, European worldview perspectives are supported by the members of editorial boards of major journals and publishers of textbooks and monographs, reviewers of proposals, decision makers in funding agencies, and the majority of professors in graduate programs. Quite often, the innovative ideas of researchers and program developers, vis-à-vis the tenets of the mestizo worldview are discouraged or criticized by the European worldview–based establishment in the social sciences. Even the views of some of the leading scholars in cross-cultural research can be misleading. The philosophical position of some of these scholars often appears to be supportive of the tenets of mestizo psychology; however, their methodology, choice of instruments, and their theoretical orientations frequently fall short. As Koivukari (1977) pointed out, what appears to be emic is often merely European etic in disguise. For example, Marin and Marin (1991) authored a book that provided suggestions for conducting research with Latino populations. The authors presented much needed suggestions for recruitment and identification of participants, recognizing intracultural diversity, for assessing willingness of participants to be involved in research; for translation of instruments; and for cultural immersion of researchers. Unfortunately, the book overlooked the importance of a mestizo perspective: the concepts of biculturalism/multiculturalism and multiraciality are not mentioned. In addition, the authors overlooked the critical need to be aware of potential investigator bias that can influence development of hypotheses, choice of theories and conceptual frameworks, research methodology, instruments for collecting data, and ways in which data are interpreted. Readers of Marin and Marin's book could mistakenly conclude that the European worldview is applicable to people of mixed heritage. Thus, this book can be properly classified as having a strong etic bias and as promoting a pseudo-emic approach.

Research methodology that is more consonant with a mixed heritage/mestizo worldview can be found in a chapter authored by Root (1992). Her recommendation was applicable to research with multicultural and multiracial peoples. She observed, "The sociopolitical context of multiraciality must be taken into consideration in designing a study, recruiting subjects, selecting and training researchers, and interpreting results" (p. 189). Vega (1992) also offered some very useful recommendations for conducting applied research with participants of diverse cultural backgrounds. These included evaluating cultural appropriateness of theoretical premises and hypotheses, field testing instruments to be used with several cultural groups, and sharing research findings with members of communities in which the data were collected. A recent paper authored by Castro and Ramirez (1996) also provides useful directions for research on sociocultural and environmental processes that reflect the mestizo worldview.

The literature reviewed above highlights the fact that we need a set of guidelines that can be followed when planning research or intervention with people of mixed heritage. Researchers and interventionists, scholars and change agents need to focus on certain critical questions that can help them determine if any study, program, published research, or intervention effort meets the standards of mestizo multicultural/multiracial worldviews:

1. Is the theoretical or conceptual framework being used by the researcher or intervenor consonant with the worldview of mixed heritage/mestizo subjects or clients? That is, does the theoretical/conceptual framework on which the study or intervention

is based reflect some of the tenets of the mixed heritage/mestizo worldview? For example, a cursory examination of the psychoanalytic perspective used by Fromm and Maccoby (1970) reveals its inappropriateness for mestizo subjects and communities; the assumption of European cultural superiority is evident. In light of the foregoing questions, the theory of psychological differentiation is also inappropriate for mestizos because this model assumes that people of traditional cultures are psychologically unsophisticated and underdeveloped.

2. Is the research methodology consonant with the culture and worldview of mixed heritage/mestizo subjects? To answer this question it is necessary to focus on several issues:

- *Selection of participants.* Does the procedure for selection of participants reflect the fact that there is great intercultural and intracultural variability among people of mixed heritage? It is not enough to classify participants as Mexican American, Native American, African American, Asian American, African Latino, or African white. Selection procedures also need to recognize the salience of generational status, gender, region of origin, phenotype, degree of multiculturalism or multiraciality, and socioeconomic status in populations involved in the research or intervention project. How does the researcher(s) or project developer(s) define and determine race, ethnicity, and culture? Did the researcher(s) take into account "theoretical sampling" (Ponterotto and Casas 1991) in which the number of subjects is not as important as what each participant contributes to understanding?

- *Group comparisons.* If groups were compared, were the samples comparable? As Campbell (1961, Campbell and Naroll 1972) noted, because of differences in living conditions, education, and socioeconomic class, it is virtually impossible to obtain samples from more than one society that are truly comparable.

- *Characteristics of instruments used for collecting the data.* Were the instruments used merely translations of instruments, techniques, and tests developed in another culture or for a non-mixed heritage/mestizo group? Are the content and structure of the instruments consonant with the tenets of the mixed heritage/mestizo worldview and with mixed heritage/mestizo psychodynamics? Are the demands that the instruments make of the subjects appropriate to their roles in the context of their cultures (i.e., many mixed heritage/mestizo adults with traditional orientations view instruments such as the Draw-a-Person Test, the Embedded Figures Test, and the Semantic Differential as childlike, meaningless tasks)?

- *Methodology used.* Was there use of multiple methods and measures? Were qualitative and quantitative designs combined? (Fielding and Fielding 1986)

3. Were the data collected in historical, social, economic, political, cultural, and religious context?
4. Were interpretations of the data made in historical, social, economic, political, cultural, and religious context? As was discussed in Chapter 3, some of the works of Oscar Lewis (1961, 1965) interpreted the data in the context of psychoanalytic theory and largely ignored the sociocultural contest in which they were collected. Segall's (1996) criticism of Triandis's concept of individualism and collectivism also shows how a holistic approach is often overlooked by researchers and interventionists: "The concepts seem to have such powerful heuristic value that some may be tempted to use them carelessly, to explain any difference that is noted to exist between groups that are labeled individualist or collectivistic, as if that is what they really are and as if all the other things are do not matter as much" (p. 542).

- Did the researcher(s) or interventionist(s) do a self-assessment for determination of possible bias? Ramirez (1994b) suggested an approach for self assessment for therapists that could also be applicable for researchers and interventionists. Root (1992) posited an important question when she asks readers of publications to ask: Who does the research? (p. 188).
- Selection of statistical procedures for data analysis. Was there use of path analysis and multiple regression techniques that are more representative of the holistic nature of the mixed heritage/mestizo perspective?

Table 5–2 provides a set of considerations (related to the mestizo appraisal standards presented above) that can be used to evaluate the

Table 5–2. How Well Does the Study or Program Focus on the Mestizo Populations?

Evaluate each of the following standards on a scale of 1 (not at all characteristic) to 5 (very characteristic)

Theory or conceptual framework
1. The theory or conceptual framework does not reflect notions of superiority in regards to culture, race, gender, genetics, physical disabilities, or sexual orientation.
2. The theory or conceptual framework emerged from the native culture or value system of the people who are being studied or on which the program is being implemented.

Participants
3. The participants reflect the intracultural diversity of the groups that are the object of the research or intervention.
4. SES, linguistic, generational status, multiracial/multicultural variables were considered in the selection of participants.
5. Groups being compared are comparable (SES, generational, and education levels are common confounds).

Instruments and Intervention Procedures
6. The content of the instrument is reflective of the mestizo multicultural/multiracial worldview.
7. The structure of the instrument is reflective of the mestizo view.
8. The demands of the instruments or procedures of the intervention made on the participants are consistent with the mestizo worldview.
9. The instruments and the procedures reflect approaches that are part of the native culture(s), for example, story telling, life histories, respect for nature, spirituality, and a sense of community and humanity.

Methodology
10. Employs multiple methods and multiple measures.
11. Uses qualitative as well as quantitative methodology.

Data Collection
12. Data are collected without deceiving, demeaning, or embarrassing participants.
13. Data collection uses participant observation and/or approaches that are potentially beneficial (empowering) to the participant (Almeida et al. 1983).
14. Data are interpreted in the context of historical, political, religious, economic, and social perspectives.

Data Analysis
15. Statistical procedures used allow findings to be placed in the context of historical, political, religious, economic, and social perspectives.

Researchers/Intervenors
16. The researchers/intervenors conduct self-analysis to determine the degree of similarity or difference between their values and worldviews and those of the participants or persons on which intervention plan is being implemented.

design, methodology and philosophical underpinnings of studies and programs that focus on mestizo populations.

We must be cognizant of the fact that most of the research methods, instruments, techniques, theories, and conceptual frameworks of the mental health professions and the social sciences are biased toward the European worldview. We should also recognize that most training programs for social scientists and mental health practitioners are based on the tenets of the European worldview as described in Chapter 1. In particular we must be cautious of European etic disguised as emic. Although several cross-cultural researchers reflect the mestizo worldview in their rhetoric, their bias toward the European worldview is evident in their choice of methodology and instruments. Some years ago, Price-Williams (1975) provided a warning that we would all do well to consider in evaluating our own work as well as that of others: "Our own categories of explanation and definition, embedded in our psychological theories, may not be appropriate when projected on some other culture" (p. 23).

SUMMARY

The choice of theories, conceptual frameworks, research methodologies, and instruments for collecting data and for providing services in intervention programs with mixed heritage peoples is critical to our understanding of the world around us and to our future as a diverse nation and world. It is important to recognize that the European worldview dominates most of the thinking, training programs, publication outlets, funding agencies, and research and intervention technologies of the social sciences and helping professions throughout much of the world. European approaches to research and intervention have produced a distorted, incomplete, and inaccurate picture of people of mixed heritage, of their communities, and of their cultures. We must be wary of etic disguised as emic: paternalistic perspectives and attitudes of cultural superiority have no place in cross-cultural research and intervention programs.

❖ 6 ❖

Coping with Diversity in the Global Community

As scientists we become so involved with our methodology that we perceive the world through one pair of methodological spectacles without even being aware that we are doing so.

—John W. Osborne (1982)

As psychology continues to move from culturally monolithic to culturally pluralistic approaches to investigate prejudice, racism, and discrimination, it may serve as a model and as an influencing force in converting our society from a culturally monolithic system to a culturally pluralistic one—a society in which prejudice, racism, and discrimination will no longer serve as the dominant factor governing interracial group relations in this country.

—Albert Ramirez (1988)

The most important thing we must do is to change our attitudes and our cosmo/vision in a way that will allow each of us to become interested in others. We need to acknowledge that we can learn much from other cultures and consider that we share the same planetary habitat. . . . When this planetary conception is accepted by psychologists the barriers that exist for integrating the psychologies of the First, Second and Third Worlds will finally be overcome. This will benefit all of us.

—Ruben Ardila (1993)

Problems related to diversity are undermining the goal that the world can eventually become a global community in which nations and peoples can live in peace, learn from each other, and cooperate to build a better world for all concerned. This chapter focuses on the need to integrate the mestizo multicultural/multiracial and European approaches and methodologies for the purpose of understanding and resolving problems related to diversity. In particular, this chapter concentrates on the psychodynamics of being multiracial and multicultural—the worldview, skills, and leadership abilities of those persons who can help a divided world grow to be a true global village.

NATURAL SCIENCE VS.
PHENOMENOLOGICAL APPROACHES

Throughout much of its history, psychology has been struggling with controversies over the nature of the research methodology and the philosophy of science that it should adopt. On one side are those who would like to see the discipline modeled after the natural sciences; on the other are those who claim that the unique nature of the phenomena studied by psychologists demands an equally unique methodology and philosophy of science. A controversy between Professors Greeno and Osborne, which surfaced in the *American Psychologist* (1982), indicated the depth of feeling associated with this issue. In a critique of a literature review on learning by Greeno, Osborne observed:

> Cognitive psychologists such as Greeno tend to conceptualize learning in terms of cognitive processes that result in overt behaviors, but humanistic psychologists conceptualize learning as a complex of organismic processes producing a change in worldview, which leads to changes in overt behavior. . . . This approach to learning ties it to the learner's way of life as it embodies his or her philosophical and religious values and life experiences. . . . There is an urgent need to keep in touch with the fullness of human nature and not become so involved with one scientific perspective, natural science, that the real-life world of human beings becomes the natural scientific world. [p. 33]

Greeno countered Osborne's comments with the following observations:

> Cognitive psychology is "guilty as charged" of adopting an approach more consistent with natural science, in which the individual and the environment are viewed from a perspective external to both and the characteristics of cognition and experience are understood to be the outcome of an interaction of the individual's mind and the situation. Phenomenologists, in contrast, consider the central problem of psychology to be understanding how individuals construct meaning for situations. Historically, sciences have progressed significantly by overcoming egocentrism of that kind, although it has been defended on ideological grounds from the Ptolemaicists in astronomy to the vitalists in biology and now by the phenomenologists in psychology. History has repeatedly shown that approach to be unproductive. [p. 333]

From the discussion in the preceding chapters, it could be concluded that the controversy between the European and mestizo, multicultural/multiracial worldviews in the social sciences and mental health professions is similar to that between the natural science and phenomenological approaches to research reflected in the dialogue between Greeno and Osborne. Another conclusion that can be drawn from discussions in the preceding chapters is that the multicultural/multiracial orientation of mestizos in the Americas embodies an amalgamation of the Native American and Afro-centric perspectives on the one hand and the European worldview on the other. Thus, both the European/multicultural/multiracial and natural science–phenomenology controversies are central to the study of multicultural/multiracial people in the Americas and the world. That is, multicultural/multiracial processes represent a combination of personality characteristics, thinking styles, and orientations to life that reflect both the European and mestizo worldviews, as well as the natural science and phenomenological perspectives on the study of psychological phenomena. To properly understand and conceptualize multicultural/multiracial processes, then, what is required are research perspectives and methodologies that are representative of both the European and mestizo worldviews. Neither a predominant natural science nor a phenomenological perspective will suffice. What is required is a combination of the two approaches, a perspective reminiscent of the dualistic philosophy of Antonio Caso (1943a) discussed in Chapter 3. As the reader will recall, Caso argued that in order to understand the reality of Mexico and its mestizo peoples, the approaches and perspectives of both science and metaphysics are required. What is needed in psychology, then, is an acceptance of the philosophical perspectives presented by Caso, as characterized by his observation that reason and intuition complement each other in the pursuit of knowledge. In addition, the helping professions also need to recognize the importance of multicultural/multiracial processes in personality development and functioning. Mental health professionals must acknowledge that multicultural/multiracial people are living proof that the natural science and the phenomenological, the mestizo and the European, can be brought together in harmony. Thus, to truly understand the phenomenon of pluralism and diversity in the Americas and the world, we need to integrate and amalgamate what has for too long been perceived as distinct.

DIVERSITY AND THE WORLD COMMUNITY

Diversity represents both the greatest blessing and the greatest challenge for humanity. The challenge is reflected in the emotion surrounding the vote for secession of Quebec from Canada, the ethnic conflicts in the former nations that were part of the Soviet Union, the conflicts in nations of post-colonial Africa, the violence in Bosnia, and the continuing conflicts in the Middle East and Ireland. In the United States, diversity continues to be a challenge to understanding and cooperation as ethnic/racial minorities continue to seek equality of opportunity and justice in a time of retrenchment in civil rights legislation and affirmative action programs. Women continue to seek equality in salaries, the opportunity to work and be educated in traditional male jobs and institutions, and the right to decide if they will carry a pregnancy to term. Lesbians and gays seek the right to marry and the right to have same-gender partnerships recognized for the purpose of insurance coverage and retirement. People with disabilities seek equal access to public services as well as equal opportunities in employment and education. Diversity, then, is at the core of some of the most serious problems affecting social, economic, and political stability in many of the nations of the world. Diversity is crucial to the survival of an effective United Nations and to the efforts toward world peace. One of the greatest dangers is that leaders, policy makers, and the body politic will conclude that diversity is incompatible with democracy.

For example, American sociologist Lance Morrow ("A Cry for Leadership" 1979), commenting on the crisis of leadership in the United States, observed that democracy and leadership are incompatible and that the nation's plural interests threaten to turn our country into a set of internal Balkan states, into hostile tribes. Bernstein (1994b) wrote a book that is sharply critical of multiculturalism and that concludes that this is a divisive concept. Lind (1995) also argued that multiculturalism is a barrier to the development of the United States as a true nation-state. The diversity fear-mongers have made their presence felt in the passage of Proposition 187 in California that limits the provision of education and social services to immigrants, and in recent efforts in Congress to limit immigration and to make English the official language of the country. Observations such as these could result in disastrous consequences: leaders of countries in the

Americas may come to conclude that the only answer to problems created by diversity lies in establishment of monocultural/monolingual, totalitarian forms of government. But how can this unacceptable conclusion be circumvented? How can problems of diversity be understood and conceptualized? How can leaders who are sensitive to diversity and effective at leading diverse groups be identified and trained?

The dynamics of multicultural/multiracial perspective embody solutions that are potentially important to controversies of scientific methodology in psychology and to those concerning political problems facing many of the nations of the world. The multicultural/multiracial perspective is the alternative to political totalitarianism. Multicultural/multiracial orientations to life reflect thinking styles, attitudes, and political solutions that represent more than one way of approaching reality, more than one approach to the solution of problems.

UNDERSTANDING THE PSYCHODYNAMICS OF MULTICULTURAL/MULTIRACIAL LEADERS

The study of multicultural/multiracial orientations of life requires a multiplicity of research approaches and methodologies. In no other area of study is the issue of diversity of research approaches and perspectives more critically important than in the study of leadership in mixed groups under conditions of conflict. The project to be described below summarizes four years of research on young multicultural/multiracial adults; the focus was on the relationship between pluralistic identity and flexibility in leadership behavior. The research methodology used represents an integration of mestizo and European worldview perspectives. It combined ethnographic, life history, and laboratory methods in the research design. Although the study was primarily focused on some of the ethnic groups of the Americas, the methodology and the conclusions drawn from the findings are applicable to other groups in the world. What follows are the principal questions addressed by the researchers during the various phases of development of the project and also a presentation of the research procedures and findings related to each of the questions posed.

How can people with multicultural orientations to life be identified? Some of the early speculation and research on multicultural/

multiracial identity development led to the conclusion that it was difficult, if not impossible, for people to develop pluralistic identities. For example, Stonequist (1964) referred to members of minority groups as "marginal," conceiving of the marginal man as "poised in psychological uncertainty between two (or more) social worlds, reflecting in his soul the discords and harmonies, repulsions and attractions of those worlds" (p. 329). According to Stonequist, the "lifecycle" of marginal men followed three stages: (1) positive feelings toward the host culture; (2) conscious experience of conflict; and (3) responses to the conflict that may be prolonged and more or less successful in terms of adjustment. Furthermore, the third stage may encourage the individual to adopt one of three roles: (a) nationalism—a collective movement to raise the group's status; (b) intermediation—promoting cultural accommodation; and (c) assimilation. Stonequist noted the possibility that some of these conditions might result in creativity, citing the case of the Jewish people, but, for the most part, his model focused on conflict and implied that the only "healthy" resolution was assimilation into the dominant culture.

Irvin Child's research (1943) with young male second-generation Italian Americans in New Haven, Connecticut, also led him to conclude that there were three types of reactions indicative of identity development in bicultural situations: (1) the rebel reaction—desire to achieve complete acceptance by the American majority group and to reject the Italian culture and associations; (2) the in-group reaction—the desire to actively participate in and identify with the Italian group while rejecting American society; and (3) the apathetic reaction—a retreat from conflict situations and avoidance of strong "rebel" or "in-group" identities. This apathetic reaction, according to Child, could be observed in individuals making a partial approach toward both cultures in an effort to find a compromise or combination as a solution to the conflict.

Madsen, in explaining the behavior of young adult Mexican Americans living in multicultural environments, subscribed to a conflict model similar to that used by Child. In his article entitled "The Alcoholic Agringado" (1964), Madsen described the traumas of cultural transfer experienced by Mexican-American males. Madsen depicted the Mexican American as standing alone between two conflicting cultural worlds and resorting to alcohol for anxiety relief. Research by anthropologist Celia Heller with Mexican-American adolescents

(1968) also concluded that these young people were limited to two monocultural choices leading either to complete identity with Mexican-American culture (which she believed resulted in delinquency) or to assimilated Anglo-American lifestyles (which, in her view, led to educational and economic success). Ramirez conducted intensive interviews with Mexican-American adolescents. His findings (1969) showed that while some Mexican-American youth experienced problems of identity, many young people in Texas and California functioned effectively in Anglo- and Mexican-American cultures and had established multicultural/multiracial identities with minimum conflict and problems of adjustment. McFee (1968) also identified bicultural orientations to life among some members of the Blackfeet Indian tribe living in bicultural reservation communities in the United States. McFee emphasized the relationship of the situational context to the development and expression of flexibility and adaptability of behavior. He hypothesized that in the course of tribal acculturation in bicultural reservation communities, a bicultural social structure that provides both cultural models (mainstream white American and Native American) is established. Thus, McFee labeled the bicultural person he had identified through his research as the "150 percent man."

Valentine's research (1971) with urban African-American youth in the United States also identified participants with bicultural orientations to life. Valentine focused on the behavioral flexibility evident in the people he observed:

> The collective behavior and social life of the black community is bicultural in the sense that each Afro-American ethnic segment draws upon a distinctive repertoire of standardized Afro-American behavior and, simultaneously, patterns derived from mainstream cultural systems of Euro-American derivation. [p. 143]

Research by Ramirez and Castañeda (1974) with Mexican-American and Anglo-American elementary school children who exhibited multicultural orientations to life indicated that these children could perform effectively and comfortably in both cultures and that they had established close friendships with peers of several groups. These children also exhibited considerable flexibility in their classroom behavior, performing effectively in situations and tasks demanding the use of widely different skills and problem-solving styles. These observations led the investigators to conclude that multicultural/multiracial children were bicognitive or cognitively flexible and that this flexibility had developed as a result of socialization in two or more cultures.

Combining the findings of their research with those obtained by McFee and Valentine, Ramirez and Castañeda (1974) arrived at a definition of multicultural/multiracial orientation to life that could be used in efforts to identify subjects with pluralistic orientations to life:

> A bicultural/multicultural person has had extensive socialization and life experiences in two or more cultures and participates actively in these cultures. That is, his/her day-to-day behaviors show active participation in two or more cultures and extensive interaction with members of these sociocultural groups. In addition, the behavior of the bicultural/multicultural person is flexible in the sense that he/she uses different problem solving, coping, human relational, communication, and incentive-motivational styles. In line with the aforementioned skills, the bicultural/multicultural person is adaptable in behavior, being able to make adjustments to a variety of different environments and life demands. [pp. 98–99]

The investigators (Ramirez et al. 1977, 1978a) presented this definition to two professors, two counselors, and two students who were all well acquainted with the majority of Latino students on the campus of a public university located on the west coast of the United States. Based on the definition provided, each judge was asked to identify four students who were high on multiculturalism and four whom they judged to have a monocultural orientation to life. The investigators selected eight (four high and four low) of these students who had been identified in the lists of at least four of the judges for further study. They conducted intensive interviews (from four to six hours) with these eight participants.

In addition to the interviews, the investigators observed the eight participants unobtrusively over a period of a week, recording their behaviors in detail as they participated in class and campus activities. The information from the interviews and observations generated a pool of items that was combined with items derived from earlier investigations as well as with items from related instruments (Ramirez 1967, Teske and Nelson 1973). This resulted in two questionnaires:

the Bicognitive Orientation to Life Scale (BOLS) and the Multi-culturalism Experience Inventory (MEI). The questionnaires were assembled, pilot-tested, reviewed by external consultants, and revised, and the same procedure was repeated three times. The resulting questionnaire for assessing multicultural experience consisted of three parts: demographic-linguistic information, personal history, and bicultural/multicultural behavior. Among the dimensions included in the latter two areas were socialization and educational experiences, interpersonal interactions, and experiences in situations related to school, political, athletic, religious, family, and recreational spheres. The following sample items were taken from each of the three parts of the questionnaire:

1. Demographic-Linguistic Information (check one)
   What was the approximate ethnic composition of the high school you attended?
   • all Latinos
   • mostly Latinos
   • Latinos and Anglos, about evenly
   • mostly Anglos
   • all Anglos
2. Personal History
   In high school my close friends were
   • all Latinos
   • mostly Latinos
   • Latinos and Anglos, about evenly
   • mostly Anglos
   • all Anglos
3. Multicultural Participation
   When I discuss personal problems or issues, I discuss them with
   • only Latinos
   • mostly Latinos
   • Latinos and Anglos, about evenly
   • mostly Anglos
   • only Anglos

(The complete Multiculturalism Experience Inventory [MEI], together with instructions for scoring, can be found in the Appendix.)

The Bicognitive Orientation to Life Scale (BOLS) was developed to provide an indication of personality flexibility. It asked respondents to register their concurrence or disagreement with statements indicative of either a field-sensitive (FS) or field-independent (FI) orientation to life. Field-sensitive (FS) individuals are more influenced by, or more sensitive to, the human element in the environment. On the other hand, field-independent (FI) individuals have an advantage in life situations that are more impersonal. They are more able to isolate parts from the whole and are less constricted by conventional uses of objects and materials. Characteristics that differentiate between FS and FI individuals, then, are those that reflect preferred modes of relating to, classifying, assimilating, and organizing the environment. Scale items express a field-sensitive orientation in the areas of interpersonal relationships, leadership style, learning style, attitudes toward authority, and interest in science versus interest in the humanities.

Corresponding items express a field-independent (FI) and a field-sensitive (FS) orientation in the same areas of behavior. The following are examples of FS and FI items: FS—I have always done well in subjects like history or psychology. FI—I have always done well in math and science courses.

Participants were asked to indicate their degree of agreement with each statement on a four-point Likert scale. Upon completion the twenty-four statements were scored on a scale from one to four with higher scores being indicative of greater concurrence with the statement. A separate field-sensitive and field-independent score was obtained by summing across the appropriate item clusters. A "bicognitive" score was derived by summing across both field-sensitive and field-independent scales. Participants who were identified as multicultural were those who obtained a high bicognitive score on the BOLS and who scored high on multiculturalism experience on the MEI. A bicultural/multicultural index was obtained for each participant by combining his/her BOLS and MEI scores.

Ramirez and colleagues (1977, 1978a) administered the BOLS and MEI to 1,046 participants with Spanish surnames in colleges and universities throughout Texas and California. From this population the researchers selected a sample of 129 participants for the next phase of their study in which they determined how bicultural/multicultural orientations to life develop.

In order to answer the second question, the investigators developed a semi-structured life history procedure, which they entitled Psychohistory Schedule for Assessing Multiculturalism (PSAM). The interviews ranged from an hour and fifteen minutes to an hour and thirty minutes and focused on five different life periods: preschool, elementary school, middle school, high school, and college. Questions centered around the following themes: language learning and usage; family and community life; school experiences; identity conflicts; perceived advantages and disadvantages of Anglo, Mexican-American, and other cultures; degree of comfort experienced while participating in Anglo, Mexican, Mexican-American, and other cultures; preference for ethnic background of marriage partner; importance of passing on cultural heritage to children; philosophy of life; career goals; and contemporary multicultural identity. The scoring system developed for the PSAM is described in Chapter 5.

Examination of the data from the interviews revealed five historical development patterns (HDPs) or paths of development of multicultural orientations to life and several variations within each of these. The 129 participants varied considerably in terms of their HDPs as reflected by the content of their life histories, as summarized in Table 6–1.

Table 6–1. Historical Development Patterns (HDPs)

N	Patterns	Defining Characteristics
18	Parallel	Extensive and continuous exposure to Latino culture (or to Latino and other minority group cultures) and mainstream culture beginning in the preschool period and continuing for at least two more life periods
73	Early Latino/gradual mainstream	Extensive, almost total exposure to Latino culture (or to a Latino culture and other minority group cultures) throughout most life periods with gradually increasing exposure to mainstream culture with increasing age
23	Early Latino/abrupt mainstream	Extensive, almost total exposure to Latino culture (or to Latino cultures and other minority group cultures) in the first two or three periods of life followed by sudden immersion to mainstream culture
11	Early mainstream/gradual Latino	Reverse of early Latino/gradual mainstream
4	Early mainstream/abrupt Latino	Reverse of early Latino/abrupt mainstream

LIFE HISTORIES

Parallel Histories

"Parallel" describes persons whose lives as children and adolescents were influenced by equally frequent and equally extensive associations with Latino (or a combination of Latino with other minority group cultures) and with mainstream United States culture.

Paula H. and her family were farm laborers in the fields of the Central Valley in California and during the years of Paula's childhood and adolescence, her family moved several times in and around the Fresno area. The neighborhoods she lived in and the schools she attended brought her into extensive contact with mainstream Anglo-American and Mexican-American children. Paula formed close friendships with peers from both cultures and visited frequently in the homes of both groups, where she interacted extensively with their parents and siblings. Paula's parents spoke Spanish at home, and she would speak Spanish with them, although she spoke to her siblings in English. Her parents had close friendships with both Anglo and Mexican-American adults. In jobs that Paula held as an adolescent and young adult, she was supervised by both Anglo and Mexican-American adults; her co-workers were members of both the Anglo and Mexican-American groups. Before she went to college most of her teachers were Anglo, but she established a close friendship with a Mexican-American woman who was her basketball coach and Spanish teacher in high school. In college, Paula maintained close friendships with Anglo and Mexican-American students, and she participated extensively in activities sponsored by both groups. She dated both Mexican- and Anglo-American men, and she belonged to clubs in which the memberships were predominantly either Mexican-American or Anglo.

Nick S. was born and reared in Phoenix, Arizona. His mother is Anglo (mainstream American) and his father is a member of a Hispanic-American family who settled in New Mexico in the seventeenth century. Nick has been close to both his father's and his mother's families (both of whom live in the Phoenix area) throughout his life; he has been conscious of his dual ethnic origins since early childhood. Although the members of his mother's and father's families differ extensively from each other in terms of language, values, and lifestyle,

Nick has always enjoyed shuttling between these two worlds, and he has become fluently bilingual in the process. His first experience with ethnic barriers took place in middle school. At the time, he was initially shunned by traditional Mexican-American students, who felt that Nick was a traitor to their group because of his close friendships with Anglo peers. His rejection by traditional Mexican Americans was short-lived, however, because Nick never ceased to try to befriend the members of this group. The experience which finally earned his complete acceptance by traditional Mexican Americans occurred midway through his first year of middle school. At the time, Nick averted a major "rumble" between Anglos, Native Americans, African Americans, and Mexican Americans by serving as a mediator between them and by dispelling rumors. Nick was perceived as fair and impartial by all groups, and he managed to pull the student body of his school together by forming a United Nations club on campus. He held several positions of leadership, serving as a class officer throughout his high school years. In college, Nick was highly respected by Mexican Americans, Native Americans, Anglos, and African Americans. He chaired several committees in student government and served as an effective spokesperson when students had complaints to present to the faculty and administration. The following excerpts from his life history testify to Nick's pluralistic philosophy of life:

> I find that all cultures, groups, and individuals have something unique and genuine to offer to me. I have learned that if I really listen, everyone is trying to teach me something that I should know about myself. I don't think I shall ever stop learning although there have been several times in my life when I have thought that nothing will ever surprise me or challenge me again, but, sure enough, I meet someone new or I visit a new city or a country I have never been to before and new doors open up in my mind.

Early Latino/Abrupt Mainstream

The early Latino/abrupt mainstream category was typical of persons who experienced nearly exclusive associations or functioning in Latino culture early in life and who were later thrust into extensive contact with Anglo mainstream culture.

Ricardo S. was born in Mexico, and his family moved to El Paso when he was five years old. Initially, the family lived in a tenement located in a section of town where everyone was of Mexican descent. He spoke Spanish exclusively both at home and in the neighborhood; he had no associations with Anglos during his first three years in the United States. When he was eight years old, his parents moved to a small town in Indiana where they were the only Mexican-American family. Initially, Ricardo felt lost and alienated, but he gradually mastered English and eventually gained popularity with his peers in school and in the neighborhood. At home, his parents would speak to the children in Spanish, but Ricardo and his siblings started to speak English exclusively once they had learned the language. After graduating from high school, Ricardo went to live with his uncle and aunt in El Paso and attended the University of Texas at El Paso. Initially, the move from Indiana to Texas was a shock: once again he felt alienated and lonely. After his first year in college, he decided to go to a Spanish-language institute in Mexico City; this experience had a profound effect on his life. He returned from Mexico speaking fluent Spanish and deeply interested in Mexican culture; this, in turn, led to his decision to study archaeology. Upon his return, he established close friendships with Mexican, Mexican-American, and Anglo students. He assumed the role of mediator and spokesperson for Mexican American students on campus, often negotiating their demands with members of the university administration.

Early Latino/Gradual Mainstream

The early Latino/gradual mainstream pattern describes the lifestyles of persons who experienced early familiarity with Latino culture and gradually gained increasing exposure to mainstream culture.

Robert M. was born in the United States in a small town situated in the Rio Grande Valley of Texas. In the years prior to his going to school, he rarely interacted with Anglo peers or adults. Robert spoke Spanish exclusively. His only exposure to English prior to attending school was through television, books, and magazines. The school he attended for the first two years had an all Mexican-American student body, but the teaching staff was made up of both Anglo and Mexican Americans. His first sustained exposure to Anglo adults was in the first grade, where his teacher was Anglo. Prior to starting the third grade, Robert's parents purchased a home in a neighborhood which was made up of both Anglo and Mexican-American families; his first sustained exposure to Anglo peers was in the new neighborhood. He gradually developed close friendships with Anglo peers and in late elementary school and middle school, he started visiting extensively in the homes of Anglo friends. While he became better acquainted with Anglo culture, he continued to maintain close friendships with Mexican-American peers and adults. This pattern of interaction with both groups continued into his college years.

Early Latino Native American/Gradual Mainstream

Richard Z. was born in a Native American Indian pueblo near Albuquerque, New Mexico. His father is a Latino and his mother is Hopi. During most of his childhood and early adolescence, Richard was steeped in both Latino and Hopi cultures. His grandfather was a medicine man in the pueblo, and Richard, who was close to him, learned about healing in the Indian tradition. His early years in school were spent in the company of Latinos and Indians. He was gradually introduced to mainstream culture through television, movies, and books, and by his acquaintances with Anglo teachers. He gradually came to meet more Anglo friends in his middle school years and developed many friendships with Anglos in his high school years. He was particularly fond of his track coach, who was biracial Anglo-Cherokee; it was this man who helped him to overcome a distrust that he had always had toward Anglo adults. In college, Richard was deeply involved in activities—both academic and social—with Latinos, African Americans, American Indians, Asian Americans, and mainstream Americans. He was a student assistant in the financial aid office and was well known among the students for his sincere concern and empathy for all students experiencing economic crises. His philosophy of life, as stated in his interview, reflects his multiculturalism:

> I can truly say that I am now able to look at the uniqueness of the persons who I meet and not get hung up on superficial things like physical appearance, accent, clothing, etc. This was a real challenge to me, because of my initial distrust of white people and because I had

never been around many blacks. I feel that I am now able to make a special effort to find out who the people I interact with really are, who they really are behind the masks that we all use. I also want to know how they have overcome obstacles in their lives. To me that's what its all about—meeting the challenges of life and learning from them.

Early Mainstream/Abrupt Latino

Persons categorized under the early mainstream/abrupt Latino pattern had almost exclusive contact with Anglo culture during the first few years of their lives and then experienced sudden emersion in Latino culture.

Maria J. was born in a small town in Iowa, and her nuclear family and a few relatives were the only Mexican-American residents of the town. Her parents and siblings rarely spoke Spanish, but about twice a year they would journey to a town in another part of the state where a number of Mexican-American families would get together for a day-long reunion. At these gatherings, she heard adults speaking Spanish and telling stories about Mexico and the southwestern United States. Throughout elementary and middle school, all of Maria's close friends were Anglos, and, other than her parents and some relatives, she did not have very much experience interacting with Mexican-American adults. Prior to the start of her first year in high school, Maria's family moved to a small town on the central coast of California. Maria experienced a shock because at her new the school, it was rare for Anglos and Mexican Americans to interact. In fact, it was not uncommon for the two groups to exchange insults and to engage in fights. The Mexican Americans rejected her because she did not speak Spanish; the Anglos would not accept her because she was Mexican-American. Initially, she joined a group of rebels whose members came from both groups. Gradually, by her persistence and her ability to make friends with administrators and faculty, she gained the respect of both Anglos and Mexican Americans. In her junior year, she was elected to a position on the student council and in her senior year became class president. While in college, she continued to hold positions of leadership and responsibility and often mediated between Mexican-American and Anglo groups, preventing conflict between them.

Early Mainstream/Gradual Latino

Early mainstream/gradual Latino describes a developmental trend in which the person's early life involves exclusive contact with Anglo culture followed by a gradual introduction to Latino culture.

James S. was born in an all-Anglo suburb of Houston, Texas. His parents spoke English at home; for the first six years of his life, James had no contact with Mexican-American peers or authority figures beyond his immediate family. His first exposure to Mexican-American peers was in his first year of elementary school, where he became acquainted with the few Latinos who attended his school. His contact with Mexican Americans increased in middle school and high school. He formed close friendships with Mexican-American teachers during this time. James was well accepted by both Mexican-American and Anglo groups in his last two years of high school, holding several positions of leadership in high school. He continued to be a leader in college.

The data collected through the life history interviews revealed that the identities of participants ranged from almost exclusively Latino or mainstream Anglo to indications of a strong identity with both cultural groups and, on occasion, with other groups as well. Several components emerged as important determinants of the contemporary multicultural identity (CMIs) of the participants: functionalism, commitment, and transcendence.

Fitzgerald's (1971) description of the bicultural behavior of Maori university graduates in New Zealand provided examples of functional behavior. He described his subjects as "shuttling" between two cultures but without making any corresponding changes in their cultural identities. He concluded from this that the Maoris could assume any number of social identities (i.e., certain learned roles expected of an individual outside his first culture) without assuming a corresponding cultural identity (i.e., the individual retains identity with his/her first culture).

The second important component of the CMI—the degree of commitment to the cultural groups in which the person participates—concerns the willingness of the person to invest energy and time in those groups in order to work to help improve the culture, to ensure the well-being of the members of those groups. With a high degree of CMI, the person exhibits a commitment to improving the lives of people in the groups in which he/she participates and, furthermore, commits himself/herself to improving the cultures of those groups. In addition, by playing the roles of cultural ambassador and mediator, the person demonstrates a commitment to improving relationships and understanding among the several groups in which he/she participates. In connection with commitment, Adler (1974) stated: "Multicultural man is the person who is intellectually and emotionally committed to the fundamental unity of all human beings while at the same time he recognizes, legitimizes, accepts, and appreciates that fundamental differences lie between people of different cultures" (p. 25).

Transcension, the third characteristic of CMIs, refers to the dynamics of identity formation. Adler described a person who is transcendent as follows:

> The parameters of his identity are neither fixed nor predictable, being responsive instead to temporary form and openness to change. . . . He is able, however, to look at his own original culture from an outsider's perspective. This tension gives rise to a dynamic, passionate, and critical posture in the face of totalistic ideologies, systems, and movement. . . . Intentionally or accidentally, multicultural persons undergo shifts in their psychocultural posture; their religion, personality, behavior, occupation, nationality, outlook, political persuasion, and values may in part or completely reformulate in the face of new examples. [pp. 30–31]

Adler concluded that the transcendent person has the ability to be a part of and also to stand apart from the different groups in which she/he participates.

Table 6–2 presents several CMI categories identified, along with the definitions suggested by the life histories collected. The distribution of the 129 participants among the different categories is also presented in this table.

Synthesized Multicultural

Persons identified as synthesized biculturals/multiculturals exhibited similar personality characteristics, including positive attitudes toward Latino and other minority cultures and mainstream cultures; com-

Table 6–2. Contemporary Multicultural Identities (CMI)

N	Contemporary Multicultural Identities	Defining Characteristics
39	Synthesized multicultural	Positive attitudes toward several cultures; competent functioning in more than one culture; feels accepted by members of more than one culture; feels committed to more than one culture as expressed through philosophy of life and life goals
22	Functional multicultural/mainstream orientation	Functions competently in both Latino and mainstream cultures; more comfortable and self-assured in mainstream culture; greater commitment to mainstream culture expressed through philosophy of life and life goals
49	Functional multicultural/Latino orientation	Functions competently in both Latino and mainstream cultures; more comfortable and self-assured in Latino culture; greater commitment to Latino culture expressed through philosophy of life and life goals
19	Monocultural	Functions competently and is more comfortable and self-assured in culture of origin to the exclusion of other cultures

petent functioning in both Latino, mainstream, and other cultures with an ability to "shuttle" between the cultures; evidence of close interpersonal relationships with members of different age, sex, and socioeconomic groups from different cultures; behaviors demonstrating a commitment to assisting in the continued development of the cultures they participate in; and a transcendent philosophy of life.

Laura C.-S. was born in New York City. Her mother is Puerto Rican and her father is Jewish. Her early years were spent among Puerto Rican, Jewish, and mainstream American peers. Laura grew up speaking three languages—Yiddish, Spanish, and English—and enjoyed participating in the multicultural environment of New York City. When she was 12 years old, her father accepted a job in Puerto Rico, and the family moved to the island. Initially, the move was difficult for Laura; while she spoke Spanish, she was not completely fluent in it and so felt ostracized by her classmates. However, she was able to gain acceptance because of her interest in drama and dancing. She became active in the theater and developed an intellectual interest in the use of drama and dance to enhance intercultural understanding. During her senior year, she became a volunteer in the elementary schools, where she worked with Puerto Rican children who were experiencing problems of adjustment because their families had returned to the island after living for several years on the United States mainland. In college, Laura studied ethnomusicology, and she founded a theater and dance group. The members of both these groups were from diverse ethnic, racial, and socioeconomic backgrounds. Her philosophy of life expresses her interests in encouraging intercultural understanding through the arts:

> Much of culture is expressed in dance, theater, and painting. You don't need languages to perceive the heart and soul of a culture and a people. I am also very excited about the respect and understanding that is created by participating in or observing multicultural dancing and theater. This is where the future of multicultural understanding lies; if we did diplomacy through art, all peoples would truly understand each other and we could achieve world peace.

Ray A., a Latino, was born in San Antonio, Texas, and lived there for the first few years of his life while his father was stationed at an Air Force base. When he was 5 years old, his family moved to Europe, where they lived in several countries both on and off military facilities. In his early adolescence, his family moved to Japan, and they stayed there until the end of his sophomore year in high school. Ray had established close friendships with peers from all the different countries and cities in which he had lived; he could also speak different languages fluently. He and his family returned to the United States, to a city in northern California where Ray finished his last two years of high school. During this time, he excelled in sports, was a member of the debate team, and was president of the student council and of the United Nations club. In college, Ray was viewed as a leader by both Mexican Americans and Anglos. He led a fight to keep militant Mexican-American students from preventing the nomination of a bilingual/bicultural Anglo student for the office of president of the Mexican-American student club on campus. His transcendent philosophy of life was reflected in his commitment to assisting members of all ethnic groups at his university.

Functional Bicultural/Mainstream Orientation

Although functional bicultural/mainstream people are multicultural with positive attitudes toward Anglo, Mexican-American, and other minority cultures, they perceive greater acceptance from Anglos and are more comfortable in Anglo cultural settings and evidence a greater commitment to the goals of Anglo culture. They show no evidence of having a transcendent identity—that is, they see other people and themselves as being culture bound.

Ramiro J. was born and reared in Dallas, Texas. His Latino family was well-off economically. He had lived in integrated neighborhoods and attended some of the best schools in the city. He was fluently bilingual and he had close friends who were both Mexican Americans and Anglos. He attended social and intellectual functions sponsored by members of both groups. However, Ramiro admitted to feeling more comfortable when with Anglos and when participating in Anglo cultural activities. In particular, he avoided interacting with what he referred to as the "rural, very Mexican" type. He said,

> The extreme Mexican types don't like me because they feel that I'm too stuck up, that I think I'm better than they are. I just can't deal with them, and I won't try because they don't accept my values and interests. I just feel that the Mexican type has to learn that the world is not the way they would like it to be and they have to learn to change or they are just not going to make it.

Functional Bicultural/Latino Orientation

The definition for Functional Bicultural/Latino CMI category is very similar to that of the previous category except that the person is more committed to Mexican Americans and feels more comfortable when participating in Mexican-American culture.

Andrea W. was born of Latino parents and grew up in a rural town in the Central Valley of California. Her family lived on a ranch several miles from the town in which she attended school. During early childhood, her closest friends were her siblings and cousins. During the first six years of her life, her parents spoke Spanish exclusively, but when Andrea turned 7 her parents converted from Catholicism to a Protestant religion. The majority of members of the church she attended were Anglos. From this time forward, Andrea had extensive contact with Anglos, going to Sunday school and to church retreats and attending many social functions sponsored through the church. At the same time Andrea developed close friendships with the other Latino families who were members of her church. Throughout elementary, middle, and high school, she had close friends who were Latinos and Anglos and attended functions sponsored by both groups; however, she always felt more comfortable with Latinos. This pattern held during her college years even though she participated actively in Anglo functions and had many Anglo friends; she always felt more comfortable when she was around Latinos. She explained her feelings in this way: "Mexican Americans and other Spanish-speaking peoples feel like members of my family to me. I guess Spanish makes me more comfortable. I feel it is a language of friendship and intimacy. Somehow, I can't seem to get too close to people who can't speak Spanish. Perhaps this will change in the future, but I don't think so."

A few of the participants who had been identified as multicultural by the MEI and the BOLS turned out to be predominantly monocultural. For the purposes of the study they were classified as either Predominantly Latino or Predominantly Anglo. That is, although they exhibited some competencies and had some experiences in a second culture, they would generally prefer not to participate in other cultures. Fitzgerald (1971) also identified this monocultural orientation in his work with the Maori college graduates. While all his participants knew how to conduct themselves in European functions, they occasionally chose not to do so. Fitzgerald observed: "The element of individual choice then, becomes highly significant in such acculturative settings. Identification must involve such a complicated process of decision-making in face of multiple social and cultural situations" (p. 49).

Thus, in these cases, there is no question that people not only refused to participate in activities that were not part of their first culture, but they also refused to consider developing an identity with another culture. Many of these monocultural people had at some time participated in another culture, but for one reason or another decided not to make a commitment to that culture. The component of commitment, therefore, plays a very important role in contemporary multicultural identity.

In general, the overall findings strongly indicated that the process of development of multicultural orientations to life is an organic, dynamic processes. The life history data highlighted the fact that people are continually acquiring new sociocultural skills and perspectives, identified as personality building elements or resources in Chapter 4. In addition, the participants were constantly in the process of rearranging and combining these personality-building elements and resources. (For a more complete description of the model of identity development that emerged from this research, refer to Chapter 4.)

Stage Theory of Multicultural Identity Development

Some investigators have concluded that there are identifiable and discrete stages in the multicultural/multiracial developmental process. The first stage theory was proposed by Cross (1971, 1978) in a five-stage model of nigrescence or Negro-to-black conversion. He labeled the five stages as Pre-encounter, Encounter, Immersion/Emersion, Internalization, and Internalization-Commitment. More recently Cross (1991) has elaborated on the personality characteristics representative of the five stages. Atkinson and colleagues (1989) also proposed a stage theory of racial/ethnic identity development. The researchers proposed these stages: conformity, dissonance, resistance and immersion, and introspection and integrative awareness. The last two stages of both the Cross and the Atkinson and colleagues' models are characterized by achievement of multicultural orientations to life—similar characteristics to the synthesized multiculturals described by Ramirez and colleagues (1977, 1978a). These common characteristics were a positive sense of self, a capacity to value and respect other racial and ethnic groups, a recognition of shared oppressions with a broad range of societal groups, and the will to promote change.

Jacobs (1992) studied biracial development in children using a doll-play instrument consisting of 36 dolls specifically made for the study. The dolls had various combinations of skin and hair color and distinct racial features. The interview included having the subject child participate in nine separate tasks such as storytelling incorporating the dolls and asking a child to select the dolls he/she "likes best." The investigator concluded that biracial children pass through three stages:

1. *Pre-color constancy*. In this stage the child engages in liberal play with color and demonstrates flexibility in choices of dolls for

family members. The child's use of color is nonevaluative. At this stage color is explored with no firm classification of social groups by race. Most children at the pre-color stage accurately identify their own color and playfully experiment with color in family identifications and in preference.

2. *Biracial label and racial ambivalence.* Jacobs found that most of the participants attained this stage at 4½ years of age. This stage was characterized by a fuller understanding of color meanings (especially prejudice against blackness) and the knowledge that his/her own color will not change. Ambivalence about racial status was noted at this stage with whiteness preferred and blackness rejected. In this stage the child's racial self-concept rests on two elements: knowledge that his/her color will not change (color constancy) and the co-emergence of a biracial label that the child has internalized and begins to use to construct a personal racial identity. Jacobs advised that the biracial self-concept may require the parents' presentation of a biracial label to the child such as, "You're part black and part white." Once the child accepts a biracial label, he/she tends to construct the family in ways that define membership in a biracial group that has one parent belonging in a black group and the other in a white group.

3. *Biracial identity.* This final stage was observed in 8-to-12-year-old biracial children. At this stage the child was observed to have discovered that membership in a racial group is related to, but not determined by, skin color; they determine that racial group membership is determined by parentage. Jacobs (1992) stated:

The child is not interracial because his or her father is black or his or her mother is white in color, but because the child's father belongs to the social class of black people and his or her mother belongs to the social class of white people. In Stage 3 the child's discovery that his or her parents' racial group membership and not color per se defines the child as biracial allows him or her to separate skin color and racial group membership and rate him- or herself and family members' skin color accurately. [p. 203]

Jacobs observed that racial ambivalence tended to decrease across Stage 2 and that as his participants entered Stage 3 formerly discor-

dant elements of racial identity were fully reconciled in a unified ego-identity.

Kich (1992), in studies of children, adolescents, and young adults, also identified three stages of development: (1) initial awareness of difficulties and dissonance between self-perception and others' perceptions; (2) struggle for acceptance from others (ages 8 through late adolescence); and (3) acceptance of biracial and bicultural identity (late adolescence through adulthood).

Research by Helms (1994) with African Americans supported the findings reported by Ramirez (1983) regarding the organic and dynamic nature of identity development in people of mixed heritage. She concluded:

> In earlier versions of racial identity theory, Helms (1990, 1992) as well as other identity theorists (see Atkinson et al. 1989) used the concept of stages rather than ego status to define the developmental process. However, because people tend to think of stages as being located external to the person and transitions between stages as being fixed or relatively stable, such usage encourages minimization of the dynamic aspects of the developmental process. [Trickett et al. 1994, p. 302]

The research of Phinney and her colleagues (Estrada 1994, Phinney 1989, 1990, Phinney and Devich-Navarro, in press) with African-American and Latino adolescents also confirms the dynamic, organic nature of multicultural/multiracial identity processes. Phinney and Devich-Navarro (in press) concluded

> In summary, we found that most ethnic minority adolescents combine their sense of being ethnic and American and acknowledge being bicultural, but their sense of being bicultural varies widely, depending on how they perceive the two cultures and the way they identify with each. Being bicultural does not require a weakening of identification with one's ethnic culture; most participants, about 90 percent, felt identified with both cultures. However, biculturalism is a complex and multidimensional phenomenon; there is not just one way to being bicultural. [p. 36]

Phinney and her colleagues also found that the bicultural issues faced by adolescents from the two ethnic/racial groups are somewhat different. She believed that these variations represent the different ways of being bicultural in a diverse society.

The importance of the type of multicultural identity and the path followed to the development of that identity cannot be overemphasized, but the ultimate test of effective functioning in a diverse society is behavior and leadership behavior in particular. Thus Ramirez and his colleagues (Ramirez 1983) posed two additional questions that provided a different focus to the research program: Are multicultural persons more effective than monocultural persons as leaders of groups that are culturally diverse? If multicultural people are in fact more effective as leaders in these mixed ethnic group situations, what is it that makes them so?

To answer these questions, the investigators employed a combination of mestizo and European approaches to research and data collection. They devised a simulated situation that made use of the laboratory method for studying small groups—reflective of the European worldview—and they collected their data by employing observational and interview techniques—in line with a mestizo worldview.

LEADERSHIP IN MIXED ETHNIC GROUPS

To examine the two additional questions concerning identity and leadership, the researchers (Garza et al. 1982, Ramirez et al. 1977) selected 36 male Latino college students between the ages of 18 and 23. Half were from university campuses in California and the other half from Texas campuses. These participants were tested with the BEI and the BOLS and identified as either multicultural or monocultural. They were asked to participate in an ethnically mixed discussion group composed of four males—the participant plus three confederates of the researchers who had been pre-instructed to promote a certain point of view. For the purposes of the study, confederates were introduced to the participant as fellow students and their true roles were not revealed. In order to establish an ethnically mixed group, the three confederates represented three distinct populations: Anglo, African-American, and Latino. Confederates who visibly represented their ethnic group with respect to considerations such as regional accent and physical appearance were selected.

When the participant and the three confederates arrived for the scheduled session, the two experimenters, both male, introduced themselves and asked the group members to sit in chairs arranged in a circle. The first experimenter told the group that the purpose of the research was to study decision-making processes in mixed ethnic groups and that they would be given 20 minutes to discuss a controversial problem concerning the preservation of the cultural integrity of a hypothetical, non-industrialized society. The group was told that contact has been made with a traditional society (located in a remote mountainous region in Central America) in which mortality rates and malnutrition are high, but the people have a very supportive and cohesive family life and religion. Should we intervene, offering technological knowledge with respect to food production and health care or leave them alone? Prior to providing further details about the issue, the first experimenter informed the group that a group coordinator (leader) was needed. By means of a controlled lottery, the participant was invariably selected to be the group leader. Immediately following the "selection," the first experimenter took the group coordinator (the participant) into an adjoining room for five minutes to give him further instructions on his task as group leader: he was to attempt to achieve group consensus in the ensuing discussion and to refrain from expressing his own opinion.

Meanwhile, the second experimenter assigned each confederate his role for that particular session, counterbalancing so that the African American, Anglo, and Latino would adopt either a pro-intervention, anti-intervention, or an undecided position an equal number of times. As part of the training and pilot testing phase, the three confederates had been trained at length in delivering convincing arguments for each of the three roles. While there were different confederates at the two sites, all used the same arguments and care was taken to maximize similarity of physical appearance and accent.

After the five-minute briefing, the participant and first experimenter returned to the session room, and the four group members were each provided with a "fact sheet" to consult, as needed, during the session. The fact sheet consisted of a few paragraphs describing benefits and drawbacks of daily life in the recently discovered "traditional" society. The written description included sufficient information to justify either the intervention or nonintervention position. All members were then asked to write on a slip of paper their position (intervention or nonintervention) regarding the problem. These were collected prior to the start of the actual discussion.

Present in the room and introduced at this time was a trained observer who remained in a corner to record the coordinator's behavior during the session using a modified Bales (1950) behavior observation scale. The same trained observer was used at both the California and the Texas field sites in order to achieve greater reliability. Although interrater reliability for five raters was established during the pilot testing phase, all group discussions were tape recorded to verify the accuracy of the behavioral observations. The audio recordings were also used to ensure the three confederates maintained high constancy of behavior (e.g., made the same arguments) across all sessions. The ratings of the two independent judges revealed great consistency in both the content and intensity of the confederate statements, thus precluding the possibility that variations in leader behavior were caused by variations in confederate behavior. The rating also showed high accuracy of the Bales observer.

The coordinator was reminded that the group had 20 minutes for discussion and his attention was directed to a timer that was clearly visible to all group members. Upon completion of all preliminary instructions, the first experimenter told the group to begin the discussion as soon as he left the room, and then he left. The second experimenter remained in the room to start and time the discussion and to issue five- and two-minute remaining-time warnings.

The means and standard deviations on the different leadership behaviors for the two classifications—monocultural and multicultural—are presented in Table 6–3.

The findings yielded five dimensions of group leader behaviors that participants with a greater degree of multicultural experience used more frequently than those with less multicultural experience:

1. taking charge (quicker to assume leader role; being assertive and active; assessing group process);
2. effectiveness of communication (asking for opinions, evaluations, and feelings; clarifying statements of members; clarifying issue being discussed);
3. attempting to reduce interpersonal conflict (mediating, seeking compromise solutions);
4. social sensitivity and personableness (acknowledging contributions made by members; addressing members by name);

Table 6–3. Comparison of Multicultural and Monocultural Leaders on Leadership Behaviors

	Means			
Leadership Behavior	Monoculturals (N = 19)	Multiculturals (N = 17)	F	P
1. Time in seconds to assume leadership	5.166	3.667	3.22	.08
2. Active and assertive	3.412	5.417	3.41	0.07
3. Asks members for opinions, evaluations, and feelings				
Total	9.47	15.00	13.49	.0008
Anglo	2.33	4.83	5.33	.03
African American	2.25	3.33	2.73	.11
Mexican American	3.25	4.41	6.96	.01
4. Acknowledges contributions of members				
Total	.667	1.917	3.20	.08
Anglo	.083	.333	1.71	.20
African American	.500	1.083	2.97	.10
Mexican American	1.667	1.066	3.01	.08
5. Clarifies issue under discussion	1.890	3.000	4.70	.04
6. Assesses group progress	.750	1.667	1.87	.18
7. Mediates between members in conflict	.916	2.167	2.05	.17
8. Seeks compromises or intermediate solutions	1.162	2.014	1.99	.17
9. Addresses members by first name	.261	2.251	5.13	.03
10. Shows tension and inappropriate behavior	1.21	.120	3.41	.07

5. coping with stress (fewer visible indicators of tension; absence of inappropriate behaviors).

Ratings on global leadership style indicated that high multicultural participants were more flexible, that is, these participants tended to be less autocratic and more democratic. High multicultural participants were active and assertive, but they combined these behaviors with tactfulness and personableness. Low multicultural participants, on the other hand, tended either to behave in an authoritarian fashion, rudely interrupting the members of their group by shouting them down, or to assume a very passive and laissez-faire management style, allowing time to be wasted in unproductive arguments among the group members.

Results of the post-group interviews conducted with the group leaders showed that leaders of high multicultural experience were more accurate in reporting what actually transpired in their groups; in the actual group process, 59 percent of the high multiculturals were accurate, whereas only 37 percent of the low multiculturals were accurate. When asked to speculate as to why their group had failed to achieve consensus in the allotted time, the high multicultural participants stated that they would most certainly succeed if given a second chance, and 53 percent of them gave self-responsibility attributions for their perceived failure, that is, they made statements such as "I should have concentrated more on the person who couldn't make up his mind" or "I should have asked the two people who were doing most of the arguing to try to step into each other's shoes." In contrast to this, 69 percent of the low multicultural leaders gave other directed responsibility attributions; they made statements such as "Those two guys are too stubborn and narrow-minded to ever agree with each other" or "The members of my group just can't get along with each other."

In general, high multicultural leaders appeared to have more behavioral and perspective repertories or resources available to them. They also made more effort to communicate with the Anglo and the African-American group members; they made sure that all members in the group expressed their opinions and that they all understood each others' points of view. In contrast to this, monocultural leaders would tend to communicate more with the Latino group members, often ignoring the Anglo and African-American members. Monocultural leaders were also less concerned with ensuring that points of view expressed by individual members were understood by others in their group.

The greater accuracy of reports made by multicultural leaders during the post-group interviews indicated that they better understood the dynamics of their groups. This latter finding also indicated that they were more sensitive to the group process and to the interpersonal dynamics that transpired in their groups; further, they were more open to their experiences, that is, they were less defensive (less likely to distort what actually transpired and to try to avoid blame for the group's "failure" to achieve consensus).

Advantages of Being Multicultural/Multiracial

In recent years researchers have combined mestizo and European research methodologies to investigate the psychological adjustment of multicultural/multiracial people. Hall (1992) studied adult men and women black-Japanese participants from the Los Angeles, California, area. Interviews were done using the Hall Identity Questionnaire designed by Hall. The instrument taps ethnic identity choice, demographics, ethnic composition of neighborhood and friends, racial resemblance to a particular ethnic group, involvement in political movements, and acceptance of and by particular groups. The researcher found that the participants in her study were well adjusted to their heterogeneous heritage. She concluded:

> In fact, most found their biracialism and biculturalism to be assets, as reflected in the following comments, "I've got the best of both worlds"; "It makes me more sensitive and understanding of other minorities." These black-Japanese are, indeed, the "cosmopolitan people" described by Park (1937) and the "multicultural people" considered by Ramirez et al. (1977). [p. 263–264]

Research by Kich (1992) and by Stephan (1992) also confirmed that multicultural/multiracial adults are well adjusted and do not suffer from identity crises or feelings of marginality.

Multicultural leader behaviors, and the flexibility and adaptability of multicultural/multiracial people are essential to living successfully in a diverse nation and world. Also essential is the combination of European and mestizo worldviews in research, intervention, and theory development that accurately reflect the psychodynamics of multicultural/multiracial children, adolescents, and adults.

It is the responsibility of social scientists and mental health professionals to bring to the awareness of the body politic and the academic and mental health communities the recommendation of Ruben Ardila (1993) identified in the quotation at the beginning of the chapter: we need to learn from others and from other cultures if we hope to benefit from the knowledge of First, Second, and Third World Psychologies in order to help us to better understand the diverse world in which we live and the diverse forces that drive the development of our personalities.

It is our collective responsibility to help all peoples in the world to live happily and effectively in a diverse society and a multicultural/multiracial world. Some suggestions will be provided in Chapters 8 and 9.

SUMMARY

Most people and most nations in the world are striving to come to terms with the challenges posed by diversity. At the individual level we are faced with coming to terms with our own diverse cultural and racial heritages and with the effects of diversity on our friendships, intimate relationships, and relationships with our children. Diversity at the individual level is also felt in our efforts to work cooperatively with others in an atmosphere of cooperation, understanding, and peace. In order to ensure that the challenges presented by diversity do not lead to confusion, separatism, misunderstanding, and distrust, we need to understand the psychodynamics of being multicultural/multiracial. To accomplish this goal we need to confront a long-standing but still important controversy in psychology and the social sciences: Should investigators and change agents adopt the methodology of the natural sciences or should they use the more phenomenologically oriented humanistic approaches?

The answer offered here is that if we are truly to understand diversity we need approaches to research that are in themselves reflective of diversity; we need both the mestizo (more representative of phenomenology) and the European (more representative of the natural sciences) approaches and perspectives to scientific investigation. These two perspectives and approaches were combined in a research project that identified multicultural leaders and compared the behaviors of these leaders with those of monocultural leaders in mixed ethnic groups under conditions of conflict. The approach succeeded in identifying leadership behaviors that reduced conflict in mixed ethnic group situations. The two approaches have also been combined successfully to understand the processes of multicultural/multiracial identity development. How these processes can be applied successfully to problems of diversity is the focus of the last two chapters.

❖ 7 ❖

The Mestizo Worldview
and Mental Health

It seems reasonable to think of man as existing in a "bio-psycho-social" field. This depicts an open transactional system that allows uninterrupted bidirectional flow of information and energy transactions extending from the deepest and most minute recesses of the body (intracellular metabolic processes) to the social field, encompassing cultural forces, even historical forces that contributed to shaping the culture.

—*Morton F. Reiser (1975)*

When I fell off my horse and broke my leg, I was taken to the hospital and the doctors and nurses took care of me, but I did not feel completely well again until I went to see the medicine man; he made me feel like my body was whole again.

—*a member of the Navajo nation*
(from Innovations, *Winter 1976)*

Sociocultural factors affect responses to different types of intervention.

—*Telles et al. (1995)*

The perspectives on health and illness presented above are reflective of the mestizo worldview. There are three major characteristics of this belief system: integration of mind and body (a holistic view); the quality of the relationship between the person and the physical and social environments; and the quality of the relationship between the person and the supernatural. This chapter examines each of these components in detail. In addition, the roles of the indigenous healers will be examined and their various approaches to healing identified. The final section of the chapter reviews current attempts at integrating mestizo, American Indian, African-American, and European perspectives and approaches to develop intervention and primary prevention programs.

HOLISTIC VIEWS OF HEALTH AND MALADJUSTMENT

> Mental goes by the spirit of the body. The mind is governed by the spirit of the body. If the body feels something the mind is affected. [A. Curandero quoted in A. Kiev 1968]

> Body and mind are conjoined, the core essence of a person, responding to and regulating his various activities. [Fabrega and Manning 1973]

> Health is defined as a harmonious balance between a person's physical, psychological, and spiritual entities; illness can manifest itself as disruption in a person's social, physical, or psychological life. [Chavira and Trotter 1978]

In the mestizo, multicultural/multiracial worldview of mental illness and health, the body and the mind are believed to be conjoined. Within the context of this perspective, the entire domain of human behavior is believed to be influenced by both biological and sociocultural events and forces. Thus, changes in the body are believed to have profound effects on the personality style. For example, Fabrega and Manning (1973) have observed that mestizos in the Chiapas highlands of Mexico believe that gaining weight makes the person slower, lazier, and more cautious and restrained. They also point out that among this group of mestizos, emotions play an important role in causation of illness:

> Inspection of the list of emotions that are described as pathogenic indicates that pleasantness or unpleasantness are not critical factors. Rather, their amount and persistence in the individual across time appears to be critical. Emotions and feelings are seen as inevitable, but when present they should be discouraged (in actions, talk, or thought) or neutralized (as with alcohol) so that the body at no time or during any one interval carries an excessive load. [p. 228]

These investigators also found that interpersonal relationships are believed to have a direct bearing on health: "Arguments, separations, envious coveting, love triangles, intensely satisfying exchanges, etc. all have medical relevance precisely because they give rise to excessive feeling" (p. 228).

The holistic view of health and illness characteristic of the mestizo worldview has resulted in development of theories of disease and of health care systems that are different from those of Western European cultures. For example, in the context of the mestizo worldview, disease is viewed as being closely related to everyday life and is considered to be intimately connected to the quality of family and community relationships as well as to relationships with the supernatural. Thus health care systems are seen as part of the broad context of culture. As Kleinman (1980) observed in the context of a holistic perspective of illness and health, health care is a system that is social and cultural in origin, structure, function, and significance. Figure 7–1 illustrates the complexity of health care systems that are based on holistic perspectives of health and illness.

GOOD RELATIONS WITH THE PHYSICAL AND SOCIAL ENVIRONMENTS

In the multicultural/multiracial worldview, health and illness are associated with the quality of the relationship between the person and his/her physical and social environments. As discussed in Chap-

Figure 7–1. A Diagrammatic Representation of the Spirit Hierarchy[1]

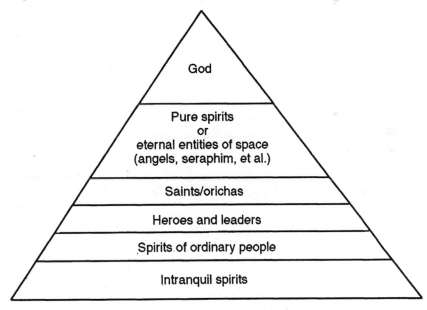

---

[1]Reprinted from Harwood 1977, p. 72 by permission of Kluwer Academic Publishers.

ter 2, in many of the religions of the native peoples of the Americas, human beings are considered to be part of the natural order of things in the cosmos. Some North and South American Indian groups as well as some African cultures (Myers 1988) share a common view. They believe that all things in the cosmos are interrelated, and that harmony and balance among all elements of the universe play a central role in illness and in health.

In many of the Native American, African, and mestizo groups in Latin America, the quality of the person's relationship with his/her social environment figures importantly in the beliefs regarding illness and health. As discussed in Chapter 4, the mestizo cultures of Latin America emphasize the importance of developing and maintaining good interpersonal relationships with others, particularly with members of the nuclear and extended families. Illness in these societies is often viewed as a consequence of conflicts with or separation from important others. Feelings of guilt are often associated with illness and maladjustment. For example, guilt over not living up to the expectations and wishes of parents and other family members is believed to result in poor health. Envy is believed to play an important role in causes of illness associated with the interpersonal domain. Rubel (1966), through his research with Mexican Americans in South Texas, identified the central role of envy in the cause of illness or maladjustment. If a person is envied by another, he/she might experience symptoms of illness or maladjustment. One of the most common illnesses in Latino cultures, *mal-de-ojo*, is believed to be caused by a form of envy. If a person's physical features (usually the face) are admired by another, usually a much older, person and the admirer does not touch the admired person by lightly running the palm of the hand over the face, the admired person can become ill. The symptoms—fever and a general feeling of malaise—can only be relieved by contacting the person who admired the patient and asking him/her to carry out the appropriate caress.

Many illnesses and problems of adjustment in mestizo cultures are believed to be caused by feelings of alienation from the family group, the community, or the culture of origin. For example, illness in young people is often associated with the acculturation process. For children and adolescents in particular, illness and maladjustment are believed to be associated with alienation from parents, grandparents, and siblings as a result of the adoption of lifestyles and value systems that differ from those of the home culture. Madsen (1964), mentioned in Chapter 3, documented several cases of acculturation alienation among young adult Mexican Americans in rural South Texas. These people had become assimilated into Anglo mainstream culture and in the process had rejected their home culture. Madsen observed that these individuals experienced considerable feelings of guilt over having abandoned their original culture and developed a dependency on alcohol in their attempts to alleviate anxiety; he thus referred to these people as alcoholic agringados. Fried (1959) also documented cases in which adults had become ill as a result of having become separated from their community and culture of origin. Indians in Peru who had migrated from their villages in the mountains to urban areas in the lowlands and who were forced to adopt the lifestyles of city dwellers tended to develop physiological and emotional symptoms. Acculturation has also been identified as one of the causes of physical and emotional illness among members of North American Indian groups (Hallowell 1951, Spindler 1952).

Disruption of good relations with the physical environment is given a central role in the explanation of causes of illness and psychological maladjustment among many of the cultures of the Indian groups in North America and in Afrocentric thought. The person who does not perform the proper ritual of atonement for killing an animal, for uprooting a plant, or for taking the fruit of a tree or a bush can become ill or experience unhappiness and lack of harmony in his/her life. Wyman and Kluckhohn (1938), for example, identified etiological factors that the Navajos believe can produce sickness: natural phenomena such as lightning, winds, thunder, and sometimes the earth, sun, or moon; and some species of animals, including bears, deer, coyotes, porcupines, snakes, eagles, and fish. Kaplan and Johnson (1967), in their research on Navajo psychopathology, discovered that illness was believed to result from possession by certain aspects of dangerous animals, natural phenomena, witches, or ghosts.

HEALTH AND GOOD RELATIONS WITH THE SUPERNATURAL

To Western man, illness is an impersonal event brought about by neutral, non-emotional natural agents such as germs, while for the Mexican American illness relates to the individual's life, his community, his interpersonal relationships and, *above all to his God*. Disease is defined not only in naturalistic, empirical symptomatic terms, but also in *magical and religious terms*. [Kiev 1968, p. 77]

One of the most important goals of the religious practices and rituals of the indigenous cultures of the Americas is that of developing and maintaining good relations with the supernatural. Leon-Portilla (1963), for example, explained that the Mayas developed an elaborate systems for measuring time, because this allowed them to predict the arrivals of the time-bearing deities and, in turn, permitted them to situate themselves under the influence of those deities whose signs were favorable. The people followed the advice of the wise men and the priests who knew the intricacies of the calendars, and they relied on these shamans to help them maintain good relations with the supernatural. Lamphere (1969) explained that the Navajos developed various chants or "sings," each chant being a system of ritual procedures designed to prevent the development of "ugly conditions" associated with the disruption of good relations with the supernatural. The belief reflected in these rituals is that the creators of the present world emerged from the "lower worlds" and taught the ancestors of the Navajos the ceremonial knowledge necessary to perform the chants. For example, the myth of the Male Shooting Way tells of two heroes (Holy Young Man and Holy Boy) who experience a series of trials and misfortunes. Various supernaturals aid the heroes by teaching them a ceremony that counteracts their troubles. Mary Crow Dog (1990) described the legend of White Buffalo Woman in the teaching role: "the story of White Buffalo Woman who brought to our people the most sacred of all thing, the Ptehincala-huhuchanunpa, the sacred pipe around which our faith revolves" (p. 247).

In the beliefs of the indigenous and mestizo peoples of the Americas, the status of a person's relations to the supernatural figures importantly in considerations of illness or maladjustment. Maladjustment or illness is believed to be a direct result of a breakdown of the good relations necessary between the person and the supernatural. In the Latino cultures, a breakdown of good relations with the supernatural is believed to occur when the person commits a transgression against God or his/her family. In many of the native cultures of North America, it is believed that disruption of good relations with the supernatural can occur as a result of contact with "ugly things"—anger, weapons, and with certain forces (associated with natural phenomena, witches, and ghosts) that have entered the body. Alienation of the individual from the supernatural can occur as a result of contact with witchcraft or by the action of snakes, bears, lightning, and so forth.

Treatment of illness and psychological maladjustment associated with the native and mestizo religions of the Americas usually involves the re-establishment of good relations between the patient and the supernatural. The treatment itself is usually carried out by those persons who are believed to have access to the supernatural. For example, in Latino culture the native curer uses prayer and encourages the patient to do penance. In addition, the patient is usually encouraged to re-establish good relations with his/her family. Among the Navajo, the singer engages in specific actions during the course of the chant that exemplify the theme of "taking in" or "applying to." The objective of these actions is to identify the patient with the supernatural and make him/her sacred. To further this effect, sacred objects derived from the spiritual world are put into contact with the patient's body to sanctify him/her.

The process of mestizoization in the Americas (as mentioned in Chapters 1 and 2) resulted in the amalgamation of the beliefs and rituals of the native religions with those of the European religions. Thus, much of the supernatural power that had been associated with a pantheistic deity in the native religions was transferred to God, Christ, the Virgin, or the saints, or even members of the clergy. However, some of the supernatural power and the "routes" of access to that power remained outside the realm of official religion and the clergy. Thus, certain individuals in the native cultures—*curanderos(as)*, shamans, spiritists, medicine men, magicians, and witches—who are believed to have access to supernatural power play a central role in the treatment of illness and prevention of disease.

CURANDEROS(AS), ESPIRITISTAS, AND MEDICINE MEN

The person who is experiencing symptoms of psychological maladjustment and/or physical symptoms of illness seeks the help of someone in the community who is believed to have supernatural power or to have access to such power. The cure is done either directly by the curer or by the curer's intercession with the supernatural. In the Americas, there are three major types of curers—*curanderos(as)*, *espiritistas*, and medicine men. The rituals and paraphernalia of these practitioners are quite diverse, but in general their curative activities fall into four major categories:

1. Confession, atonement, and absolution;
2. Restoration of balance, wholeness, and harmony through self-control;
3. Involvement of the family and community in the treatment; and
4. Communication with the supernatural.

Confession, Atonement, and Absolution

The practices of most of the native healers of the Americas are closely associated with religion because in the mestizo worldview, religion and science (and, thus, religion and healing) are seen as belonging in the same domain. Jerome Frank (1961) identified the unity of religion and healing in non-Western cultures as the major determinant of differences observed between Western and non-Western healing: "In the West psychiatry and religion are distinct enemies. In many other cultures the therapist may also be the religious agent, and use of the techniques of confession, atonement, and absolution follow naturally" (p. 121).

Since sin and guilt are among the principal causes of illness and maladjustment in the native and mestizo cultures of the Americas, confession, atonement, and absolution are frequent rituals used in treatment. In some cases, atonement is accomplished through prayer or penance; in others, it may involve cleansing the body, accomplished by brushing the body with branches of rosemary or by sprinkling it with holy water. The Puerto Rican *espiritista* is likely to make use of seances and role playing to rid the ailing individual of evil spirits as well as to call on the person's protective spirits for help in the cure. North American Indian medicine men, on the other hand, are more likely to use chanting, storytelling, and body rubs.

Restoration of Balance, Wholeness, and Harmony through Self-Control

In many of the native and mestizo cultures, illness and maladjustment are seen as end products of lack of self-control on the part of the individual. The person allows his/her feelings, emotions, or desires to run unchecked, hurting the self and others. Thus, the person who is in need of help is perceived as being out of balance and harmony, and his/her spirit is believed to be fragmented. An important aspect of treatment, then, is to teach the person self-control. This is best exemplified in the treatment rituals used by the Navajo medicine men. The ceremonies usually involve a religious tale about something gone wrong, and how, when supernatural figures are called upon, they are able to cure or correct the problem. Medicine men re-enact the stories and, through song and chanting, take on the characteristics of the supernatural being in order to cure the patient. There is, for example, a series of stories involving Coyote, who is famous for his excesses—greed, lust, envy, and trickery—often hurting himself and others through his actions. These stories help to identify human weaknesses; they show how a person can become like Coyote and indulge in excesses of lust, alcohol, drugs, and so on. After the medicine men perform the curing ceremony, they continue to counsel the patient, helping him to control his excessive behavior by reminding him of Coyote.

Self-control was also given great importance by the Nahua peoples of Mexico (see Chapter 2). There were specific scripts provided for parents so that they might give advice to their young children regarding the importance of self-control. The schools to which these children were sent later in life also made self-control one of the most important educational goals.

Restoration of balance, wholeness, and harmony in the person who is ill or maladjusted is also achieved through exorcising negative elements or spirits and protecting the person from evil forces and bad spirits. As was mentioned earlier in this chapter, illness or maladjustment is also believed to result from the casting of spells or from contact with "ugly things" or dangerous elements of one kind or another. Thus, curative rituals often involve ridding the person's body of these negative elements or confronting the evil spirit that has possessed the person or has taken temporary hold of his/her soul. These procedures are best exemplified in the work of North American Indian medicine men and Puerto Rican *espiritistas*. The following description of the treatment of a 15-year-old girl by a Puerto Rican *espiritista* was taken from *Innovations* (Fields 1976a,b). The girl's presenting problem was violent arguments with her father, to which she would react by leaving the house and wandering the streets without being aware of her identity or surroundings. The patient was taken to a seance led by an *espiritista*.

This girl was allowed to abreact in the seance while in trance possession, screaming unintelligible words, fainting, having convulsion-like movements of a sexual nature. The medium and two women of the group saw that she did not hurt herself and assisted her to make the ritual movements of hands warding off the spirits. After she came out of the trance, an assistant medium in turn entered into a trance and confronted her with a "good spirit," who said: "Do you think that you are a big girl? Even though you are well developed, you are still young. Don't you know what could happen to a girl like you in the streets?" Members supported the medium saying: "Yes, something evil could happen to you on the streets."

The girl was not impressed by these admonitions, and the medium entered into a deeper trance, breathing more quickly and speaking in another pitch of voice reflecting his changed trance state, speaking this time as a "bad spirit": "I am your bad spirit, I am going to get you in trouble. I like what happens on the streets, you are not going to get rid of me. I go where you go." The group echoed his remarks. The girl panicked, seemingly became aware of the possible consequences of her own impulses, and said: "Leave me alone, leave me, become spirits of light and progress." The group joined in, reciting the Lord's Prayer to reinforce the influence of the "good spirit." [Fields 1976a, p. 10]

Involvement of Family and Community in the Treatment

Restoration of good relations between the person who needs help and his/her social environment is believed to be so important that in some cultures treatment is not felt to be effective unless family and community members are involved. While family and community participation is more common in the treatment procedures and rituals of the North American Indians, it is also used by *curanderas* and *espiritistas* in Latino cultures. In some cases the patient is treated at home in the context of family, but more usually family members and close friends accompany the patient to the place where the treatment is carried out—a *centro*, a *hogan*, or the *curandero*'s home. Involvement of the family and the community in treatment serves to re-establish good relations between these people and the person who is ill or maladjusted. Thus, wholeness and harmony with family, community, and culture are restored. An important by-product of involvement of family and community in treatment is that the participants usually make a commitment to support the patient and to assume responsibility for his/her gradual reintegration into family and culture. An example of the important role family and community members can play in the treatment program of the medicine men is described in a case history in *Innovations* (Fields 1976b):

> Edward Yazzi is a Vietnam veteran, and like many of his buddies, had trouble adjusting to civilian life when he returned home. He gained weight, had frequent nightmares about killing and being killed, and complained that his "mind was messed up." The medicine man Yazzi consulted recommended a three-day ritual which is one of the ceremonies traditionally included in the rubric of the "Enemy Way." A major ceremony such as that of the Enemy Way involves the gathering of many friends and relatives. They share in the prayers of blessing for the restoration of the patient and receive blessings from the ceremony themselves. Emphasis is on the unity of experience. To be sick is to be fragmented. To be healed is to become whole and to be whole one must be in harmony with family, friends, and nature. Navajo healing rituals involve family, friends, and nature. They usually take place in a hogan, a simple, eight-sided earthen dwelling which has religious significance as a kind of microcosm of the Navajo spiritual world. In the hogan prayers are chanted with ritual objects that are taken from the natural world of the reservation: juniper branches, bird feathers, dyes from berries and barks. Every ceremony involves a religious tale about something going wrong, and how, when supernatural figures were called upon, they were able to cure or correct the problem. The medicine man re-enacts the story, and through song and chanting, becomes the supernatural being in order to cure the patient. There is a strong aes-

thetic component in the ritual ceremonies. A catharsis, purging, or removal of a symptom does not seem to arise from anything like the Christian confessional or talking therapies, but rather out of highly stylized, ritualized art form in which the patient participates as a protagonist, often with his family and friends. For Edward Yazzi, the troubled veteran, for example, a three-day "squaw dance" was prescribed. This is one of the ceremonies traditionally included in the rubric of the "Enemy Way." Instead of striving for insight, the medicine man may ritualistically confront an "evil one" who took the mind of the person he wants to help. He will say, "I want the mind that you stole." The medicine man, by identifying with the holy person, takes on special powers, and through the supernatural figure in the religious tale is believed to be able to cure the ailing patient. [p. 15]

Communication with the Supernatural

One of the most important skills or abilities—and one that is believed to set the native healer apart from other members of his/her sociocultural group—is the ability to communicate with the supernatural. The healer is either believed to be able to communicate with the spirit world directly or to facilitate communication between the person who needs help and the supernatural world. People who have this ability have been given the name of *shaman* by social scientists. Harner (1973) provided a definition of a shaman: "A shaman may be defined as a man or woman who is in direct contact with the spirit world through a trance state and has one or more spirits at his command to carry out his bidding for good or evil. Typically, shamans bewitch persons with the aid of spirits or cure persons made ill by other spirits" (p. 85).

Treatment activities related to contact with the spirit world are based on the belief in the concept of soul, that is, a belief that all living things have souls that are immortal. The belief is that the soul retains the personality, knowledge, and motivations of the individual or living thing to which it belonged in life. Under the proper conditions, these souls can contact and affect persons living in the physical world. The activities of the souls are similar to the activities of the living beings to which they belonged on earth; therefore, spirits are believed to be both good and evil. They can either heal or create illness.

Through his investigations of Puerto Rican spiritism, Harwood (1977) has identified a spirit hierarchy (see Figure 7–1). Spirits are ranked according to their moral perfection; those occupying different moral ranks are also believed to reside on separate spatial planes. He described this spiritual hierarchical arrangement:

> The lowest level of the spirit hierarchy, which is conceived as starting only a few inches above the earth, is inhabited by spirits that departed from bodies in an unsettled state (*espiritos intranquilos*). These spirits may be bound to earth through a special attachment to the living which grows either out of inordinate love or an unmet obligation (e.g., an unpaid debt). Spirits may also occupy this lowest rank because they have failed to fulfill their spiritual potential in life. People who have died prematurely (especially through suicide, or fatal accident, or violent crime) fall into this category, as do those who have devoted their lives to material pursuits. To enable these "little elevated" spirits *(espiritos poco elevados)* to quit the earthly ambiance and ascend to the next spiritual rank, incarnate spirits (i.e., the living) must perform certain services in their behalf. These services, which include reciting prayers, lighting candles, and offering flowers, are spoken of as "giving the spirit light" (*darle la luz al espirito*). If not "given light," these restless spirits may become subjugated to earthly malefactors (*brujos*—sorcerers), who use them in harming enemies. [pp. 72–73]

Healers who communicate directly with the supernatural engage in both diagnostic and treatment activities. During the initial consultation, the healer usually has two objectives: to determine the identities of the patient's protective spirits and to pinpoint the client's problems and diagnose their causes. A frequent practice in diagnosing a client's condition involves the medium's calling upon a spiritual guide to make contact with other spirits who are influencing the client. The spirits contact the client through dreams or through the healer. Diagnoses of both physical and spiritual etiology are frequent, and conjoint treatment involving physician and healer may result.

The treatment procedures followed by many Puerto Rican spiritualists or mediums include the following:

- Exorcism is part of most *espiritista* sessions. It is done to remove harmful spiritual influences that clients may have brought with them to the meeting or that they may take away with them when they leave. The ritual is performed by fumigating the client with cigar smoke or sprinkling him/her with holy water.

- The medium then interrogates the spiritual agent until he or she admits responsibility for the client's problems and begs the victim's forgiveness.
- Giving the spirit light is done by the medium giving the client a program of rituals designed to elevate the offending spirit to a higher level in the hierarchy and thus permanently remove its harmful effects. The program usually consists of reciting a particular prayer several times daily or performing other tasks which are believed to be helpful in elevating the spirit from the lowest rung on the hierarchy, for example, offering flowers, candles, or other ritual paraphernalia. Sometimes the client must restore disrupted relationships with his/her family in order to succeed in elevating the offending spirit.

MODELS FOR UNDERSTANDING AND PROMOTING MENTAL HEALTH IN THE AMERICAS

In summarizing the material covered in this chapter up to this point, it can be concluded that in order to represent the mestizo worldview properly, a holistic health/illness model is needed: an integrated model that views the mind and body as conjoined and that conceives of health and illness as being affected by biological, sociocultural, and supernatural factors and forces. Fabrega and Manning (1973) observed that an integrated/holistic model of this type is consistent with the most recent knowledge derived from research on psychosomatic medicine. Holistic/integrated models have also been found to be consonant with recent developments in behavioral health (Matarazzo 1982). Reiser's (1975) review of neurobiological research also supported a holistic/integrated model of health/illness. In fact, Reiser proposed a model reflective of the fact that people live in a biopsychosocial field. Figure 7–2 is based on a diagram presented by Reiser, but it includes modifications made by the author in order to include the supernatural realm.

A holistic/integrated model such as that described above demands development of health care models for intervention and primary pre-

Figure 7–2. A Mestizo-European Model of Health/Illness[2]

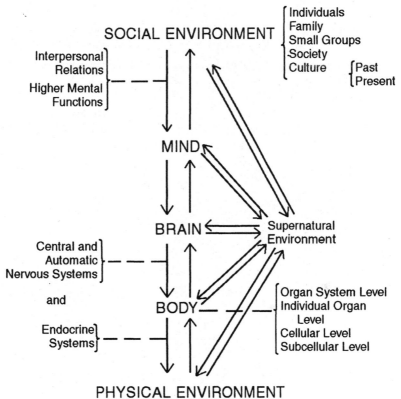

[2]Adapted from Reiser 1975, p. 493. Reprinted by permission of Lippincott-Raven Publishers.

vention that are themselves integrated and holistic. Such a health care model must incorporate the different domains that are part of the mestizo view of illness and health. Figure 7–3 was taken from Kleinman (1980) and modified by the author in order to include the supernatural domain.

Several efforts have been made to develop procedures for the health care of mestizo peoples in the Americas. Most of these efforts have attempted to integrate Native American, mestizo, African, and European approaches to treatment and diagnosis. The philosophical frame-

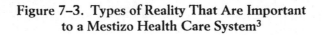

**Figure 7–3. Types of Reality That Are Important
to a Mestizo Health Care System[3]**

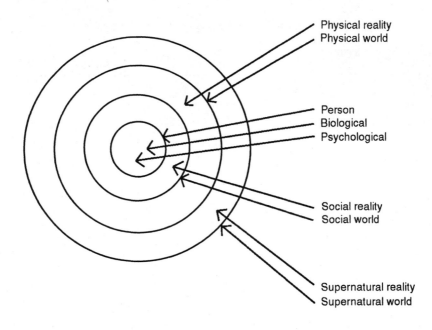

---

[3]Adapted from Kleinman 1980. Reprinted by permission of the University of California Press.

work for these integrative approaches was provided in part by the writings of E. Fuller Torrey (1973), whose work led to the recognition of the importance of shared worldview in diagnosis and treatment. With respect to the therapist's being able to name what is wrong with the patient, Fuller Torrey stated,

> The very act of naming it has a therapeutic effect. The patient's anxiety is decreased by the knowledge that a respected and trusted therapist understands what is wrong. The identification of the offending agent (childhood experience, violation of taboo) may also activate a series of associated ideas in the patient's mind, producing confession, abreaction, and general catharsis. This is the principle of Rumpelstiltskin. Based upon personality studies of the Brothers Grimm in the

early nineteenth century, the principle illustrates the magic of the right word. [p. 16]

Some of the most important attempts to integrate mestizo and European approaches in diagnostic and intervention strategies involve training professional mental health practitioners to use some of the diagnostic and healing procedures employed by *curanderas*, *espiritistas*, and medicine men. Kreisman (1975) described treatment of Mexican-American patients with schizophrenia at the Denver General Hospital where conventional therapy was adapted to the model of *curanderismo*. The White Cloud Center at the University of Oregon Medical School sponsored a project (Manson 1982) that encouraged physicians and medicine men to share knowledge and work together to integrate approaches for treating North American Indian patients. In another project, at the New Jersey College of Medicine and Dentistry, attempts were made to encourage health and mental health professionals to employ some of the procedures of the Puerto Rican *espiritistas*.

Vivian Garrison (1979), an anthropologist who has worked closely as a consultant and co-therapist with mental health professionals and paraprofessionals suggested, "interventions might be more acceptable [to the Puerto Rican patient] if they resemble some of the spiritualist diagnostic process in which a series of questions are stated to be affirmed or denied." She also listed other kinds of approaches that might be in keeping with Puerto Rican expectations and that would probably contribute to more effective therapy for them:

- a walk-in service with a short-term treatment pattern; extensive use of paratherapeutic techniques such as home visits and environmental intervention;
- the use of paraprofessionals; the "helper" therapy principle involving someone in the care and treatment of others who has himself been helped;
- role-playing and "acting out" rather than "talking out" techniques; and
- limitation of goals of therapy to more immediate relief of symptoms and problem solving rather than long-term personality reconstruction.

One of the best examples of integration of European and native healer approaches is an intervention project developed at the Rosebud Reservation in South Dakota designed by Sioux medicine men in collaboration with Western psychologists and entitled "Identity Through Traditional Lakota Methods" (Mohatt and Blue 1982). Attneave (1974) also reported on a successful two-way referral system between Indian Health Service Staff and traditional healers in an Eskimo village.

Research by Rogler (Rogler and Cortes 1993) has suggested an analysis of culture-specific help-seeking pathways for Puerto Ricans living in New York City. Supporting the conclusions made by Attneave (1969) in her work with urban Native Americans, the investigator observed that psychosocial and cultural factors, including the client's social network, are influential in the decision making processes regarding the help-seeking behaviors of a person who is experiencing problems of adjustment. The client is viewed as having an orientation toward well-being that is encapsulated within a group or kin structure. Thus, if a client drops out of therapy it may not necessarily be a negative indicator but may indicate that positive changes have taken place in her/his social network during the course of treatment.

Working with Latino families in San Antonio, Texas, Cervantes and Oscar Ramirez (1995) emphasized the importance of mestizo spirituality in family therapy: "Thus a mestizo spirituality can be defined as a perspective that allows for an introspective attitude fostering culturally sanctioned inclinations towards wholeness, harmony and balance. This attitude is embedded within a consciousness that understands learning one's life history, diversity and multicultural struggle" (p. 230). The authors also emphasized that the philosophy of *curanderismo* (faith healing) is an important mind-set for the therapist/healer involved in understanding of the intricate, yet natural, connection to the healing process in the family.

Carrasco et al. (1996) focused on values relating to gender role definition in the psychotherapy approaches they employ with Latino male sex offenders. They concluded that the concept of father dominance in the family and male dominance in Latino culture in general has two components—filial obedience and love/responsibility. The authors observed that it is filial obedience, particularly as it applied to step-daughters, that is related to sexual abuse and other dysfunctional relationships in families of sex offenders. Values relating to machismo (male dominance) are discussed and explained to the clients in therapy. Values are redefined and gradually the offender is helped to accept the love/responsibility that legitimizes the power of the role of the father within the family. Therapy focuses on the positive elements of the macho self-concept, replacing the distorted *machista* (chauvinistic) perspective.

Yang (1989), observing that Asian Americans tend to somatize, channeling stress and tension into bodily symptoms such as headaches, dizzy spells, digestive problems, and insomnia, recommended the use of acupuncture as part of mental health approaches to treatment. Sue and Zane (1987) indicated that credibility and giving are both essential concepts when counseling Asian Americans. Credibility concerns the client's perception of the therapist as an effective and trustworthy helper. It derives from the prestige that is attached or attributed to factors such as age, expertise, and sex in interpersonal relationships in traditional Asian cultures. Giving, which involves using therapeutic techniques that ensure that clients feel a direct benefit from therapy almost immediately, derives from the gift-giving ritual that is frequently a part of interpersonal relationships among both Asians and Asian Americans. Carlin (1986), focusing on problems of refugees, described the use of community support groups that preserve the language, custom, and traditions of the native cultures.

The efforts to integrate the mixed heritage and European worldviews in mental health intervention approaches and training for mental health professionals represent a good beginning, but we need models that are comprehensive in order to better serve the mental health needs of multicultural/multiracial people. Some of these are described below.

As early as the late 1960s, Carolyn Attneave (1969) recognized the need to encourage and reinforce the reciprocal support of Native American extended families living in urban environments as a treatment model for Native Americans and others of mixed heritage. She entitled her model of treatment "network therapy." Ross Speck (Speck and Attneave 1974) evolved a system of therapy for people who suffered from schizophrenia that involved resocialization of the family unit (because the patients had often become isolated from friends, relatives, and neighbors) to strengthen healing bonds. His goal was to establish a self-help therapeutic community. Speck and Attneave (1974) collaborated to establish a model, which they entitled "social network therapy," that employed approaches used by medicine men (discussed earlier in this chapter), specifically the involvement of

family and community in treatment to restore wholeness and harmony in the client. They introduced the concepts of "retribalization,"
by which they meant that they were restoring a vital element of relationship and pattern that had been lost to the family and community. This social network consisted of the nuclear family and all of
the kin of each member, as well as the friends, neighbors, work associates, and significant helpers from churches, schools, social agencies,
and institutions who were willing to help. This group, or network,
served to revive or create a healthy social matrix, which would then
deal with the distress and predicaments of the members far more
effectively, quickly, and enduringly than any outside professional
could ever hope to do. Speck and Attneave (1974) described the treatment of Claude, a patient suffering from a "paranoid psychosis" in
the Jones family.

> Implementation of the model consisted of three sessions at two-week
> intervals. Session 1 involved assembling some 50 participants includ-
> ing the client, family members, and other community members along
> with team members and observers. The conductor or intervenor began
> by asking all the participants to undergo nonverbal warm-up exercises.
> The intervenor then spoke for 10 minutes, describing the social net-
> work model. The remainder of the session was devoted to identification
> of possible goals for Claude—separation from symbolic attachments to
> his parents, breaking the "speed-shooting" habit, and development of
> plans for school and work. The conductor formed eight subgroups,
> each composed of six or seven persons. Spokespersons were selected
> for each of the groups; these reported back to the entire group on the
> issues they had discussed regarding the goals identified, that is, what
> is contributing to Claude's drug use.
>
> In the second session, after several issues were identified, the con-
> ductor suggested that a committee called the Claude Committee be
> formed to deal with the issues that the majority of the spokespersons
> had suggested. They were instructed to discuss, and take responsibility
> for, helping Claude with the three goals that had been identified. In the
> third session a Parent Committee was formed for Claude's parents
> because they refused to recognize that their behavior had had a role in
> Claude's problems. Termination came when during the two weeks fol-
> lowing the third session, the two committees were able to accomplish
> the tasks for which the network had been assembled. Claude found a

satisfactory job. He moved to an adjoining state and lived with relatives who had attended the network meetings. Separated from his peer group who were habitual drug users and removed from the relationship with his parents, he stopped using drugs.

Rogler and colleagues (1989) described a community program developed in the South Bronx in New York City to serve troubled Puerto Rican adolescents. The major goal of the program was to counteract the stressful effects of single-parent households and family disorganization by providing symbolic families for the clients. The symbolic families consisted of up to fifteen adolescents currently living in the client's neighborhood. Each symbolic family was headed by neighborhood teenagers who played the roles of symbolic mother, father, aunt, and uncle. The symbolic family members received intensive training in psychological therapy and clinical skills and became the primary caretakers and therapists of the participants, assuming many of the roles and functions that the children's biological families had abdicated or lost.

Szapocznick and colleagues (1978a) and Szapocznick and Kurtines (1993) adapted a European treatment family therapy approach, that of Salvador Minuchin (1974), for use with people of mixed heritage living in the Miami area. Their approach employed a focus on family values and bicultural process, an approach pioneered with Latino school children (Ramirez and Castañeda 1974) in Southern California and Texas. They selected family therapy as the treatment of choice because of the strong family orientation of the cultures of people of mixed heritage. The family therapist assumed a position of authority within the family in order to restore and reinforce essential elements of the traditional value system. In addition they combined a bicultural effectiveness training (BET) program, an approach conducted in twelve conjoint sessions. In BET the initial change strategy was temporarily to defuse family conflict by placing the focus of both the intergenerational and intercultural differences on values conflict. The family's perception of the conflict was reframed; this was accomplished by providing the family with a transcultural perspective that emphasized the communality between parents and their children and by de-emphasizing the generational differences (e.g., by teaching that each member has a valued position or point of view that was culturally determined).

The second strategy of BET was to establish new cross-alliances between family members and cultures. This was done through exercises designed to make both parents and adolescents more comfortable with both cultures. Through these exercises parents were encouraged to accept and understand the value of certain aspects of American culture represented by the child; adolescents were encouraged to accept and understand the value of certain aspects of the Hispanic culture represented by their parents.

Multiracial models. Specialized support groups (King and DaCosta 1996) have been developed to address some of the unique experiences of biracial and multiracial people such as the feeling of being "in-between" and other problems of adjustment that develop as a result of the way the concept of race is constructed in society. Root (1996) has identified four general goals of biracial identity that are addressed by these social support groups: (1) accept both sides of racial heritage, (2) have the right to decide how they want to identify themselves racially, (3) develop strategies for coping with social resistance or with questions about their racial identity so that they no longer feel that there is something wrong with them, and (4) identification as a new racial group—the biracial person feels a strong kinship to other biracial persons. The individuals move fluidly between racial groups but also view themselves apart from these reference groups without feeling marginal because they have generated a new reference group. One of these social support groups described by King and DaCosta (1996), the HAPA Issues Forum, a student/community group of multiracial Japanese Americans was formed to address the changing demographics of the Japanese-American community, primarily high out-marriage rates and the presence of many multiracial children.

Members of HAPA are actively challenging reconstructing race via four strategies. They (1) live their political agenda every day to "resist" and "redo" racial categories, actively identifying themselves as biracial in everyday life, (2) encourage people who interact with them to see them as biracial, (3) create an image of the mixed race person in the traditional Japanese community by educating that community, and (4) ensure that mixed-race people play a vital role in the traditional Japanese community. King and DaCosta (1996) also describe the activities of mixed-race African-American support groups. These groups are not focused on dialogue with only one group; instead they form coalitions with other multiracial people. These groups provide social support for their members and describe the "mixed" experience to the general community. The common goal of these groups is to encourage a transition in members from being "in-between" to being "all"—multicultural.

A NEIGHBORHOOD-BASED, CULTURE-RESPONSIVE MODEL FOR MULTICULTURAL/MULTIRACIAL STRESS

Ramirez (1983) proposed a community-based model—the Neighborhood-Based, Culture-Responsive (NCBR) model, which was designed to address the adjustment problems of adolescents and at the same time to provide intervention and primary prevention benefits for parents, siblings, and other members of the clients' community. Figure 7–4 provides an overview.

Step One: Ethnography

The first step in implementation of the Neighborhood-Based, Culture-Responsive (NBCR) model is to do a thorough ethnography of the community in which it is going to be used. The specific goals of the ethnography follow.

Assessment. The degree of the politics of conflict, vis-à-vis the different value systems, belief systems, and lifestyles in the community must be assessed. Castañeda (1984) observed that politics of conflict in communities can interfere with the development of bicultural/ multicultural orientations to life. In particular, Castañeda argued that it is the acculturating individual's perception of the politics of the conflict and institutional awareness of this conflict that is the important determinant of the extent to which the person is willing to accept values, beliefs, and lifestyles different from those of his/her group of origin. Multicultural/multiracial stress is greatest in those communities with considerable separation and conflict among the different ethnic/ racial groups or in those where traditional and modern values are in conflict (such as disagreement over issues of abortion, gay/lesbian rights, welfare, and immigration). The politics of conflict in a community make it difficult for its residents to develop multicultural/multiracial orien-

**Figure 7–4. A Neighborhood-based, Culture-Responsive
Mental Health Model for Children and Adolescents**

ADJUSTMENT PROBLEMS OF CHILDREN AND ADOLESCENTS
RELATED TO ACCULTURATION STRESS

(IDENTITY CONFUSION; CONFLICTS WITH PARENTS,
AUTHORITIES, AND PEERS;
DRUG ABUSE; TEEN PREGNANCIES; SCHOOL DROP-OUT;
RACIAL AMBIVALENCE; GROUP VIOLENCE, ETC.)

↓

ASSESSMENT OF PSYCHOLOGICAL PROBLEMS AND DEGREE
OF MULTICULTRALISM/MULTIRACIALISM IN LIFE ORIENTATION

1. MULTICULTURAL EXPERIENCE INVENTORY
2. BICOGNITIVE ORIENTATION TO LIFE SCALE
3. FAMILY ATTITUDE SCALE
4. TRADITIONALISM-MODERNISM INVENTORY

IDENTIFICATION OF RESOURCES IN FAMILY,
COMMUNITY, AND CULTURE

↓

ETHNOGRAPHIC APPROACHES
PUBLIC HEALTH, RELIGION, CULTURAL/COMMUNITY SUPPORT GROUPS,
FAMILY, SCHOOL AND NATIVE HEALERS

INTERVENTION AND PRIMARY PREVENTION
1. ESTABLISHMENT OF COMMUNITY SUPPORT AND REFERRAL
   NETWORKS USING RESOURCES IDENTIFIED ABOVE
2. THERAPY
   A. FAMILY/COMMUNITY GROUPS
   B. PEER GROUPS
3. SUPPORTING AGENCIES ALREADY PROVIDING SUPPORT AND
   REFERRAL SERVICES
4. FORMER CLIENTS AND THEIR FRIENDS AND FAMILY MEMBERS
5. CONSULTATION WITH SCHOOL PERSONNEL
6. EDUCATION/SUPPORT GROUPS

↓

GOALS
1. GREATER ADAPTABILITY AND FLEXIBILITY THROUGH BICOGNITIVE
   FUNCTIONING
2. MULTICULTURAL/MULTIRACIAL IDENTITY

tations to life; this is particularly the case for adolescents who are in constant interaction with peers and adults of different groups.

Resources. Spiritual, cultural, community, and familial resources that can be used in the intervention and prevention model need to be identified. As discussed earlier in the chapter, the family, community, and culture play important roles in mixed heritage approaches to healing. Therefore, it is important to identify and incorporate existing support systems in community, family, and culture.

Support and Referral Networks. Information that can help to establish support and referral networks must be obtained. That is, ethnographic information can lead to identification of needed relationships between the agencies and support sources that already exist in the family, community, and culture. Informal ties can be formalized for greater effectiveness; new ties can be developed by encouraging better communication links between various sources of support and by eliminating barriers and misunderstandings that discourage cooperation. This component of the ethnography is critical because the referral network is seen as the major source of client referrals as well as a source of support services that can help in the implementation of the model. Agencies, institutions, organizations, and individuals in the referral and support network will also help to identify and train the people who will be primarily responsible for implementing the model.

Consultation. The consultant (Lopez 1996) behaves as a multicultural educator and ambassador to work with teachers, mental health professionals, and medical care providers as well as with providers of other services. By encouraging a greater match between teaching styles and approaches to service delivery and the learning styles and values of adolescents and their families, the clients can be made to feel less alienated and are thus less likely to drop out of school.

Leader-Models. The multicultural/multiracial paraprofessional leader-models must be identified by approaching institutions of higher education, churches, and volunteer groups in the community. Actual implementation of the intervention component of the program will be affected by people who are native to the community and who are themselves multicultural/multiracial. These persons have experienced and resolved multicultural/multiracial stress problems similar to those with which the clients and their families are struggling. These people will lead intervention groups for clients, do client assessment, encourage maintenance of the referral and support networks, and serve as multicultural/multiracial models for clients in the community.

Variables Related to Successful Outcomes. The attitudes, perceptions, coping strategies, or orientations to life that determine successful multicultural/multiracial adjustments in the community can be revealed through the ethnography. What are the characteristics of multicultural individuals in the community? Which behaviors and values are associated with flexibility of behavior? What are the characteristics of the families and peer groups who cope successfully with politics of conflict and the diversity of the community?

Step Two: Client Assessment

The second step in implementation of the Neighborhood-Based, Culture-Responsive (NBCR) Model is a complete assessment of the clients who are referred for intervention. This involves development of a mestizo personality profile. Three instruments are administered to the prospective client to arrive at this profile: the Multiculturalism Experience Inventory, the Bicognitive Orientation to Life Scale, and the Family Attitudes Scale. The results of the profile permit the client and leader-model to plan an individualized intervention program and to identify the goals to be accomplished through the program.

Step Three: Implementation and Assessment

The third step involves implementation and assessment of the intervention program; the intervention program is a combination of procedures and techniques derived from both the mestizo and European worldviews. The description that follows summarizes the major goals and the procedures used by the leader-models to accomplish these. Intervention is done in family/community and peer groups through same-gender and mixed gender group sessions.

Family/Community Network Sessions. The activities of the family/ community network sessions clarify values and roles in the young person's home and community life. Activities and procedures also help to identify value differences that may be associated with specific intrapersonal and interpersonal conflicts (identified by comparing Family Attitude Scale responses by adolescents and those of their parents and other authority figures). Participants in these sessions should include all available family members and four people (two of whom are invited by the parents and two by the young person) who are not part of the immediate family. Parents and the client are free to invite anyone in the community, including members of the extended family, native healers, clergy, school personnel, boy- or girlfriends, and so forth. Some of the objectives and activities of the family/community network sessions are presented in Table 7–1.

Peer Group Sessions. Peer group sessions are conducted with eight participants of the same gender or with four male and four female participants. The peer group sessions, like the family network sessions, are designed to achieve values and role clarification, to develop perspectives for understanding values reflected by institutions, and to develop mestizo interpersonal and institutional skills. The sessions also seek to improve relationships with peers and to establish a sense of community among the participants.

The Same-Gender Peer Group sessions will include eight intervention group participants and group leaders (of the same gender as the participants). Language(s) in which the session will be conducted will depend on the preferences of the members (see Table 7–2).

Four male and four female participants and one male and one female group leader will comprise the Mixed-Gender Peer Group session. Again language(s) in which sessions are conducted will depend on the preferences of the members (see Table 7–3).

Assessment of Client's Progress. To assess the degree of progress being made by the adolescent client in the intervention component of the model, the Multiculturalism Experience Inventory and the Bicognitive Orientation to Life Scale and the Family Attitude Scale can be re-administered at various times during the course of implementation of the program. Progress is measured by the resolution of value and lifestyle conflicts (external and internal), and by the degree of participation in the cultures represented in the community (as determined by information obtained from Step 1).

Step Four: Client Follow-Up

The fourth and final step involves encouraging former clients to assist in the implementation of the intervention and prevention programs. Clients who have benefited from the model are encouraged

Table 7–1. Family/Community Network Sessions

Goals	Activities Directed by Group Leader
1. Values clarification for young person and parents	Analysis of differences in values; discussion of members' perceived advantages and disadvantages of mixed heritage and mainstream cultures; parents' perceptions of school; adolescent's perceptions of school
2. Role clarification for adolescent and parents	Same as above; also discussion of each member's description of the ideal son/daughter, parent, teacher, student
3. Improved communications between parents and adolescent	Description of family structure and transactional patterns from group leader's observations; assignment to community members to serve as *padrinos* (cultural brokers or facilitators) in relationships between adolescent and parents, between adolescent and the school and other institutions, and between parents and the school and other institutions; group leader's facilitation of communication between parents and adolescent in the sessions
4. Development of multicultural skills in adolescent and parent	Setting of behavioral goals by adolescent for more extensive participation in mainstream and mixed heritage traditional cultures; assignment of community members to serve as *padrinos*
5. Development of positive behavioral health orientations	Group leader initiates discussion regarding individual and family health. Discussion focuses on belief systems and values regarding health (illness in mixed heritage and mainstream cultures and on how family conflicts and multicultural/multiracial stress can affect health); establishment of health goals

to serve as apprentices to group leader-models and to receive training in doing consultation with peer groups, institutions, and the referral-support networks.

Some aspects of the NCBR model have been incorporated into a primary prevention program for Latino adolescents that is being implemented in Southern California. The CLARO program (Flores

Table 7–2. Same-Sex Peer Group Sessions

Goals	Activities Directed by Group Leader
1. Clarification of values	Analysis of values and cognitive style differences; discussion of leader's and members' personal experiences with conflict; role playing of conflict situations which have meaning to group members
2. Clarification of role	Same as above; discussion of ideal son/daughter, multicultural/multiracial person, father, mother, teacher, employer, employee
3. Understanding values reflected by institutions	Same as above with addition of discussion of ideal school, family, and community; group leader initiates discussion of how to identify values reflected by institutions such as the schools; members establish individual goals for understanding institutions in which they have experienced conflict and, with the help of the group, devise plans to achieve these goals; assignment of community *padrinos* consultation plans; reports of degree of success or failure in achieving goals; development of new plans with help of group members
4. Development of multicultural/multiracial interpersonal and institutional behavior	Group leader describes personal experiences in developing a multicultural/multiracial orientation to life; members examine own multicultural/multiracial profiles and establish goals and implement plans to improve their multicultural/multiracial skills in relating to institutions and individuals; group members serve as *padrinos* for each other and as consultants to each other
5. Development of positive behavioral health orientations	Group leader initiates discussion concerning multicultural/multiracial behaviors; focus is on development of skills to take advantage of services offered by mental health clinics and mental health services through schools, churches, and other community agencies; setting of health goals

Table 7–3. Mixed-Gender Peer Group Sessions

Goals	Activities Directed by Group Leader
1. Development of understanding of how value and cognitive style conflicts can create interpersonal conflict with members of the opposite sex in the same ethnic group	Analysis of value and cognitive style differences; group leader's analysis and discussion of members' personal experience; role playing of actual conflict situations; discussion of male's perceptions of ideal female and female's perceptions of ideal male. Discussion of definitions of machismo (Carrasco et al. 1996)
2. Development of understanding of how value conflict can create interpersonal conflict with members of the opposite sex in other ethnic groups	Same as above; also discussion of perceptions of male and female roles in other cultures
3. Clarification of role	Analysis of FAS and TMI responses; members' perceived differences in male and female roles in other cultures
4. Development of positive behavioral health orientation in interpersonal relationships	Discussion of ways in which relationships with others can affect health and psychological adjustment

1996) employs supportive, culturally based groups and activities to assist Latino adolescents to define their identities and to provide alternative solutions to the problems they face in an urban multicultural environment. The program assists participants to cope with feelings of alienation, lack of information, poor living conditions, language barriers, racial discrimination, unemployment, and poverty. Facilitators are trained to lead support group discussions that focus on identity, on definition of the male role, on gang violence and drugs and alcohol, on nonviolence, on the mestizo heritage, on bilingualism, on cultural differences and similarities, and on spiritual preparation.

The mestizo spiritual component of the NCBR model has been incorporated into family therapy with Latino families in San Antonio, Texas, by Cervantes and Ramirez (1995). The authors observed:

> We view family therapy as a natural method with which to integrate spirituality, given its theoretical roots of system balance, family focus,

and family intervention. Mestizo spirituality is a base of knowledge that recognizes a unique perspective and psycho-spiritual themes to guide clinical practice with Mexican-American families. [p. 241]

SUMMARY

The models and perspectives reviewed above indicate that there are significant advances being made in combining the mixed heritage/ mestizo and European approaches and worldviews in the development of mental health programs. These efforts are testimony to the fact that a multiracial/multicultural psychology is becoming a reality.

The mestizo worldview, vis-à-vis illness/health and health care, is characterized by being integrated or holistic rather than dualistic. In the context of the mestizo worldview, health and illness are related to the quality of the person's relationship to the social and physical environments as well as to the quality of his/her relationship with the supernatural. Native healers and shamans are believed to have access to the supernatural and their activities are directed at restoring balance, wholeness, and harmony in life; identification with the supernatural; protection from the supernatural; and reintegration of the client or patient with the family, culture, and community.

Recent advances and knowledge in psychosomatic medicine and behavioral health are based on mestizo models of health/illness and health care. Models for the delivery of mental health services to mestizos in the Americas need to be congruent with the holistic/ integrative view of health and illness. In the context of this holistic view, the use of a combination of European and mestizo approaches and techniques can lead to effective treatment practices and to the encouragement of development of pluralistic identities in people who live in multicultural environments.

❖ **8** ❖

Assessing and Developing Multicultural/Multiracial Orientations to Life: A Guide for Self-Assessment and Growth

Countless number of times I have fragmented and fractionalized myself in order to make the other more comfortable with my behavior, my words, my loyalties, my choice of friends, my appearance, my parents and so on. And given my multiracial ancestry, it was hard to keep track of all the fractions, to make them add up to one whole. It took me over 30 years to realize that fragmenting myself seldom served a purpose other than to preserve the delusions this country has created around race.

—*Maria P. P. Root (1996)*

People without the experience of resolving ambiguity, of moving from marginal status to center, or of expanding definitions beyond traditional constraints in order to really see what in fact exists often cannot adapt competently to marginality or ambiguity, much less to a person who embodies ambiguity.

—*George Kitahara Kich (1996)*

[A]ctive involvement in religious activity has helped African Americans sustain their sense of competence and agency. Our humanistic focus stressed the individual's capacity to have personal causal impact through the exercise of intentions.

—*Adelbert H. Jenkins (1995)*

What does your mind seek?
Where is your heart?
. . . Can anything be found on earth?
—*From a Nahuatl poem, quoted in Leon-Portilla (1963)*

The questions posed by a Native American poet living in the Valley of Mexico in the fifteenth century are relevant today. The questions speak to us as we seek purpose and meaning in a diverse society; as we try to understand our family relationships, our relationships with friends, with colleagues at the work place, our intimacy relationships, our relationships with children and adolescents, and as we seek to know who we are and what we want out of life. Specifically the questions relate to the following challenges in life:

- We seek to understand the impact of personal and family histories in our development.
- We attempt to understand relationships with people of different backgrounds or relationships with people who have different sexual orientations, political views, religions or lifestyles.
- We try to help multicultural/multiracial children as they attempt to understand themselves in a society with rigid definitions of race, ethnicity, gender, sexuality, class, and religion.
- We attempt to come to grips with our position on affirmative action, abortion, welfare, gay rights, capital punishment.
- We attempt to determine how we can play useful and meaningful roles as educators, mentors, parents, and concerned citizens who can make the world a better place in which to live.

As asserted in Chapter 6, in order to cope with the challenges of diversity and to take full advantage of the opportunities it offers, we need to develop multicultural/multiracial orientations to life. We need to become educators, leaders, peer counselors, and ambassadors who can help to embrace a new world view—a combination of the mestizo and the European worldview and a new world order, one in which our humanity and spirituality are much more in evidence.

This chapter explores the processes of multiracial/multicultural development in adults. It also offers self-assessment guidelines to help the reader identify his/her stage of multicultural/multiracial development, and to articulate goals that can enhance that development.

At this point the reader is probably questioning whether he/she has to be a member of an ethnic/racial minority group to develop a multicultural/multiracial orientation to life. The answer is definitely no. The critical requirement for seeking and developing a multicultural/multiracial orientation to life is, first of all, the willingness to learn from others and to be open to diversity. Beyond that there is the need for a desire to take diversity challenges, making it possible to arrive at integration of personality resources and perspectives on life learned from other peoples and groups. Cross (1991) referred to this growth process as internalization-commitment, and Ramirez identified it as synthesis (1983, 1994b). The principal requirement for development of multicultural/ multiracial orientations to life, then, is a state of mind, a philosophy of life and not a certain genetic makeup or specific racial/ethnic origins.

Another important requirement for multicultural/multiracial development has to do with the experience of differentness, of otherness, of being marginal. Most of us experience these feelings at some time in our lives and they serve to give us empathy for those who are experiencing exploitation and exclusion for any reason, be it racial/ethnic phenotype, a physical challenge, a sexual orientation, or religious beliefs or values.

The degree of differentness experienced by people varies in type and degree. Some people are made to feel different in society because of phenotype (i.e., skin color or physical appearance). For others it is accent in language, and for still others it is thinking style, physical disabilities, religion, or sexual orientation. The basis for some people's minority status is visible while that of others may not be as evident. "Type" refers to why the rejection and oppression are occurring, and "degree" refers to the extent of rejection and oppression experienced.

Albert Ramirez (1988) and Janet Helms (1994) argued convincingly that we cannot overlook the fact that race is the most common reason why people are discriminated against, ostracized, perceived as having less social power and influence, and exploited in society—race is thus the nth degree of discrimination, prejudice, and oppression. The phenotype of having dark skins and stereotypical African, Latino, Asian, or Native American features is likely to evoke (in most areas of the world) more rejection and hostility than, say, being light skinned and speaking English with an accent or being light skinned and non-English-speaking, or having values that are different from those commonly held or a sexual orientation different from the majority. It is a question of type and degree, but the underlying experience is still differentness, otherness, marginality.

Persons who strive to develop a multicultural/multiracial orientation to life are seekers, searchers in life who are trying to understand themselves, those around them, and the society in which they live.

Jenkins (1995) views this life search as proactive, as helping us to make a difference in the circumstances that confront us. Jenkins stated, "I have argued that this capacity for agency, along with inherent strivings for psychological 'competence,' has enabled most African Americans to enhance their personal growth in spite of the social obstacles they face" (p. 271). Research by Ramirez and his colleagues (1977, 1978, 1994b) focused on three aspects of multicultural/multiracial orientations to life that reflect the agency and competence that Jenkins described: educator, peer counselor, and ambassador.

MULTICULTURAL/MULTIRACIAL PERSONS AS EDUCATORS, PEER COUNSELORS, AND AMBASSADORS

As a multicultural/multiracial educator, a person makes information about the cultures, groups, and individuals he/she is familiar with available to others. The objectives are to promote understanding and self-esteem and to help eliminate damaging stereotypes that obstruct mutual understanding and cooperation. Another principal objective of the educator role is to encourage people to open their learning-experience filters (see Chapter 4) to diversity so that they can enhance their pool of multicultural resources for multicultural/multiracial personality development and functioning. An important characteristic of the multicultural leaders observed in the leadership study described in Chapter 6 was that they were open to the opinions of others in their groups, even if these opinions did not agree with their own. They also tried to arrive at compromise positions that did not make any member of the group feel excluded or devalued. Their behavior and attitude was also marked by optimism, by the enduring hope that people, no matter how different they were from each other, could eventually work cooperatively and could come to understand each other.

The role of peer counselor exemplifies a second characteristic of multicultural/ multiracial life orientations. As a peer counselor the person empathizes with and helps others who are coping with diversity issues and problems with which they themselves have successfully overcome in the past. They provide a support system for people in diversity and acculturative crises and help to establish support groups for this purpose. Root (1996) described the formation of biracial groups such as the HAPA Issues forum that characterizes the role of peer counselor.

The most important role that characterizes multicultural/multiracial orientations to life is that of multicultural ambassador. It is based on the premise that if people of different cultures, races, and worldviews are brought together in an atmosphere of cooperation and understanding then the development of multicultural/multiracial worldviews and orientations to life will occur naturally. As multicultural/multiracial ambassador the person functions as facilitator and catalyst in multicultural/multiracial development. Some of this behavior was observed in the leaders described in Chapter 6. They established an accepting, non-threating social atmosphere in which group members could hear each other's views and in which they could learn from one another.

The multicultural ambassador is firmly committed to the goal of multicultural/multiracial development because she/he views this development as incorporating the best from what all individuals and groups have to offer. Ramirez (1983, 1994b) and Hall (1992) found that people with multicultural/multiracial orientations to life perceived being multicultural/multiracial as assets. They felt that they lived richer, fuller lives and that they had the best of all cultural worlds.

ADULT DEVELOPMENT OF MULTICULTURAL/MULTIRACIAL ORIENTATIONS TO LIFE—TWO CASE HISTORIES

The two case histories that follow are the true stories of clients selected from the author's private practice files. The multicultural/multiracial odysseys of the two people demonstrate the trials and travails as well as the triumphs of those who work toward developing multicultural/multiracial orientations to life.

Raul's Search: A Journey Assisted by Multicultural/Multiracial Art

Raul was born and reared in a medium-sized city in Central Texas. He was the oldest of five children of parents who were multiracial—Latino, Native American, and African American. He remembered that there had been much discord between his parents when he was growing up. His father had been a heavy drinker and had engaged in multiple extramarital affairs. His father stayed away from home for days at a time. His mother held down two jobs to make ends meet, and Raul, as the oldest child in the family, was forced into the role of parent when he was in early adolescence. He remembered resenting the responsibilities thrust on him and the frustration that he felt in not being able to spend time with his friends. He also remembered that his siblings rebelled against his attempts to be a disciplinarian and the one who assigned the responsibilities for housekeeping and other home and family duties. He felt that the resentment of his siblings had kept him from being able to feel close to them.

Raul's memories of childhood and adolescence were dominated by feelings of ambivalence about his multiracial origins. The city in which he grew up was mostly segregated, with much discrimination against minorities and a limited multiracial community. There was no distinct Native American community, and Latinos, whites, and African Americans lived in different areas of the city. Whites were the dominant group with respect to numbers, as well as economically and politically. He experienced only a thin veneer of ethnic tolerance and liberalism in the community and its schools. He had attended an elementary school that was all Latino, but the middle and high schools he had attended were superficially integrated: the student population was diverse, but the teachers and school administrators were white. In addition, few members of minority groups were in the college-bound classes and, with the exception of team sports, the different groups of students rarely interacted with each other. Biracial dating was discouraged both in the community at large and in the school. Raul felt rejected by the Latino and African-American women because he was multiracial. White girls invariably turned him down when he approached them for dates. Raul's experiences with rejection left a lasting wound on his psyche and also contributed to his racial ambivalence.

All this was exacerbated by his duties at home, which left him with little time to socialize with peers. He became socially isolated. Another factor that contributed to his racial ambivalence were his facial features (phenotype), which fit the stereotypes that most people held of Latinos, African Americans, and Native Americans.

Because he was encountering serious academic problems in high school, his parents sent him to South Texas (the United States–Mexico border region) to live with maternal relatives during his final two years in school. While he was able to do better academically at the new school, and while he remembered benefiting from the emotional support from extended family members, he also encountered rejection from classmates and other peers, this time from Latino students who criticized him for being "too white" because he could not speak Spanish fluently and because he spoke English without an accent. This further heightened his racial ambivalence.

Upon graduation from high school Raul was drafted and eventually sent to Vietnam. His experiences left him with many of the symptoms of post-traumatic stress disorder, but he also adopted a more spiritual perspective, engaging in daily prayer and regular church attendance. At the same time as he encountered prejudice from some white soldiers, he found acceptance among African Americans, Latinos, Native Americans, and Asian Americans (particularly Philippinos). Also he encountered other multiracial people for the first time in his life. He found acceptance from Vietnamese women who responded positively to his multiracial phenotype and multicultural values. He remembered his experiences with Asians as being positive and was even accepted by their families. He was able to learn to communicate in Vietnamese.

When he was discharged from the Army he returned to his hometown and his feelings of racial ambivalence were reawakened. While in Southeast Asia he had become interested in art and had taken lessons in sculpting and painting. He attended college when he returned home, but discovered that the did not have the patience to take the required courses. He found a job in a print shop and he continued to learn art on his own and began to work on his artwork on weekends and evenings.

Raul dated African-American, Latina, and white co-workers, but was most attracted to White women. In particular he reported that he enjoyed the looks of envy that he would get from other men when he walked into a public place with a white woman who was blonde and had blue eyes. However, his relationships with white women all failed, and this is the primary reason he sought therapy. In particular he was concerned that he tended to fall in love with women who could not love him in return. Further, he felt that his tendency to be jealous undermined his relationships as did his feelings of pessimism: "When things were going well in the relationship I kept telling myself that this was too good to be true; that something was bound to go wrong soon." He was also troubled by the feeling that most of the white women with whom he would become intimate were using him because they found his looks and cultural background exotic.

Also bothersome to Raul were his relationships with his siblings. Whenever he would try to get close to them he felt that there was a barrier between them. He felt that they resented him because he had been unduly autocratic and strict with them.

Raul was also feeling confused about the themes that he wanted to pursue in his artwork. He felt attracted to Latino, African, and Native American art but was ambivalent about these interests. He was reluctant to exhibit his work and would show it only to his girl-friends, best friends, and family members. This ambivalence was re-lated to his uncertainty about his identity. He said, "I feel like a man without a group, without a country." He never felt comfortable with any individual or group of people: "I always feel different, like an outsider."

Raul was 35 years old when he sought therapy. At that time he was in considerable turmoil because a girlfriend of two years had recently broken up with him. He was experiencing symptoms of depression and anxiety and also suffering from flashbacks and dreams that were related his traumatic experience in combat in Vietnam.

The therapist introduced Raul to multicultural psychotherapy (Ramirez 1994b) and to a program to help him to develop a multi-cultural/multiracial orientation to life. These steps included:

A Guided Self Assessment. After the initial interview Raul was given a copy of the Multicultural Experience Inventory (MEI) (see Appen-dix) and asked to complete it and bring it with him to the next ses-sion. The analysis of his MEI is shown in Figure 8–1.

The therapist directed Raul's attention to the responses he had given to items 1–8 and to some of his responses to Part I. These re-flected his history and gave clues as to his Historical Development Pattern (as discussed in Chapter 6).

The second set of items they discussed related to Contemporary Multicultural Identity (see Chapter 6). These were items 9–26, which helped to identify those individuals and groups with which Raul had been most involved in recent years and the extent of his involvement and the types of activities he engaged in. The therapist also informed Raul that his responses to some of the CMI items (9–26) were po-tentially revealing of his ability to function effectively in activities (celebrations, crisis situations, family activities, and religious/spiri-tual events) that are unique to these individuals and groups. Some of Raul's responses to Part I were also indicative of his CMI.

Figure 8–1. Raul's Multicultural Experience Inventory

Next to each item, circle the number of the response that best describes your past and present behavior.

1 = mostly my ethnic group
2 = my ethnic group and minorities other than that of my own ethnic group
3 = my ethnic group, whites, and other minorities, about equally
4 = whites and minorities other than my own ethnic group
5 = mostly whites

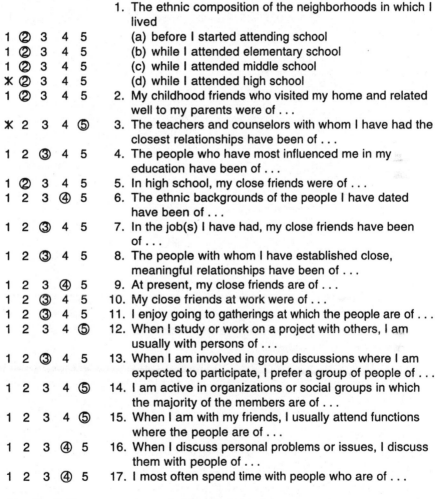

		1. The ethnic composition of the neighborhoods in which I lived
1 ② 3 4 5		(a) before I started attending school
1 ② 3 4 5		(b) while I attended elementary school
1 ② 3 4 5		(c) while I attended middle school
✗ ② 3 4 5		(d) while I attended high school
1 ② 3 4 5		2. My childhood friends who visited my home and related well to my parents were of . . .
✗ 2 3 4 ⑤		3. The teachers and counselors with whom I have had the closest relationships have been of . . .
1 2 ③ 4 5		4. The people who have most influenced me in my education have been of . . .
1 ② 3 4 5		5. In high school, my close friends were of . . .
1 2 3 ④ 5		6. The ethnic backgrounds of the people I have dated have been of . . .
1 2 ③ 4 5		7. In the job(s) I have had, my close friends have been of . . .
1 2 ③ 4 5		8. The people with whom I have established close, meaningful relationships have been of . . .
1 2 3 ④ 5		9. At present, my close friends are of . . .
1 2 ③ 4 5		10. My close friends at work were of . . .
1 2 ③ 4 5		11. I enjoy going to gatherings at which the people are of . . .
1 2 3 4 ⑤		12. When I study or work on a project with others, I am usually with persons of . . .
1 2 ③ 4 5		13. When I am involved in group discussions where I am expected to participate, I prefer a group of people of . . .
1 2 3 4 ⑤		14. I am active in organizations or social groups in which the majority of the members are of . . .
1 2 3 4 ⑤		15. When I am with my friends, I usually attend functions where the people are of . . .
1 2 3 ④ 5		16. When I discuss personal problems or issues, I discuss them with people of . . .
1 2 3 ④ 5		17. I most often spend time with people who are of . . .

✗ = South Texas experience (with grandparents)
◯ = Central Texas experience (with parents)

Figure 8–1. (*continued*)

Next to each item below, circle the response that best describes you.
1 = Extensively
2 = Frequently
3 = Occasionally
4 = Seldom
5 = Never

① 2 3 ✖ 5   18. I attend functions that are predominantly white in nature.

✖ 2 3 ④ 5   19. I attend functions that are predominantly of minority groups other than my own.

✖ 2 3 ④ 5   20. I attend functions that are predominantly of my own ethnic group in nature.

① 2 3 ✖ 5   21. I visit the homes of whites.

① 2 3 ✖ 5   22. I invite whites to my home.

✖ 2 3 ④ 5   23. I visit the homes of persons of my ethnic group (other than relatives).

✖ 2 3 ④ 5   24. I invite persons of my ethnic group (other than relatives) to my home.

✖ 2 3 ④ 5   25. I visit the homes of minorities other than of my own ethnic group.

✖ 2 3 ④ 5   26. I invite persons of minorities other than those of my own ethnic group to my home.

○ presently
✕ while in the service

Four additional items assessed Raul's perceived degree of comfort, acceptance, and identity with the different groups that have had an impact on him as well as those that are currently influencing his multicultural/multiracial development. He was also asked to identify the three goals that he considered to be most important to his future multicultural/multiracial development, as shown in Figure 8–2.

Analysis of the responses to the MEI and the additional multicultural/multiracial development questions provided a focus to the next step of Raul's journey of self discovery—his life history.

A Life History. The therapist guided Raul through a life history by following the outline presented later in this chapter. The information clarified his CMI and, along with the findings of the MEI, indi-

Figure 8–2. Raul's Response to the Additional MEI Items

1. Indicate the degree of comfort you feel when you are with
    1 = Very comfortable
    2 = Somewhat comfortable
    3 = Sometimes comfortable/Sometimes not
    4 = Somewhat uncomfortable
    5 = Very uncomfortable

Whites	1	2	③	4	5
Latinos	1	②	3	4	5
African Americans	1	②	3	4	5
Native Americans	1	②	3	4	5
Asian Americans	①	2	3	4	5

2. Indicate the degree of acceptance you feel when you are with
    1 = Very accepted
    2 = Somewhat accepted
    3 = Sometimes accepted/Sometimes not
    4 = Somewhat unaccepted
    5 = Very unaccepted

Whites	1	2	3	④	5
Latinos	1	2	③	4	5
African Americans	1	②	3	4	5
Native Americans	①	2	3	4	5
Asian Americans	①	2	3	4	5

3. Indicate the degree to which you are identified with
    1 = Very identified
    2 = Somewhat identified
    3 = Sometimes identified/Sometimes not
    4 = Minimally identified with
    5 = Not at all identified with

Whites	1	②	3	4	5
Latinos	1	2	③	4	5
African Americans	1	②	3	4	5
Native Americans	1	2	③	4	5
Asian Americans	1	②	3	4	5

4. Identify the three goals that are most important to your continued multicultural/multiracial development.
    a. To put less importance on physical appearance when I relate to women.
    b. To feel more comfortable in using the art of different cultures in my work.
    c. To show my work to strangers.

cated that some of Raul's confusion and ambivalence had origins in the unusual historical development patterns he had followed throughout his life. These patterns were parallel with abrupt exposure to Whites in his middle and high school years in Central Texas and his abrupt exposure to traditional Latinos during the last two years of high school in South Texas.

In the first part of his life, his family had lived in government-subsidized housing, which was racially and culturally diverse with respect to people of color. During this time his Historical Development Pattern was Early Parallel, with equal exposure to his own primary cultural group (urban Latino) and to other groups of color, including African American, Native American, and Asian. In his middle school years he had his first experience with whites, an abrupt and intensive one (Early Parallel/Abrupt White). This was followed by an equally abrupt rural Latino experience (Early Parallel/Abrupt Rural Latino) when he was sent to live with relatives in the community on the United States–Mexico border region of South Texas.

Next, his life history showed a parallel experience when he was inducted into the armed forces and lived in environments in which he had extensive contact with African Americans, Native Americans, Filipinos, members of other biracial groups, and whites. This was followed by an abrupt exposure to Vietnamese culture when he became intimately involved with Vietnamese women and participated in the activities of their families.

Findings from the MEI and Life History provided information as to Raul's Contemporary Multicultural Identities. In the initial stages of his life he was a preferred Latino and a functional African American and Asian American. During his middle school and early high school years, he became a functional white and continued being a functional Latino, African American, and Asian American. During the time he was living in South Texas, he became even more functional as a Latino and as a bicultural/biracial white/Latino. In the service and prior to the Vietnam experience, he became a more functional African American, Latino, white, Filipino, Asian, and Native American. When he went to Vietnam he became even more functional in Asian culture. Returning to the United States he became a more functional Latino, African American, white, and Native American, and had fewer interactions with Asians.

Identifying Barriers
to Multicultural/Multiracial Development

Drawing on the life history and MEI data, Raul reached certain valuable insights, particularly with respect to barriers that were impeding his multicultural/multiracial development.

- He was able to understand the nature of his cultural/racial ambivalence and how this was impacting his life, particularly with respect to his ambivalence toward the mixed cultural themes in his troubled artwork and his relationships with women. He learned that he was reluctant to show his work that reflected his multicultural/multiracial origins. He had not yet come to terms with the fact that he was a multicultural/multiracial person, and thus was reluctant to exhibit his work because it revealed who he really was, and he might have to deal with the questions of what and who he was.
- He also arrived at the insight that his relationships with women had been dominated by his previous experiences with white women. He was using women as status symbols and as attempts to make up for the rejection he had experienced from them in the past. His perceptions that white women wanted to have relationships with him because he was "exotic" was projection on his part because he himself was using white women for similar reasons. He came to recognize that phenotype was unimportant in relationships and that it was the degree of match with a person's values and orientation to life that would determine if he could have harmonious and meaningful relationships with them. This also applied to his friendships.
- He was also able to understand why his siblings were ambivalent toward him. He had been too harsh a disciplinarian, because he blamed them for his not being able to have more time to date and to play with peers.

The next step in Raul's quest was to determine how these barriers could be overcome so that these would no longer interfere with his multicultural/multiracial development. He established goals for overcoming these barriers and met with positive results:

- He realized he could achieve self-discovery as a multicultural/ multiracial person if he experimented with multicultural/multiracial themes in his artwork. He was encouraged to find a support system for this endeavor. He discovered an international art institute in which he could take courses and meet others who were multiracial and multicultural (whites as well as people of color) and who could be his colleagues. The acceptance and positive feedback he received for his work in this setting reduced his ambivalence, and he began reading extensively about African, Native American, and Latino art. His unique style of combining the three different cultural traditions brought him acclaim and recognition. He overcame the barrier of reluctance to exhibit his artwork.
- He began dating women with whom he felt comfortable, particularly women he met at the international art institute he was attending. His previous tendency to emphasize phenotype in intimacy receded and he became less self-conscious about feeling used in relationships. His feelings that a relationship would fail or that he was not receiving as much love as he was giving lessened considerably.
- He was able to make amends to his siblings for his harsh approach to child rearing and his autocratic managerial approach to assigning household duties. He and his siblings were able to discuss their experiences of being multircial/multicultural, and they established much stronger bonds.

Progress toward Becoming a Multicultural/Multiracial Educator, Peer Counselor, and Ambassador

As a multicultural/multiracial educator, Raul eventually became an instructor in the institute of international art where he had been a student, and he developed a sense of community with the other instructors as well as the students at the school.

Raul became a multicultural/multiracial peer counselor when he served as a mentor for adolescents in the old neighborhood in which he grew up, sharing his own struggles with them. He joined the Big Brothers Program and organized a support group for artists who were expressing their cultural and racial identity struggles through their artwork.

Raul spearheaded an effort to establish a multi-day workshop-conference that included African, Latino, Native American, Filipino, Asian, and other biracial/multiracial artists and allowed them to discuss multicultural/ multiracial art themes and the representation of art themes that reflected the international and intranational struggles for equality and social justice. In this way he served as a multicultural/ multiracial ambassador.

Jill: Self-Understanding through Autobiography and Spirituality

Jill was born in Boston, Massachusetts, and lived on the East Coast until she moved to Texas as a young adult. The only child of second-generation White European immigrants, Jill recalled that her parents' relationship was strained and that she never saw them express affection toward each other. Her father was a traveling salesman and spent a lot of time on the road. Jill remembered that her mother had been controlling, critical, and restrictive. She discouraged Jill's childhood friends from visiting in their home and would not allow Jill to spend time away from home either. Even as an adult, when Jill and her mother moved to Texas following her father's death, the strictness and restrictiveness continued. Jill remembered that when she was attending college, her mother would not allow her to go to parties or football games with her friends.

Jill had a close relationship with her father, who often served as a buffer to her mother's strict child rearing and her controlling tendencies, but his long absences were difficult for Jill. After her father's death and following her graduation from college, she escaped her mother's controlling tendencies by joining the Peace Corps. She remembered this time in her life as a liberating experience. She traveled extensively and she made friends who were of different ethnic/racial groups and religious backgrounds. It was also during her time in the Peace Corps that she began to develop an interest in spirituality and particularly in how spirituality is reflected in world literature.

While in the Peace Corps Jill met and married a Japanese-American man. Both their families opposed the union and Jill's mother did not attend the ceremony or acknowledge their marriage. Her husband's family, although initially opposed, eventually accepted the marriage.

Jill remembered that this was the first time in her life that she felt she had a supportive family environment and a group of friends who loved her and accepted her as she was. Nevertheless, Jill and her husband faced prejudice from people in the community in which they lived in Texas, because they were a biracial couple. Their children were subjected to racial slurs and rejection. In time the pressures on the family took their toll and this resulted in marital problems and eventually in divorce.

Divorce was a devastating experience for Jill; her husband was the first person to whom she had become emotionally attached since her father, so her sense of loss was great. She also felt she had lost the supportive group of friends and family who were part of her husband's extended family. She was overwhelmed as she found herself having to become mother and father to her young children. She had to give up her goal of earning a Ph.D. Prior to her divorce she had been able to get her masters degree in world literature and the religions of the world, and she had hoped to be able to continue her graduate work on this topic.

Jill found employment in an inner city high school, where she taught literature and world history. She felt that she had to struggle to keep her students interested in the subject matter, and discipline problems in the classroom made things difficult for her, particularly in the years prior to her retirement. She recalled that her experiences at the school provided mixed feelings. In spite of the frustrations she encountered, she did not ask for a transfer because she enjoyed working with a diverse group of students and she felt proud that she was able to interest some of her students in the subjects in which she was interested.

Adjustment to retirement was difficult for Jill. She had too much time to reminisce and this eventually led to self-blame. She also became painfully aware that she did not have a close relationship with her children and grandchildren, and she blamed herself for this. She was confused about her feelings toward her mother and ex-husband. She felt guilt regarding her withdrawal from Catholicism after her marriage and her adoption of her husband's religion, Buddhism. These feelings were exacerbated as she began to write her autobiography, which she hoped to leave as a legacy for her children and grandchildren. She thought that through this work they could better understand the many trials and travails she had experienced in life, in lieu of making amends that she felt she could not do more directly.

When Jill came to therapy she was distressed because she was suffering from writer's block. She had succeeded in writing the chapters about her early childhood years and about her relationship with her father in particular, but she was stymied in her attempts to write the chapter about her mother.

Jill, like Raul, participated in multicultural counseling and she also followed the program for development of multicultural/multiracial orientation to life:

A Guided Self-Assessment. After the initial session she completed the MEI and brought it with her to the second session, where she and the therapist reviewed and discussed her responses, which are shown in Figure 8–3.

Jill and the therapist first reviewed her responses to items 1–8 and to some of the items of Part I, which are primarily historical and gave clues to her Historical Development Pattern. As her responses regarding her childhood and adolescent years show, most of her interpersonal contacts had been with mainstream middle-class white Americans and with members of white European ethnic groups, with only minimal contact with African Americans and Latinos (primarily Puerto Ricans). She had contact with people of different religions such as Jews, Protestants, and Catholics (Early white Catholic/Gradual white Protestant, Jewish, and Latino), experience that may have been the root of her interest in the different forms of spirituality expressed in literature and in studying the religions of the world.

Jill's responses to additional questions, as shown in Figure 8–4, reveal her perceived degree of comfort and identity with the different groups that had influenced her life in the past, as well as those that are currently influencing her multicultural/multiracial development. The responses to item 9–23 and some items of Part I related directly to Jill's Contemporary Multicultural Identity and prompted a discussion regarding her view that her responses might have been different had she responded to the MEI at other times in her life, for instance, during the early years of her marriage, when she had been close to her husband, his extended family, and their friends (many of whom were biracial and multiracial). The therapist encouraged Jill to complete an MEI for this time in her life as well.

Jill's Life History. During the first part of her life Jill's diversity experiences included contact with mainstream Whites as well as those who were more recent immigrants in urban areas of the East Coast

Figure 8–3. Jill's Multicultural Experience Inventory

Next to each item below, circle the response that best describes your past and present behavior.

1 = mostly my ethnic group
2 = my ethnic group and some minorities
3 = my ethnic group and minorities, about equally
4 = mostly minorities

				1. The ethnic composition of the neighborhoods in which I lived
①	2	3	4	(a) before I started attending school
1	②	3	4	(b) while I attended elementary school
1	②	3	4	(c) while I attended middle school
1	②	3	4	(d) while I attended high school
1	②	3	4	2. My childhood friends who visited my home and related well to my parents were of . . .
①	2	3	4	3. The teachers and counselors with whom I have had the closest relationships have been of . . .
①	2	3	4	4. The people who have most influenced me in my education have been of . . .
1	②	3	4	5. In high school, my close friends were of . . .
1	②	3	4	6. The ethnic backgrounds of the people I have dated have been of . . .
1	2	③	4	7. In the job(s) I have had, my close friends have been of . . .
1	2	③	4	8. The people with whom I have established close, meaningful relationships have been of . . .
1	②	3	4	9. At present, my close friends are of . . .
1	2	③	4	10. My close friends at work were of . . .
1	2	③	4	11. I enjoy going to gatherings at which the people are of . . .
①	2	✗	4	12. When I study or work on a project with others, I am usually with persons of . . .
1	2	③	4	13. When I am involved in group discussions where I am expected to participate, I prefer a group of people of . . .
①	2	3	✕	14. I am active in organizations or social groups in which the majority of the members are of . . .
1	②	3	✕	15. When I am with my friends, I usually attend functions where the people are of . . .
1	②	3	✕	16. When I discuss personal problems or issues, I discuss them with people of . . .
①	2	3	✕	17. I most often spend time with people who are of . . .

✕ before retirement

Figure 8–3. (*continued*)

Next to each item below, circle the response that best describes you.

1 = Extensively
2 = Frequently
3 = Occasionally
4 = Seldom
5 = Never

①	2	3	✖	18. I attend functions that are predominantly of my ethnic group.
✖	2	3	④	19. I attend functions that are predominantly of minority groups.
①	2	3	✖	20. I visit the homes of people (not relatives) of my ethnic group.
✖	2	3	④	21. I visit the homes of people of minority groups.
①	2	3	✖	22. I invite people (other than relatives) of my ethnic group to my home.
✖	2	3	④	23. I invite people of minority groups to my home.

○ currently
✕ during marriage

and only minimal contact with African Americans and Latinos. She had experience interacting with people of different religious groups and attended a variety of services and religious celebrations such as bar mitzvahs and baptisms.

The second major phase of her life involved the move to Texas with her mother after her father's death. This was the first time that Jill had come into contact with Latinos, Native Americans, Asian Americans, and African Americans. These interactions continued during the next major phase of her life when she joined the Peace Corps. While serving in the Peace Corps, Jill traveled extensively in Latin America, Europe, and India. This allowed her to explore her interests in the religions and literature of the world more extensively.

Her next major life phase was her marriage to a Japanese American. It was at this time that she became actively involved in Japanese-American culture as well as in the biracial/ multiracial cultures of some of her husband's relatives and friends who were married to African Americans, Latinos, Chinese, and Koreans. It was during this period that she became inactive in the Catholic Church and became a practicing Buddhist.

Figure 8–4. Jill's Response to the Additional MEI Items

1. Indicate the degree of comfort you feel when you are with
    1 = Very comfortable
    2 = Somewhat comfortable
    3 = Sometimes comfortable/Sometimes not
    4 = Somewhat uncomfortable
    5 = Very uncomfortable

White Catholics	①	2	3	4	5
White Non-Catholics	1	2	③	4	5
Biracial/Multiracial People	1	2	3	④	5
Japanese Americans	1	2	3	④	5
Latinos	①	2	3	4	5
African Americans	①	2	3	4	5

2. Indicate the degree of acceptance you feel when you are with
    1 = Very accepted
    2 = Somewhat accepted
    3 = Sometimes accepted/Sometimes not
    4 = Somewhat unaccepted
    5 = Very unaccepted

White Catholics	①	2	3	4	5
White Non-Catholics	1	2	③	4	5
Biracial/Multiracial People	①	2	3	4	5
Japanese Americans	①	2	3	4	5
Latinos	1	②	3	4	5
African Americans	1	②	3	4	5

3. Indicate the degree to which you are identified with
    1 = Very identified
    2 = Somewhat identified
    3 = Sometimes identified/Sometimes not
    4 = Minimally identified with
    5 = Not at all identified with

White Catholics	①	2	3	4	5
White Non-Catholics	1	2	3	4	⑤
Biracial/Multiracial People	1	2	3	④	5
Japanese Americans	1	2	3	④	5
Latinos	1	2	③	4	5
African Americans	1	2	③	4	5

4. Identify the three goals that are most important to your continued multicultural/multiracial development.
    a. To be able to discuss biracial issues and mixed-ethnic marriage issues with my children and grandchildren.
    b. To renew friendships with the biracial/multiracial and Asian people I met when I was married.
    c. To become an active member of both the Buddhist and Catholic religions.

Following divorce she lost most contacts with Asians and biracial/ multiracial people, as well as with other Buddhists. She returned to Catholicism. Most of her contacts were with mainstream whites and with Latino and African-American colleagues in the inner city school in which she taught. Contacts with Latinos and African Americans were less frequent and less intense after her retirement.

Historical Development Patterns

Jill started as early white with a gradual introduction to Jewish, Protestant, and other white European groups. This was followed by an abrupt introduction to Latino, African-American, and Native American cultures when she moved to Texas. She also had an abrupt introduction to Japanese-American culture when she married.

Contemporary Multicultural Identities

Currently Jill is predominantly white and functional Latino and African-American. In the past, when she was married and a practicing Buddhist, she was more synthesized, because she felt that she was a member of both the mainstream white group and the Asian group, particularly Japanese-American and biracial/multiracial groups.

Barriers to Multicultural/Multiracial Development

From the Life History Information and the MEI Jill arrived at the following insights regarding barriers toward multicultural/multiracial development:

- She had unresolved feelings of anger toward her mother and ex-husband. Her feelings toward her mother were contributing to her writer's block. Her feelings toward her husband had kept her from continued involvement in Buddhism (which she had enjoyed) and from having contacts with some of the Asian and biracial/multiracial friends whom she had met through her husband and his family.
- Her unresolved ambivalence toward biracial relationships because of the racism her children encountered as well as the prejudice she and her ex-husband experienced as a biracial couple

interfered with her being able to discuss biracial/multiracial issues with her children and grandchildren.
- Her feelings of guilt regarding her decreased involvement in Catholicism at the time of her marriage and her concern that the breakup of her marriage was a punishment from God.

To eliminate the barriers she identified during therapy, Jill took several proactive steps:

- She participated in multicultural therapy to deal with her feelings of anger toward her mother and ex-husband and her feelings of ambivalence regarding her biracial marriage and the biracial/multiracial identities of her children and grandchildren.
- She confronted the hurt she had encountered in her mother's lack of acceptance of her marriage and the discrimination her children, ex-husband, and she had encountered from the mainstream white community.
- She began to re-establish relationships with Asian and biracial/multiracial friends and to become involved in both the Catholic and Buddhist religions.
- She began to pursue additional graduate work related to her academic interests in religions and cultures of the world.
- And finally she initiated discussions with her children and grandchildren using the autobiography she was writing as a focus. In this way she could explain how she had felt about the rejection and critical stance of her mother and the racism and rejection experienced by her ex-husband and herself, and how she had felt powerless to help her children as they were dealing with rejection and racial ambivalence.

Jill also made progress toward becoming a multicultural/multiracial educator, peer counselor, and ambassador.

In the role of a multicultural/multiracial educator, Jill enrolled in a university extension creative writing class. For writing assignments she wrote about joining the Buddhist religion and about her friendships with Latinos and African Americans in the Peace Corps and with colleagues and students in the high school in which she taught. She wrote about her experiences in teaching students of different ethnic groups.

After reading some of her essays in class Jill was approached by several fellow students who revealed their problems regarding biracial/multiracial relationships and marriages and problems they were encountering in multicultural/multiracial employment settings. Jill was able to listen and to share some of her insights and experiences with them, thus serving as a multicultural/multiracial peer counselor.

With the help of some of the biracial/multiracial friends with whom she had reestablished contact and with some of the students in her creative writing course, Jill established a Buddhist-Catholic Study Group. The group was multicultural/multiracial in its composition and included Latinos, Asians, African Americans, biracial peoples, and whites. Members of the group discussed their experiences in attempting to integrate different orientations to Christianity: Native American and European belief systems as represented in Latino Catholicism, African-American and white spiritual belief systems as reflected in black churches, and white and Buddhist as represented in Asian-Christian churches. Jill was able to draw on her knowledge of world literature and international theology to serve as a multicultural/multiracial ambassador for the group.

Raul's and Jill's case studies can serve as models for the reader's efforts to assess his/her degree of multicultural/multiracial development, to identify barriers to development, to evolve goals to overcome barriers, and to develop the roles of multicultural/multiracial educator, peer counselor, and ambassador.

A SELF-ASSESSMENT GUIDE

The following exercise is designed to help the reader understand his/her own multicultural/multiracial orientation to life. It also seeks to help the reader identify goals for continued development and to eliminate any barriers which might interfere with the attainment of these. Procedures for assessment and for encouraging development of multicultural/multiracial orientations to life have emerged from the psychotherapy/counseling and research experiences of the author.

First a word of caution. From reading the case histories of Jill and Raul, the reader is well aware that multicultural/multiracial development programs need to be tailored to individual needs, life experiences, and life goals. The programs involve months of guided self study and effort to change. The procedures presented here should be considered to be general guidelines only.

The First Step: Assessment

The reader is encouraged to photocopy and complete the MEI in Appendix A.

Analysis of MEI responses:

- Historical Development Pattern section. The reader should review his/her responses to items 1–8. These responses help to identify tentatively a Historical Development Pattern (HDP) or Patterns (see Chapter 6). Depending on the reader's personal experiences, modifications may have to be made in the HDP as was the case for Raul and Jill. This is only a preliminary determination of HDP. A more permanent determination is possible after the Life History is completed. Answers to these questions also give an indication as to the degree of extensiveness and intensiveness of the reader's diversity experiences, which can be explored in more detail in doing the self-life history.
- Contemporary Multicultural Identity section. Now the reader is asked to examine responses to items 9–26 (if a person of color) or items 9–23 (if White). From these responses the reader will be able to arrive at a tentative determination of her/his Contemporary Multicultural Identity (CMI). Again modifications may have to be made of the categories presented in Chapter 6, but the reader can guide himself/herself with the definitions offered there. A more conclusive identification of CMI can be made after the Life History has been concluded.

Some follow-up questions might also help the reader with the tentative identification of the HDP and CMI. These are as follows:

1. Indicate the degree of comfort you feel when you are with (various ethnic groups).
2. Indicate the degree of acceptance you feel when you are with (various ethnic groups).
3. Indicate the degree to which you are identified with (various ethnic groups).

4. Identify the three goals that are most important to your continued multicultural/multiracial development.

The analysis of responses to the MEI and the four follow-up questions should give focus to the life history by helping the reader to identify the critical life periods in which diversity was experienced. Referring back to Raul's and Jill's case studies can help to identify some of these critical life periods. As a review, in the case of Raul, the critical life periods were as follows:

1. Childhood-early adolescence was a time when he lived with his family in federally subsidized housing projects in an urban community in Central Texas.
2. His early high school years provided his first encounter with mainstream white peers and his perceived rejection by white, Latina, and African-American women.
3. During his later South Texas high school years with his mother's family, he experienced an abrupt immersion into traditional Latino culture of the U.S.–Mexico border region and perceived rejection by traditional Latinos and by Latinas in particular.
4. His experiences in the armed services and in Vietnam led to mixed relationships with whites and positive relationships with Latinos, Native Americans, African Americans, Asians, and biracial people.
5. In Vietnam there was also an abrupt immersion in Asian culture.
6. After Vietnam, as a printer and multicultural artist in urban Central Texas, he again perceived rejection by white women, but he established close friendships with co-workers of different backgrounds.

For Jill the different critical life periods were as follows:

1. During childhood-early adulthood she lived with her parents on the East Coast and was first introduced to different religions of mainstream whites and immigrant European groups.
2. After the move to Texas she developed an interest in spirituality and world literature in her college work. She also experienced abrupt immersion in Latino, African, and Asian cultures.

3. In the Peace Corps she had interaction with people of different religious backgrounds, races, and ethnic groups, and experienced international travel.
4. Her marriage gave her an introduction to Japanese-American culture, Buddhism, and biracial friends, and also the experience of prejudice because of her biracial marriage.
5. Divorce saw her return to the Catholicism and to the mainstream White community, and separation from Asian-American and biracial friends and from Buddhism.
6. When she was teaching, Jill was exposed to the diversity of the student body and colleagues in an inner-city school.
7. After retirement Jill had to rely on her children and grandchildren for help and support, yet did not feel emotionally close to them. She also felt the loss of the support she had experienced in the Asian-American/biracial community and the Buddhist religion.

Consider these case studies as examples and identify and list the critical time periods in your life when you had major encounters with diversity. Next answer some basic questions about your family background and early socialization experiences to lay the groundwork for examining those critical life periods:

Family questions include:

Origins

- the ethnic/racial background of your mother's family
- the ethnic/racial background of your father's family
- the ethnic/racial background of your extended family (include relatives by marriage).

Family Attitudes toward Diversity

- How did your parents respond when you asked them questions about your ethnic/racial, religious, or language background?
- Did your parents encourage openness of learning-experience filters, that is, did they view differences as positive and as a source of potential learning and growth?
- How did they respond when you asked about other groups?
- Did you hear negative stereotypes or ethnic/racial slurs in your home? If you did, how did they affect you?

Early Visitors and Visits

- Who were the adults who visited in your home?
- Who were your childhood friends who visited in your home and in whose homes you visited?

Neighborhoods in Which You Lived with Your Family

- What was the ethnic/racial composition of the neighborhood(s) you lived in?
- What were the social-political-economic-spiritual characteristics of that region(s) of the state, country, or world?
- What was the degree of segregation, the presence of glass ceilings, and the availability of models who represented diversity and biracial relationships?
- What were the characteristics of the pre-school(s) you attended, and of the teachers, administrators, or other educational personnel who influenced you?
- What were the influences of the religions/spiritual groups that you had contact with or the churches and groups that your parents or friends belonged to?

History, Music, and Travel

- What were the historical stories, folklore, music, nature of entertainment, or travel to which you were exposed?

Influential Adults

- Who were the adults who were influential in your life: day care personnel, extended family, clergy, co-workers of parents, friends of parents, any housekeepers, baby-sitters, or others who worked around your home who had an influence on you?

Self-Awareness

- When and how did you first become aware of the fact that you were different from others in regard to age, gender, skin color, eye color, hair, physique, disabilities, or sexual orientation? How did the experience(s) affect you?

- Did you experience rejection? Were you made to feel different because of the way you looked, the languages you spoke, or your socioeconomic class or gender?

School Environments

- Were you influenced by the social atmosphere and policies (Castañeda's politics of values conflict) of the schools you attended?
- Did these schools encourage learning about your group as well as other groups? Were your languages, cultures, religions, groups, or races valued?
- Did the school atmosphere encourage or discourage cross-race/ethnic friendships, dating, and other activities?
- What were the effects of extracurricular activity such as University Interscholastic League competition or competition in sports, participation in church groups, summer camps, or community groups (scouts, summer employment groups, etc.)?

Focus on Critical Life Periods Identified Earlier in This Chapter:
   Consider each of the critical life periods in which you experienced diversity, and ponder the following questions for each:

- What was the nature of the diversity experience(s)?
- Were they parallel, gradual, or abrupt?
- What positive and negative experiences were associated with these experiences?
- What cultures, groups, religions, spiritual experiences, and people did you learn about?
- What did you learn—what values, languages, skills, problem-solving approaches and so on?
- How did the experience(s) change you? Do these changes still have an influence on your lifestyle?
- Did any barriers for multicultural/multiracial development emerge from any of the diversity experiences?
- Have you been a multicultural/multiracial educator, peer counselor, or ambassador? How?
- What influence have these experiences had on your multicultural/multiracial development?

Barriers to Multicultural/Multiracial Development Identified

The reader is encouraged to identify and list any potential barriers to development of diversity orientations to life from each of his/her critical life periods. For example, in Raul's case history, his abrupt experience with whites in high school led to rejection by white women, which in turn had an impact on his intimacy relationships as an adult. The same was true with respect to his abrupt introduction to traditional Latino culture when he was sent to live with relatives in South Texas. This experience left him with ambivalence toward Latino culture and the Spanish language and also toward Latinas whom he perceived as having rejected him.

Potential Goals for Multicultural/Multiracial Development

Examination of both the HDPs and CMI(s) allows the reader to assess how she/he is functioning as a multicultural person at the present time, how he/she has functioned in the past, and how she/he might want to function, thus helping to identify any goals the reader might have as to future multicultural/multiracial development. For example, in the case of Raul, his current CMI made it obvious to him that he was isolated from others who might also have multicultural and multinational artistic interests. For Jill it was the realization that after her divorce she had distanced herself from sources of support and life interests such as the Buddhist religion and her Asian and biracial friends.

STRATEGIES FOR OVERCOMING THE BARRIERS

Once the reader is able to identify those barriers to multicultural/ multiracial development that are present in his/her life, she/he can begin to develop strategies to overcome these, much as Jill and Raul were able to do. It is well to keep in mind that for most barriers, the insight as to nature and origin may not be sufficient to create change; behavioral and cognitive changes will also be necessary.

For example, the well-known psychologist Albert Ellis recalled (Corey 1995) that when he discovered that he had an exaggerated fear of speaking in public, he had to adopt both philosophical as well as behavioral strategies for change. The philosophical change involved telling himself that whenever he was to shy too speak up in a group or in a class, he was depriving others of his unique and personal views on issues or problems. The behavioral change involved making a contract with himself in which he agreed never to leave a group or public gathering until he had forced himself to ask a question or make a comment. It was both the philosophical and behavioral changes that eventually helped him to overcome shyness. The strategies that Ellis describes are also necessary for multicultural/multiracial development: insight, attitudinal, and behavioral changes are all needed.

GOALS FOR CONTINUED MULTICULTURAL/MULTIRACIAL EDUCATOR, PEER COUNSELOR, AND AMBASSADOR DEVELOPMENT

In the process of identifying goals for continued multicultural/multiracial development, the reader should keep in mind the three major roles of the multicultural/multiracial person: educator, peer counselor, and ambassador. The reader needs to ask the following questions:

- What can I do to introduce others to what I have learned through my diversity experiences and to the general cause of pluralism in society?
- How can I help others whose multicultural/multiracial development is blocked by barriers similar to those that I have succeeded in overcoming? How can I help to prevent development of barriers for others (primary prevention)?
- How can I help to promote synthesis/amalgamation by serving as a catalyst by bringing people of different backgrounds, values, and worldviews together in a spirit of cooperation and understanding that can promote synthesis and amalgamation?

SUMMARY

This chapter has focused on multicultural/multiracial developmental processes. It presented two case histories of people who made the journey successfully. It also provided some general guidelines so that the reader can do a self-analysis and initiate the multicultural/multi-racial journey him/herself. The concluding chapter combines a focus on individuals with a focus on society and its institutions: What role do politics, education, and the mass media play in the development of an atmosphere that can be favorable to the development of multi-cultural/multiracial educators, peer counselors, and ambassadors in all parts of the world and in all walks of life? That is the major challenge of the twenty-first century: how to live, work, and relate harmoniously in a multicultural world.

❖ 9 ❖

Living, Working, and Relating in a Multiracial/ Multicultural World

Europe's task is no longer, nor will it ever be again, to rule the world, to disseminate by force its own concepts of welfare and what is good, to impose its own culture upon the world or to instruct it in its proper course. Europe has one final possibility, if it so desires: it can reclaim its finest spiritual and intellectual traditions, and go back to the roots of those traditions and look for what they have in common with other cultures and other spheres of civilization, and join forces with them in a search for the common minimum necessary to guide us all so that we may live side by side on one planet and confront jointly whatever threatens our lives together.

—Vaclav Havel (1996)

Furthermore it would appear necessary that the individual's perception of the politics of conflict be understood, for it may also be an important determinant of the character and form of acculturation. Most important and perhaps paradoxical, it seems that a democratic society is confronted with the need for impartial attention to the two belief systems (traditional and modern) in the evolution of public policies and institutions. There is a need for the application of democracy in the domain of cultural differences. Throughout the world, this need is as pressing today as when the American Constitution was created.

—Alfredo Castañeda (1984)

Today all of us are unquestionably a part of a global society, but the common membership does not produce cultural uniformity around the globe. The challenge now facing us is to live in harmony without living in uniformity. . . . We need to share some values such as commitment to fundamental human rights and basic rules of interaction, but we can be wildly different in other areas such as life-styles, spirituality, musical tastes and community life.

—Jack Weatherford (1994)

In this book, adapted from a 1983 version, I have updated and expanded a mestizo multicultural/multiracial paradigm for the social sciences and the helping professions. This perspective, a product of the unique history and experiences of the Americas, provides a blueprint for living, working, and relating in a diverse world. The mestizo multicultural/ multiracial perspective offers limitless opportunities to individuals and to society in a world that is rapidly shrinking because ethnic/racial lines are becoming increasingly blurred and because of the development of global economics, world politics, and communications technology.

OPPORTUNITIES FOR GROWTH

Development of adaptability and flexibility. The mestizo multicultural/ multiracial model of development emphasizes participation in diversity challenges, which provide opportunities to learn from experiences with different peoples, societies, and cultures. These interactions provide the person with a repertoire of personality-building elements or resources that can help him/her to be effective in many different life situations and with varied groups, cultures, and peoples. The multicultural leaders studied in the research reported in Chapter 6 were able to borrow from an extensive and diverse pool of leadership behaviors. These behaviors made them more effective than monocultural leaders who lacked diverse resources as they faced the task of trying to help a mixed ethnic/racial group to reach consensus on an emotion-laden problem. Diverse experiences and challenges also give us the opportunity to synthesize and amalgamate personality-building elements and worldviews from different sources in order to develop multicultural/ multiracial identities and orientations to life. In Chapter 8 we were able to see that Raul's and Jill's behavior as multicultural ambassadors helped them to develop comfortable and effective multicultural/ multiracial orientations to life.

Overcoming ethnocentric, sexist, and other general notions of superiority. The elimination of prejudices and perspectives of superiority encourage the opening of learning-experience filters and elimination of barriers that can keep us from learning from other persons, societies, and cultures. The self-life history and MEI discussed in Chapter 8 provide awareness of potential barriers to the development of multicultural/multiracial orientations to life. These techniques also give ideas as to how to overcome barriers by taking advantage of the opportunities for multicultural/multiracial development offered by diverse environments and the teachings of multicultural/multiracial educators and peer counselors.

The possibility of establishing meaningful and harmonious relationships with those who are different from us. This orientation enables friendships, working partnerships, and intimacy with people of different racial/ethnic backgrounds, classes, gender groups, sexual orientations, religions, and physical disabilities. It allows the opportunity to become true citizens of the world. Part and parcel of this is the development of multicultural/multiracial leadership skills: to communicate effectively and to get people of different backgrounds to work cooperatively to achieve common goals. The leadership research discussed in Chapter 6 identified some of the multicultural/multiracial leadership skills that helped leaders to function more effectively even in situations in which it was not possible to achieve consensus among group members.

The opportunity to participate in the roles of multicultural educators, peer counselors, and ambassadors, which help us to serve as facilitators for the development of a true global village. What we learned from the life history research described in Chapter 6 is that people with multicultural/multiracial orientations to life disavow egocentrism and a general "me" orientation; they recognize that we are all in this together. They exhibit the personality characteristic that Peter Adler (Chapter 6) has described as transcendent: feeling a part of, and apart from, different groups and cultures. This characteristic makes them more objective as they examine different cultures and groups and identify those values, belief systems, and behaviors that prevent them from being able to work toward common goals of peace and understanding.

Identification and awareness of the "true" self by recognizing and overcoming the pressures for conformity that we feel are imposed on us by people, by institutions, and by society in general. The self-life history discussed in Chapter 8 provides the opportunity to recognize our most important values and styles of life and also helps us to identify our life mission. In Chapter 8, the cases of Jill and Raul show how this is facilitated by the life history and the use of the MEI. The mestizo multicultural/multiracial paradigm can also help transform a divided world into a global village by way of the following:

- Encouraging the adoption of the philosophy of cultural democracy. This philosophy offers the opportunity for societal institutions, particularly educational institutions, to enable individuals to make informed choices regarding individual identity. Individuals do not have values, languages, and cultures imposed on them and thus can follow their own path to identity development without being forced to choose because of conformity pressures. As the quotation by Castañeda introducing this chapter emphasized, societal institutions need to be aware of the politics of conflict so that their citizens do not come to see traditional and modern belief systems as opposites and as conflicting, but as the possibility of combining them as reflected in the lifestyles of people who are multicultural and multiracial.

- Encouraging adoption of worldwide economic policies to provide people in different parts of the world with an equal opportunity to achieve their potential in life through education, adequate health care, and prenatal care. The Asian-Indian economist Sen (1995), in his book entitled *Inequality Reexamined*, proposed an economic theory reflective of a mestizo multicultural/multiracial paradigm. It is a theory based on liberty, equality, and sense of community (the bond of solidarity that unites human beings and a proposed intuitive sense of that bond). Sen argued that we should all be equally placed to fulfill our potentials, and we should be equally free to choose goals for which we might strive. He argued that democratic forms of government and a free press have made it possible to reduce possibilities of famine, to increase the levels of education, and to increase life expectancies for people in countries that are less technologically developed.

- Encouraging the development of approaches to research that combine European and mestizo traditions to make it possible to better understand and to solve those problems that stand in the way of world peace, social justice, and global community. Combining different perspectives of science and research methodology—Eastern, Western, African, Native American, and Latino—to arrive at multimodal approaches to research and personality change can help assure that people live meaningful lives in peace and harmony. For example, in Chapter 7 we saw how treatment philosophies and approaches emanating from the mestizo and European worldviews can lead to more effective approaches to psychotherapy and counseling.

But what of those who say that multiculturalism is dangerous and divisive? That it supports reverse discrimination and imposes political correctness?

IS MULTICULTURALISM DANGEROUS?

In recent years, some scholars, talk show hosts, newspaper columnists, and other English-only advocates have warned of the dangers of multiculturalism. These prophets of doom have raised the specters of reverse discrimination, political correctness, separatism, and conflicts as exemplified in the warring Balkan states. The columnist Bernstein, in his book *Dictatorship of Virtue*, went so far as to refer to multiculturalism in terms of combat: "The multiculturalist fortress is empty. We should not flee. The battle is ours" (p. 346). I hope that through the presentation of the mestizo multicultural/multiracial paradigm in this book I have been able to show that Bernstein is wrong and that the multiculturalism is not a fortress; rather, it is a global village made up of the hearts, minds, and hopes of most of the people of the world. I counter that people who are cultural and or genetic mestizos, such as Jill and Raul, as well as the international business person, the statesperson, the teacher, the therapist, the parents of biracial children, and the person who has friends, an intimate partner, or a spouse who has been reared with different values, lifestyles, and worldviews, provide promise. For these people diversity is not a war or a fortress to be assaulted. It is an everyday reality and a challenge for the development of greater self knowledge, growth, and understanding of the human condition.

The prophets of multicultural doom have failed to understand the multicultural/multiracial literature. As early as 1903, the African-American sociologist and civil rights leader, W. E. B. DuBois, articulated the goals of multicultural/multiracial development as applied to African Americans. Indeed these same goals hold for all peoples of the world: amalgamation as individuals merge their double self (such as African-American and American) into a better and truer self.

DuBois outlined his hope for African Americans: "In this merging he wishes neither of the older selves to be lost. He would not Africanize America, for America has much to teach the world and Africa. He would not bleach his Negro soul in a flood of white Americanism, for he knows that Negro blood has a message for the world. He simply wishes to make it possible for a man to be both a Negro and an American" (p. 17).

I have attempted to show in this book that this same message of merging has been reiterated by the contemporary multicultural/ multiracial scholars whose work has been reviewed in this book, including Cross, Parham, Sue and Sue, Root, Hall, Jenkins, Buriel and Ramirez, and Castañeda. In the quote from Al Castañeda that opens this chapter, we can see that the conflicting messages we hear are caught up in a politics of conflict between two opposing sets of values, two worldviews. Whether we refer to these as modern or traditional, as mestizo or North American–Western European is not important. The fact is that the conflict creates confusion and ambivalence.

As I examined some of my own experiences in the preparation of this edition, I became aware that this confusion and the "two-ness" described by DuBois was reflected in my own experiences. I can appreciate the impact of my formative years spent growing up in the United States–Mexico border community of Roma, Texas, were positive for the multicultural/multiracial process. I was able to see cooperation and mutual respect in action among members of three different groups: Mexicans, mainstream middle-class Anglo Americans, and Latino Americans. I saw values of these three groups merge to form multicultural/ multiracial perspectives. I saw their different problem-solving, communication, and human relational styles amalgamating to form new ways of approaching problems in life, and approaches for overcoming misunderstandings and for preventing conflict. I saw a new language emerging as English and Spanish mixed so that words from both languages combined to form sentences; I heard new words created from combining parts of words from both the languages.

I saw business practices and political styles adapted to reflect bicultural/multicultural styles for doing business and for advertising. I attended schools in which children who lived in Mexico sat in classes with those born in the United States. As I interacted with the children from Mexico I was able to see that even though only a river separated us and we shared the same religion and the same language, many of the ways our families did things and some of our values and perceptions of the world were different.

The confusion and the joy of diversity intensified when a joint Mexican-U.S. project, the Falcon Dam, on the Rio Grande River, was initiated only ten miles from Roma. This project brought Anglo engineers, technicians, contractors, and their families into the area. For the first time I was able to interact with Anglo peers, not just teachers and school administrators. As a member of the football team I experienced the synthesis of language and values first hand; all our signals in the huddle were called in Spanish, so the Anglo team members quickly learned enough Spanish to keep from "blowing" the plays, while those of us who were Spanish speaking improved our English language skills in order to better communicate with the new immigrants and their parents.

In retrospect I am able to see how the life experiences and values of my parents helped me to be more accepting and respectful of those who were different. My father had attended St. Mary's University in San Antonio, Texas, in the late 1920s and early 1930s. There he formed friendships with students who were from different countries in Latin American, with mainstream Anglo Americans, and with Americans of Polish, German, and French descent. The fact that he had played on the St. Mary's baseball team helped him to become acquainted with people of different backgrounds.

In Roma he owned and managed a store. There I was able to see first hand how he related to the traveling salesmen who included Jewish Americans and mainstream Anglos as well as the drivers who brought in the merchandise by truck, who were usually African Americans. My father treated all of these people with respect and showed a genuine interest as he listened to their perspectives on life and learned of their life experiences.

My mother had been an elementary school teacher in Rio Grande City, Texas, a community just fourteen miles from Roma, yet one that had been the site of a United States Army fort since before the Civil War. Soldiers of all ethnic and racial groups had been stationed there. Many women from Rio Grande City formed biracial families as they met and married men stationed there. Some of the biracial people who were products of these marriages were close friends of my mother. They had been her teaching colleagues. Through her I got to know, and to become friends with, them and their children.

When I left the Rio Grande Valley to attend the University of Texas at Austin, the multicultural/multiracial coping techniques, values, and perspectives I had learned helped me to adapt to the new environment and to form meaningful friendships in the University of Texas and Austin communities. These helped me to succeed academically. While most of these experiences were positive, I did encounter racism and prejudice. It was difficult to overcome the influences of the traditional culture of my early socialization; that socialization prescribed that I accept things as they were and not challenge authority and that I overlook negative experiences. I remember the first time I heard Cesar Chavez speak on behalf of the farm workers. I was teaching at California State University in Sacramento in 1964. At first I perceived him as a troublemaker who was exaggerating the plight of the farm workers in order to get the attention of the media. I had to struggle against the traditional values with which I had been reared, which called for support of established authority and the status quo. But gradually, as I became more aware of the validity of the issues that Chavez was talking about, and when I witnessed the march of the farm workers as it culminated at the steps of the state capitol in Sacramento, I changed my mind. I was also influenced by the Chicano, African-American, Asian-American, and Native American student movements on college campuses and by the ethnic studies programs that grew out of these movements. I began to explore my own life history and to examine my values. At this same time I began to do research with adolescents who were developing bicultural orientations to life. Those experiences, along with the civil rights movement, helped to change my life and to have a significant impact on my academic and clinical interests.

I have tried to incorporate into the chapters of this book the lessons I learned in the course of my personal multicultural/multiracial journey and through my life experiences, research, and clinical practice. In *Savages and Civilization: Who Will Survive?* Jack Weatherford (1994) observed, "We must recognize . . . the value of all people because we may need the combined knowledge of all cultures if we are to overcome the problems that now threaten to overwhelm us" (p. 291). I have experienced firsthand what Weatherford is writing about, and I have seen it in the lives of my students, research participants, and clients.

The mestizo, multicultural/multiracial world orientation to life will make it possible for us to combine the knowledge of different peoples and different cultures. The world of the future will require both traditional and modern values. It will need worldviews and diverse problem solving approaches. We must be able to relate to others on a personal level, as well as use the communications technology that will be available to us; we will need to speak different languages, to use different ways of relating to others; we must learn how to put ourselves in the shoes of other people and to see the world through their eyes.

As citizens, social scientists, educators, and helping professionals, we must be multicultural ambassadors who reach out to others and to their worlds. We will have to bring people together to work collaboratively on issues and problems that threaten our future. We will need to facilitate the process of learning from each other by keeping our learning/experience filters open, and we must also facilitate synthesis and amalgamation so that we can truly combine the knowledge of different peoples and different cultures as Weatherford (1994) recommended. As cultural/racial mestizos we can play a crucial role in shaping the future.

❖ A P P E N D I X ❖

Multicultural/Multiracial
Experience Inventory (MEI) *

The MEI was developed to assess an individual's type of Historical Development Pattern and Contemporary Multicultural Identity. Originally designed for people of color, it has been modified so that it can be used to inventory the multicultural/multiracial experiences of whites. Both of these instruments share a common survey of demographic information (Part I). The response choices and scoring procedures and the two instruments (for people of color and for whites) are presented here.

---

*This version of the MEI represents the most recent revisions suggested by research findings, so it differs slightly from the version administered to Jill and Raul (see Chapter 8).

❖ 245 ❖

PART I

Multicultural/Multiracial Experience Inventory (MEI)

1. Name _____

2. Address _____ City, State, Zip _____

3. Gender _____

4. Age _____ Date of birth ____/____/____

5. Place of birth (city/state/country) _____

6. Father's place of birth (city/state/country) _____

7. Mother's place of birth (city/state/country) _____

8. Ethnic background of the following persons (if applicable):

	Yourself	Father	Mother	Stepfather	Stepmother
Mexican American/ Latino					
African American					
Asian American					
Native American					
White/ Anglo					
Multiracial (Specify)					

9. In what country were each of the following family members born?

	U.S.	Other/Specify
You		
Your father		
Your father's father		
Your father's mother		
Your mother		
Your mother's father		
Your mother's mother		

10. What is your religious background?_____

11. How active are you in your religion?
___ Very ___ Quite a bit ___ Somewhat ___ A little ___ Not at all

12. How many years have you lived in the United States? _____

13. Have you lived in a country other than the U.S.?
____ Yes. Which country(ies)?_____
For how many years? _____
____ No.

14. Have you lived in a state other than the one in which you attended school?
____ Yes. Which state(s)?_____
For how many years? _____
____ No.

15. Where did you spend the first 15 years of your life? (list all of the places)

_____

_____

16. Where do you consider "home" (community/state/country)?

_____

16a. Would you describe this community as
___ rural
___ semi-rural
___ semi-urban
___ urban

17. What language(s) does (did) your father speak? _____

18. What language(s) does (did) your mother speak? _____

19. What language(s) do (did) your parents speak at home? _____

20. What language(s) do you speak? _____

21. What is your marital status? _____

22. If you have had committed relationships, what were the ethnic background(s) of your partner(s)? _____

PART II AND SCORING PROCEDURE
(FOR PEOPLE OF COLOR)

Part II of the MEI is composed of two types of items: Type A items are scored so that a response of "almost entirely my ethnic group" or "almost entirely whites" (alternatives one and five, respectively) receives one point; responses of either "mostly my ethnic group with a few people of color from other groups" or "mostly whites with a few people of color" (alternatives two and four) receive two points; responses of "mixed (whites, my ethnic group, and people of color, about equally)" (alternative three) receive three points; hence higher scores are indicative of a greater degree of multiculturalism. Some Type A items are historical (reflect Historical Development Pattern or HDP) and others assess contemporary functioning and identity (reflect Contemporary Multicultural Identity or CMI).

All Type B items are CMI. Type B items are answered using a Likert-type format ranging from "Extensively" to "Never." Responses of "Extensively" or "Frequently" are assigned two points. All other responses are assigned one point. Items 1–8 are HDP items and items 9–26 are CMI items. A total Multicultural score (MC) is obtained by summing the HDP and CMI total scores.

To determine which scores can be considered to constitute high, medium, or low MC, the characteristics of the region of the country, community, and institution(s) as well as of the population(s) being studied have to be taken into consideration. Environments also vary with respect to opportunity for MC development and expression.

HDP score——33 maximum
CMI score——54 maximum
Total MC——87 maximum

Multicultural Experience Inventory (for People of Color)

Type A Items

Next to each item, circle the number of the response that best describes your past and present behavior:

1 = almost entirely my ethnic group
2 = mostly my ethnic group with a few people of color from other groups
3 = mixed (whites, my ethnic group, and people of color, about equally)
4 = mostly whites with a few people of color
5 = almost entirely whites

1. The ethnic composition of the neighborhoods in which I lived

1 2 3 4 5   (a) before I started attending school
1 2 3 4 5   (b) while I attended elementary school
1 2 3 4 5   (c) while I attended middle school
1 2 3 4 5   (d) while I attended high school
1 2 3 4 5   2. My childhood friends who visited my home and related well to my parents were . . .
1 2 3 4 5   3. The teachers and counselors with whom I have had the closest relationships have been . . .
1 2 3 4 5   4. The people who have most influenced me in my education have been . . .
1 2 3 4 5   5. In high school, my close friends were . . .
1 2 3 4 5   6. The ethnic backgrounds of the people I have dated have been . . .
1 2 3 4 5   7. In the job(s) I have had, my close friends have been . . .
1 2 3 4 5   8. The people with whom I have established close, meaningful relationships have been . . .
1 2 3 4 5   9. At present, my close friends are . . .
1 2 3 4 5   10. My close friends at work are (were) . . .
1 2 3 4 5   11. I enjoy going to gatherings at which the people are . . .
1 2 3 4 5   12. When I study or work on a project with others, I am usually with persons who are . . .
1 2 3 4 5   13. When I am involved in group discussions where I am expected to participate, I prefer a group of people who are . . .
1 2 3 4 5   14. I am active in organizations or social groups in which the majority of the members are . . .
1 2 3 4 5   15. When I am with my friends, I usually attend functions where the people are . . .
1 2 3 4 5   16. When I discuss personal problems or issues, I discuss them with people who are . . .
1 2 3 4 5   17. I most often spend time with people who are . . .

Type B Items

Next to each item below, circle the response that best describes you:
1 = Extensively
2 = Frequently
3 = Occasionally
4 = Seldom
5 = Never

1 2 3 4 5   18. I attend functions that are predominantly white in nature.

1 2 3 4 5   19. I attend functions that are predominantly of minority groups other than my own.

1 2 3 4 5   20. I attend functions that are predominantly of my own ethnic group in nature.

1 2 3 4 5   21. I visit the homes of whites.

1 2 3 4 5   22. I invite whites to my home.

1 2 3 4 5   23. I visit the homes of persons of my ethnic group (other than relatives).

1 2 3 4 5   24. I invite persons of my ethnic group (other than relatives) to my home.

1 2 3 4 5   25. I visit the homes of minorities other than of my own ethnic group.

1 2 3 4 5   26. I invite persons of minorities other than those of my own ethnic group to my home.

HDP _____
CMI _____
Total MC _____

Multicultural Experience Inventory (Modified for Whites)

Type A Items

Next to each item, circle the number of the response that best describes your past and present behavior, using this scale:

1 = almost entirely my ethnic group
2 = mostly my ethnic group with a few people of color
3 = mixed (my ethnic group and people of color, about equally)
4 = mostly people of color with a few people of my ethnic group
5 = almost entirely people of color

					1. The ethnic composition of the neighborhoods in which I lived
1	2	3	4	5	(a) before I started attending school
1	2	3	4	5	(b) while I attended elementary school
1	2	3	4	5	(c) while I attended middle school
1	2	3	4	5	(d) while I attended high school
1	2	3	4	5	2. My childhood friends who visited my home and related well to my parents were . . .
1	2	3	4	5	3. The teachers and counselors with whom I have had the closest relationships have been . . .
1	2	3	4	5	4. The people who have most influenced me in my education have been . . .
1	2	3	4	5	5. In high school, my close friends were . . .
1	2	3	4	5	6. The ethnic backgrounds of the people I have dated have been . . .
1	2	3	4	5	7. In the job(s) I have had, my close friends have been . . .
1	2	3	4	5	8. The people with whom I have established close, meaningful relationships have been . . .
1	2	3	4	5	9. At present, my close friends are (were) . . .
1	2	3	4	5	10. My close friends at work were . . .
1	2	3	4	5	11. I enjoy going to gatherings at which the people are . . .
1	2	3	4	5	12. When I study or work on a project with others, I am usually with persons who are . . .
1	2	3	4	5	13. When I am involved in group discussions where I am expected to participate, I prefer a group of people who are . . .
1	2	3	4	5	14. I am active in organizations or social groups in which the majority of the members are . . .
1	2	3	4	5	15. When I am with my friends, I usually attend functions where the people are . . .
1	2	3	4	5	16. When I discuss personal problems or issues, I discuss them with people who are . . .
1	2	3	4	5	17. I most often spend time with people who are . . .

Type B Items

Next to each item below, circle the response that best describes you:
1 = Extensively
2 = Frequently
3 = Occasionally
4 = Seldom
5 = Never

1 2 3 4 5   18. I attend functions that are predominantly of my ethnic group.
1 2 3 4 5   19. I attend functions that are predominantly of minority groups.
1 2 3 4 5   20. I visit the homes of people (not relatives) of my ethnic group.
1 2 3 4 5   21. I visit the homes of people of minority groups.
1 2 3 4 5   22. I invite people (other than relatives) of my ethnic group to my home.
1 2 3 4 5   23. I invite people of minority groups to my home.

HDP _____
CMI _____
Total MC _____

ADDITIONAL ITEMS

The following items are being field tested by the author and, thus, are not included in the MEI scoring procedure:

1. Indicate the degree of comfort you feel when you are with

1 = Very comfortable
2 = Somewhat comfortable
3 = Sometimes comfortable/sometimes not
4 = Somewhat uncomfortable
5 = Very uncomfortable

Whites	1	2	3	4	5
Latinos	1	2	3	4	5
African Americans	1	2	3	4	5
Native Americans	1	2	3	4	5
Multiracial peoples	1	2	3	4	5
(Specify) _____					
People with physical disabilities	1	2	3	4	5
(Specify) _____					
Gay and Lesbians	1	2	3	4	5
(Specify) _____					

Others	1	2	3	4	5
(Specify)					

2. Indicate the degree of acceptance you feel when you are with

1 = Very accepted
2 = Somewhat accepted
3 = Sometimes accepted/sometimes not
4 = Somewhat unaccepted
5 = Very unaccepted

Whites	1	2	3	4	5
Latinos	1	2	3	4	5
African Americans	1	2	3	4	5
Native Americans	1	2	3	4	5
Multiracial peoples	1	2	3	4	5
(Specify)					
People with physical disabilities	1	2	3	4	5
(Specify)					
Gay and Lesbians	1	2	3	4	5
(Specify)					
Others	1	2	3	4	5
(Specify)					

3. Indicate the degree to which you are identified with

1 = Very identified
2 = Somewhat identified
3 = Sometimes identified/sometimes not
4 = Minimally identified
5 = Not at all identified

Whites	1	2	3	4	5
Latinos	1	2	3	4	5
African Americans	1	2	3	4	5
Native Americans	1	2	3	4	5
Multiracial peoples	1	2	3	4	5
(Specify)					
People with physical disabilities	1	2	3	4	5
(Specify)					
Gay and Lesbians	1	2	3	4	5
(Specify)					
Others	1	2	3	4	5
(Specify)					

4. Identify the three goals that are most important to your continued multicultural/multiracial development.

❖ REFERENCES ❖

A cry for leadership (1979). *Time* 114(6):24–28.

Adler, P. S. (1974). Beyond cultural identity: reflections on cultural and multicultural man. In *Topics in Culture Learning*, vol. 2, ed. R. Brislin. Honolulu: University of Hawaii, East-West Culture Learning Institute.

Ainslie, R. C. (1995). *No Dancin' in Anson: An American Story of Race and Social Change*. Northvale, NJ: Jason Aronson.

Almeida Acosta, E. (1996). *Epistemological, theoretical, and methodological bases for community social psychology*. Paper presented at the XXVI International Congress of Psychology, Montreal, Canada, August.

Almeida Acosta, E., and Sanchez, M. E. (1985). Cultural interaction in social change dynamics. In *Cross-Cultural and National Studies in Social Psychology*, ed. R. Diaz-Guerrero. Amsterdam: North Holland.

Aramoni, A. (1972). Machismo. *Psychology Today*, January, pp. 69–72.

Ardila, R. (1982). International psychology. *American Psychologist* 37: 323–329.

——— (1986). *La psicologia en America latina. Pasado-presente y futuro.* Mexico, D. F.: Siglo Veintuno Editores.

——— (1993). Latin American psychology and world psychology: Is integration possible? In *Indigenous Psychologies: Research and Experience in Cultural Context*, ed. U. Kim and J. W. Berry. Newbury Park, CA: Sage.

Atkinson, D. R., Morten, G., and Sue, D. W. (1989). *Counseling American Minorities: A Cross-Cultural Perspective*, 3rd ed. Dubuque, IA: William C. Brown.

Attneave, C. L. (1969). Therapy in tribal settings and urban network intervention. *Family Process* 8:192–210.

——— (1974). Medicine men and psychiatrists in the Indian Health Service. *Psychiatric Annals* 4(49):53–55.

Bales, R. F. (1950). *Interaction Process Analysis: A Method for the Study of Small Groups*. Cambridge, MA: Addison-Wesley.

Barker, R. (1968). *Ecological Psychology*. Stanford, CA: Stanford University Press.

Basic Behavioral Science Task Force of the National Advisory Mental Health Council (1996). *American Psychologist* 51(7):722–731.

Benitez, F. (1975). *In the Magic Land of Peyote*. Austin, TX: University of Texas Press.

Bernstein, R. (1994). *Dictatorship of virtue.* New York: Knopf.

Betancourt, H. (1994). *Culture, ethnicity and gender in cognitive (attribution) processes and violence in intergroup conflict and violence.* Paper presented at the meeting of the Mexican Society of Social Psychology and the International Society of Cross-Cultural Psychology, Merida, Mexico, October.

Betancourt, H., and Lopez, S. R. (1993). The study of cultural, ethnicity, and race in American psychology. *American Psychologist* 28:629–637.

Birman, D. (1994). Acculturation and human diversity in multicultural society. In *Human Diversity*, ed. E. J. Trickett, R. J. Watts, and D. Birman. San Francisco, CA: Jossey-Bass.

Black, C. E. (1972). Dynamics of modernization. In *Social Change*, ed. R. A. Nisbet. New York: Harper.

Bond, H. M. (1927). Some exceptional Negro children. *The Crisis* 34: 257–280.

Branch, T. (1988). *Parting of the Waters: America in the King Years 1954–63.* New York: Touchstone.

Bruner, J. S., Oliver, R. R., and Greenfield, P. M. (1966). *Studies in Cognitive Growth.* New York: Wiley.

Buriel, R. (1987). Ethnic labeling and identity among Mexican Americans. In *Children's Ethnic Socialization*, ed. J. S. Phinney and M. J. Rotherom. Beverly Hills, CA: Sage.

——— (1993a). Acculturation, respect for actual differences, and biculturalism among three generations of Mexican American and Euro American school children. *Journal of Genetic Psychology* 145(4):531–543.

——— (1993b). Childrearing orientations in Mexican American families: the influence of generation and sociocultural factors. *Journal of Marriage and Family* 55:987–1000.

Buriel, R., Calzada, S., and Vasquez, R. (1982). The relationship of traditional American culture to adjustment and delinquency among three generations of Mexican American male adolescents. *Hispanic Journal of the Behavioral Sciences* 14:41–55.

Campbell, D. T. (1961). The mutual methodological relevance of anthropology and psychology. In *Psychological Anthropology*, ed. F. L. K. Hsu. Homewood, IL: Dorsey.

Campbell, D. T., and Naroll, R. (1972). The mutual methodological relevance of anthropology and psychology. In *Psychological Anthropology*, ed. F. L. K. Hsu. Cambridge: Schenkman.

Carlin, J. E. (1986). Child and adolescent refugees: psychiatric assessment and treatment. In *Refugee Mental Health in Resettlement Countries*, ed. C. L. Williams and J. Westermeyer. New York: Hemisphere Publishing Corporation.

Carrasco, N. (1990). *The relationship between parental support and control and adolescent self esteem in Mexican, Mexican-American and Anglo-American families*. Dissertation, University of Texas at Austin.

Carrasco, N., Garza-Louis, D., and King, R. (1996). The Hispanic sex offender: machismo and cultural values. In *Yearbook for the Sex Offender: Correctional, Treatment and Legal Practice*. Plymouth, MA: Spring.

Caso, A. (1924). *El problema de Mexico y la ideologia nacional (The problems of Mexico and National Ideology)*. Mexico, D. F.: Cultura.

———— (1934). *Nuevos discurosos a la nacion Mexicana (New Perspectives on Mexico as a Nation)*. Mexico, D. F.: P. Robredo.

———— (1943a). *La existencia como economia y como caridad: Ensayo sobre la esencia del cristianismo (Economics and Charity in the Human Existence: An Essay on the Essence of Christianity)*. Mexico, D. F.: Secretaria de Educacion Publica.

———— (1943b). *Mexico: Apuntamientos de cultura patria (Mexico: Perspectives on the National Culture)*. Mexico, D. F.: Imprenta Universitaria.

Castañeda, A. (1984). Traditionalism, modernism, and ethnicity. In *Chicano Psychology*, 2nd ed., ed. J. L. Martinez and R. H. Mendoza. Orlando, FL: Academic Press.

Castro, A. (1996). *Mexican-American values and their impact on mental health care*. Dissertation. Austin, TX: University of Texas at Austin.

Castro, A., and Ramirez, M. (1996). *The Latino representation in the psychological literature: a 25-year review of 6 APA journals*. Unpublished paper. Austin, TX: University of Texas at Austin.

Cervantes, J. M., and Ramirez, O. (1995). Spirituality and family dynamics in psychotherapy with Latino children. In *Ethnicity and Psychology*, ed. K. P. Monteiro. Dubuque, IA: Kendall/Hunt.

Chavez, A. J. (1985). *The religious call in early adult development: seven life studies of Mexican-American sisters*. Dissertation, Wright Institute Graduate School of Psychology, Berkeley, CA.

Chavira, J. A., and Trotter, R. T. (1978). *The gift of healing*. Unpublished monograph. Edinburg, TX: Pan American University.

Chazaro Flores, S., and Almeida Acosta, E. (1985). Nahuatl families: families in transition. In *Cross-Cultural and National Studies in Social Psychology*, ed. R. Diaz-Guerrero. Amsterdam: North Holland.

Child, I. L. (1943). *Italian or American? The Second Generation in Conflict*. New Haven, CT: Yale University Press.

Cole, M., and Scribner, S. (1974). *Culture and Thought*. New York: Wiley.

Coles, R. (1975). *The Old Ones of New Mexico*. Garden City, NY: Anchor.

Collins, M. (1954). *Cortes and Montezuma*. New York: Avon.

Corey, G. (1995). *Theories and Techniques of Psychotherapy and Counseling*. Pacific Grove, CA: Brooks-Cole.

Cox, B., Macaulay, J., and Ramirez, M. (1982). *New Frontiers: A Bilingual Early Childhood Program*. Worthington, OH: Science Research Associates.

Crevecoeur, J. H. St. J. (1904). *Letters from an American Farmer*. New York: Fox, Duffield.

Cronbach, L. J. (1975). Beyond the two disciplines of scientific psychology. *American Psychologist* 30:116–127.

Cross, W. E., Jr. (1971). The Negro to Black conversion experience: towards a psychology of Black liberation. *Black World* 20(9):13–27.

——— (1978). The Cross and Thomas models of psychological nigrescence. *Journal of Black Psychology* 5(1):13–19.

——— (1991). *Shades of Black: Diversity and African American Identity*. Philadelphia: Temple University Press.

Crow Dog, M., and Erodes, R. (1990). *Lakota Woman*. New York: Harper Perennial. .

Cuellar, I. B., Arnold, B., and Maldonado, R. (1995). Acculturation rating scale for Mexican-Americans—II. A revision of the original ARSMA scale. *Hispanic Journal of the Behavioral Sciences* 17:275–304.

Cuellar, I. B., Harris, L. C., and Jasso, R. (1980). An acculturation scale for Mexican American normal and clinical populations. *Hispanic Journal of Behavioral Sciences* 2:199–217.

Culler, R., and Diaz-Guerrero, R. (1982). *The webwork: a new approach in describing individual support networks*. Unpublished manuscript.

Darder, A. (1991). *Culture and Power in the Classroom: A Critical Foundation for Bicultural Education*. New York: Bergin and Garvey.

Dershowitz, A. (1971). Jewish subcultural patterns and psychological differentiation. *International Journal of Psychology* 6:223–231.

Diaz-Guerrero, R. (1955). Neurosis and the Mexican family structure. *American Journal of Psychiatry* 112:411–417.

——— (1972a). Una escala factorial de premisis historico-socioculturales de la familia Mexicana (An attitudes scale of the historico-socio-cultural premises of the Mexican family). *Revista interamericana de psicologia* 6:3–4.

——— (1972b). *Hacia una teoria historica-bio-psico-socio-cultural del comportamiento humano* (*Toward a Historical-Bio-Psycho-Socio-Cultural Theory of Human Behavior*). Mexico, D. F.: Editorial Trillas.

——— (1977). Mexican psychology. *American Psychologist* 33:934–944.

——— (1992). The need for an ethnopsychology of cognition and personality. *Psychology: Journal of Human Behavior* 29:19–26.

Diaz-Loving, R., Reyes-Lagunes, I., and Diaz-Guerrero, R. (1995). Some cultural facilitators and deterrents for the development of psychology: the role of graudate research training. Special Issue. National development of psychology: factors facilitating and impeding progress in developing countries. *International Journal of Psychology* 30(6):681–692.

Dollard, J. (1935). *Criteria for the Life History with Analyses of Six Notable Documents*. New Haven, CT: Yale University Press.

Driver, H. E. (1969). *Indians of North America*. Chicago: University of Chicago Press.

DuBois, W. E. B. (1898). The Negroes of Farmville, Virginia: a social study. Washington, DC: *Bulletin of the Department of Labor* 14:1–44.

—— (1903). *The Souls of Black Folk*. New York: Bantam, 1989.

—— (1967). *The Philadelphia Negro*. New York: Schocken.

Duran, D. (1964). *Historia de las indias de nueva espana y islas de tierra firme (History of the Indigenous Peoples of New Spain and the Tierra Firme Islands)*. New York: Orion.

Erikson, E. H. (1963). *Childhood and Society*, 2nd ed. New York: Norton.

Escovar, L. A. (1980). *Design for a Course on Social Psychology in Latin America*. Miami, FL: Latin American and Caribbean Center, Florida International University.

Estrada, A. X. (1994). *Re-examining what it means to be bicultural*. Paper presented at the Second Annual California State University System Wide Research Competition, Oakland, CA, April.

Fabrega, H., and Manning, P. K. (1973). An integrated theory of disease in the Chiapas Highlands. *Psychosomatic Medicine* 35:223–239.

Fals Borda, O. (1987). *Investigacion-accion participativa en Colombia (Participative Action Research in Columbia)*. Bogota, Columbia: Punta de Lanza.

Fancher, R. T. (1995). *Cultures of Healing: Correcting the Image of American Mental Health Care*. New York: W. H. Freeman.

Fanon, F. (1967). *Black Skin, White Masks*. New York: Grove.

Felix-Ortiz, M., Newcomb, M. D., and Myers, H. (1994). A multidimensional measure of cultural identity for Latino and Latina adolescents. *Hispanic Journal of Behavioral Sciences* 16(2):99–115.

Fernandez-Marina, R., Maldonado-Sierra, E. D., and Trent, R. D. (1958). Three basic themes in Mexican and Puerto Rican family values. *Journal of Social Psychology* 48:167–181.

Fielding, N. G., and Fielding, J. L. (1986). *Linking Data*. Beverly Hills, CA: Sage.

Fields, S. (1976a). Folk healing for the wounded spirit: I. Storefront psychotherapy through seance. *Innovations* 2:3–11.

—— (1976b). Folk healing for the wounded spirit: II. Medicine men: purveyors of an ancient art. *Innovations* 3:12–18.

Fitzgerald, T. K. (1971). Education and identity—a reconsideration of some models of acculturation and identity. *New Zealand Council of Educational Studies* 45–47.

Flores, M. (1996). *The CLARO program*. Unpublished manuscript.

Foster, G. M. (1948). *Empire's Children: The People of Tzintzuntzan*. Mexico, D. F.: Imprenta Nuevo Mundo.

———— (1952). The significance of anthropological studies of the places of origin of Spanish immigrants to the New World. In *Acculturation in the Americas*, ed. S. Tax. Chicago: University of Chicago Press.

Franco, S. L. (1996). *Neuropsychological Test Performance of Mexican American and Anglo American High School Students from Communities of the U.S.-Mexican Border Region of South Texas*. Dissertation, University of Texas at Austin.

Frank, J. D. (1961). *Persuasion and Healing*. Baltimore: Johns Hopkins Press.

Fried, J. (1959). Acculturation and mental health among Indian migrants in Peru. In *Culture and Mental Health*, ed. M. K. Opler. New York: Macmillian.

Fromm, E., and Maccoby, M. (1970). *Social Character in a Mexican Village: A Socio-Psychoanalytic Study*. Englewood Cliffs, NJ: Prentice-Hall.

Galton, F. (1869). *Hereditary Genius: An Inquiry into its Locus and Consequences*. London: Clay.

Gamio, M. (1922). *Introduction, sintesis y conclusiones de la obra: La poblacion del valle de teotihuacan (Introduction, Synthesis and Conclusions: The People of the Teotihuacan Valley of Mexico)*. Mexico, D. F: Secretaria de Educacion Publica.

———— (1931). *The Life Story of the Mexican Immigrant*. New York: Dover.

Garcia, E. E. (1977). The study of early childhood bilingualism: Strategies for linguistic transfer research. In *Chicano Psychology*, ed. J. L. Martinez. New York: Academic.

Garrison, V. E. (1979). *Inner-city Support Systems Project*. (Project No. MH28467.) Bethesda, MD: National Institute of Mental Health.

Garza, R. T. (1977). Personal control and fatalism in Chicanos and Anglos: conceptual and methodological issues. In *Chicano Psychology*, ed. J. L. Martinez. New York: Academic Press.

Garza, R. T., and Lipton, J. P. (1982). Theoretical perspectives on Chicano personality development. *Hispanic Journal of Behavioral Sciences* 4(4): 407–432.

Garza, R. T., Romero, G. J., Cox, B. G., and Ramirez, M. (1982). Biculturalism, locus of control, and leader behavior in ethnically mixed small groups. *Journal of Applied Social Psychology* 12(3):227–253.

Gergin, K. J. (1976). Social psychology as history. *Journal of Personality and Social Psychology* 26:309–320.

Gillin, J. (1952). Ethos and cultural aspects of personality. In *Heritage of Conquest*, ed. S. Tax. Glencoe, IL: Free Press.

Gollnick, D. M., and Chinn, P. C. (1990). *Multicultural Education in a Pluralistic Society*, 3rd ed. New York: Merrill.

Gottman, J. M. (1994). *What Predicts Divorce? The Relationship between Marital Processes and Marital Outcomes*. Hillsdale, NJ: Erlbaum.

Greeno, J. C. (1982). Response to "The hegemony of natural scientific conceptions of learning." *American Psychologist* 37:332–334.

Guerra, F. (1971). *The Pre-Columbian Mind*. New York: Seminar Press.

Gurin, P., and Epps, E. G. (1975). *Black Consciousness, Identity, and Achievement*. New York: Wiley.

Guthrie, R. V. (1976). *Even the Rat was White: A Historical View of Psychology*. New York: Harper & Row.

Hall, C. C. I. (1992). Please choose one: ethnic identity choices for biracial individuals. In *Racially Mixed People in America*, ed. M. P. P. Root. Newbury Park, CA: Sage.

Hall, G. S. (1904). *Adolescence: Its Psychology and its Relations to Physiology, Anthropology, Sociology, Sex, Crime, Religion, and Education*, vol. 1 and 2. New York: Appleton.

Hallowell, A. I. (1951). The use of projective techniques in the study of the sociopsychological aspects of acculturation. *Journal of Protective Techniques* 15:27–44.

Harner, M. J. (1973). *Hallucinogens and Shamanism*. New York: Oxford University Press.

Harwood, A. (1977). Puerto Rican spiritism: description and analysis of an alternative psychotherapeutic approach. *Culture, Medicine, and Psychiatry* 1(1):69–95.

Havel, V. (1996). The hope for Europe. *The New York Review of Books*, June 20, pp. 38–40.

Heller, C. S. (1968). *Mexican American Youth: Forgotten Youth at the Crossroads*. New York: Random House.

Helms, J. E. (1990). *Blacks and White Racial Identity: Theory, Research, and Practice*. Westford, CT: Greenwood.

——— (1992). *A Race Is a Nice Thing to Have: A Guide to Being a White Person or the White Persons in Your Life*. Topeka, KS: Content Communications.

——— (1994). The conceptualization of racial identity and other "racial" constructs. In *Human Diversity*, ed. E. J. Trickett, R. J. Watts, and D. Birman. San Francisco, CA: Jossey-Bass.

Herbart, J. F. (1897). *Lehrfuch zur Psychologie*, trans. M. K. Smith. New York: Appleton.

Herskovitz, M. J. (1947). *Man and His Works*. New York: Knopf.

Herstein, R. J., and Murray, C. (1994). *The Bell Curve: Intelligence and Class Structure in American Life*. New York: Free Press.

Holtzman, W. H. (1979). Culture, personality development, and mental health in the Americas. *Interamerican Journal of Psychology* 13:27–49.

Holtzman, W. H., Diaz-Guerrero, R., and Swartz, J. D. (1975). *Personality Development in Two Cultures*. Austin, TX: University of Texas Press.

Iscoe, I. (1982). Toward a viable community health psychology. *American Psychologist* 37(8):961–965.

Jacobs, J. H. (1992). Identity development in biracial children. In *Racially Mixed People in America*, ed. M. P. P. Root. Newbury Park, CA: Sage.

Jenkins, A. H. (1995). *Psychology and African Americans*. Needham Heights, MA: Allyn & Bacon.

Jensen, A. R. (1969). How much can we boost IQ and scholastic achievement? *Harvard Educational Review* 39:1–123.

Johnson, D. J. (1992). Developmental pathways: toward an ecological theoretical formulation of race identity in Black–White biracial children. In *Racially Mixed People in America*, ed. M. P. P. Root. Newbury Park, CA: Sage.

Kagan, S., and Buriel, R. (1977). Field dependence–independence and Mexican-American culture and education. In *Chicano Psychology*, ed. J. L. Martinez. New York: Academic.

Kaplan, B., and Johnson, D. (1967). The social meaning of Navajo psychotherapy. In *Magic, Faith, and Healing*, ed. A. Kiev. New York: Free Press.

Keefe, S. E., and Padilla, A. M. (1987). *Chicano Ethnicity*. Albuquerque: University of New Mexico Press.

Kelly, J. G. (1971). Toward an ecological conception of preventive interventions. In *Research Contributions from Psychology to Community Mental Health*, ed. J. Carter, Jr. New York: Behavioral Publications.

Kich, G. K. (1992). The developmental process of asserting a biracial, bicultural identity. In *Racially Mixed People in America*, ed. M. P. P. Root. Newbury Park, CA: Sage.

———— (1996). In the margins of sex and race: difference, marginality, and flexibility. In *The Multicultural Experience*, ed. M. P. P. Root. Thousand Oaks, CA: Sage.

Kiev, A. (1968). *Curanderismo (Faith Healing Practices)*. New York: Free Press.

King, C. K., and DaCosta, K. M. (1996). Changing face, changing race: the remaking of race in the Japanese American and African American communities. In *The Multicultural Experience*, ed. M. P. P. Root. Thousand Oaks, CA: Sage.

Kleinman, A. (1980). *Patients and Healers in the Context of Culture*. Berkeley: University of California Press.

Klor de Alva, J. J. (1972). *Introduction to Mexican Philosophy*. San Jose, CA: San Jose State College.

Kluckhohn, F. R., and Strodbeck, R. (1961). *Variations in Value Orientations*. New York: Row Peterson.

Koivukari, M. (1977). *Fundamental Issues of the Cross-Cultural Approach and Its Methodology in Psychology*. Reports for the Department of Psychology, University of Jyvaskyla, Finland.

Kreisman, J. J. (1975). The curandero's apprentice: A therapeutic integration of folk and medical healing. *American Journal of Psychiatry* 132: 81–83.

La Farge, O. (1947). *Santa Eulalia, the Religion of a Cuchumatan Indian Town*. Chicago: University of Chicago Press.

LaFramboise, T. (1983). *Assertion Training with American Indians*. Las Cruces, NM: ERIC Clearinghouse on Rural Education and Small Schools.

LaFramboise, T., Coleman, H. L. K., and Gerton, J. (1993). Psychological impact of biculturalism: evidence and theory. *Psychological Bulletin* 114:395–412.

Lamphere, L. (1969). Symbolic elements in Navajo ritual. *Southwestern Journal of Anthropology* 2:279–305.

Lane, C. (1994). The tainted sources of "The Bell Curve." *The New York Review of Books*. December 1, pp. 14–19.

Lee, D. (1976). *Valuing the Self: What We Can Learn from Other Cultures*. Englewood Cliffs, NJ: Prentice-Hall.

Leon-Portilla, M. (1963). *Aztec Thought and Culture: A Study of the Ancient Nahuatl Mind*. Norman, OK: University of Oklahoma Press.

——— (1973). *Time and Reality in the Thought of the Maya*. Boston: Beacon.

Lewis, D. L. (1993). *W. E. B. DuBois: Biography of a Race, 1868–1919*. New York: Henry Holt.

Lewis, O. (1951). *Life in a Mexican Village: Tepoztlan Restudied*. Champaign-Urbana, IL: University of Illinois Press.

——— (1959). *Five Families: Mexican Case Studies in the Culture of Poverty*. New York: Basic Books.

——— (1961). *The Children of Sanchez: Autobiography of a Mexican Family*. New York: Random House.

——— (1964). *Pedro Martinez*. New York: Random House.

——— (1965). *La Vida: A Puerto Rican Family of the Culture of Poverty—San Juan and New York*. New York: Random House.

Lind, M. (1995). *The Next American Nation: The New Nationalism and the Fourth American Revolution*. New York: Free Press.

Lopez-Austin, A. (1975). *Textos de medicina nahuatl (Texts of Nahuatl Medicine)*. Mexico, D. F.: Universidad Nacional Autonoma de Mexico.

Lopez, M., Hicks, R. E., and Young, R. K. (1974). The linguistic interdependence of bilinguals. *Journal of Experimental Psychology* 102:981–983.

Lopez, V. (1996). *A multicultural approach to consultation*. Poster presented at the School of Education, University of Texas at Austin.

Madsen, W. (1964a). The alcoholic agringado. *American Anthropologist* 66:355–361.

——— (1964b). *Mexican Americans of South Texas: Studies in Cultural Anthropology*. New York: Holt, Rinehart & Winston.

Mannoni, O. (1960). Appel de la fédération de France du FLN. *El Moudjahid* 59:644–645.

Manson, S. M., ed. (1982). *New Directions in Prevention among American Indians and Alaskan Native Communities*. Portland, OR: National Center for American Indian and Alaskan Native Mental Health Research.

Mar, J. (1988). *Chinese-Caucasian Interracial Parenting and Ethnic Identity*. Unpublished dissertation. Amherst, MA: University of Massachusetts.

Marcia, J. E. (1980). Identity in adolescence. In *Handbook of Adolescent Psychology*, ed. J. Adelson. New York: Wiley.

Marin, G., and Marin, B. V. (1991). *Research with Hispanic Populations*. Newbury Park, CA: Sage.

Martin-Baro, I. (1985). *Accion e ideologia (Action and Ideology)*. San Salvador: Universidad Centro Americana.

Matarazzo, J. D. (1982). Behavioral health's challenge to academic, scientific, and professional psychology. *American Psychologist* 37:1–14.

McClelland, D. C. (1961). *The Achieving Society*. Princeton, NJ: Van Nostrand.

McFee, M. (1968). The 150% man, a product of Blackfeet acculturation. *American Anthropologist* 70:1096–1103.

Means, R. (with Wolf, M. J.) (1995). *Where White Men Fear to Tread: The Autobiography of Russell Means*. New York: St. Martin's.

Minuchin, S. (1974). *Families and Family Therapy*. Cambridge, MA: Harvard University Press.

Mohatt, G., and Blue, A. W. (1982). Primary prevention as it relates to traditionality and empirical measures of social deviance. In *New Directions in Prevention among American Indians and Alaskan Native Communities*, ed. S. M. Manson. Portland, OR: National Center for American Indian and Alaskan Native Mental Health Research.

Monte, C. F. (1994). *Beneath the Mask: An Introduction to Theories of Personality*, 3rd ed. New York: Holt, Rinehart & Winston.

Montero, M. (1979). *Aportes methodologicos de la psicologia social del desarrollo de comunidades (Methodological premises of a social psychology of community development)*. Paper presented at the XVII Congress of the Interamerican Society of Psychology, Lima, Peru, July.

——— (1980). *Fundamentos teoricos de la psicologia comunitaria (Theoretical foundation for a community psychology)*. Unpublished manuscript.

Myers, L. J. (1988). *Understanding an Afrocentric World View: Introduction to an Optimal Psychology*. Dubuque, IA: Kendall/Hunt.

Navarro, A. (1995). *Mexican American Youth Organization*. Austin: University of Texas Press.

Negy, C. (1993). Anglo- and Hispanic-American performance on the Family Attitude Scale and its implications for improving measurements of acculturation. *Psychological Reports* 73:1211–1217.

Nisbet, R. A. (1953). *Quest for Community*. New York: Oxford University Press.

———— (1970). *Tradition and Revolt*. New York: Vintage.

Ortega y Gasset, J. (1946). *The Modern Theme*, translated by James Cleugh. New York: Norton.

Osborne, J. W. (1982). The hegemony of natural scientific conceptions of learning. *American Psychologist* 37:330–332.

Padilla, A. M. (1977). Child bilingualism: insights to issues. In *Chicano Psychology*, ed. J. L. Martinez. New York: Academic.

———— (1980). The role of cultural awareness and ethnic loyalty in acculturation. In *Acculturation: Theories, Models and Some New Findings*, ed. A. M. Padilla. Boulder, CO: Westview.

———— (1995). Synopsis of the history of Chicano psychology. In *Ethnicity and Psychology: African-, Asian-, Latino- and Native-American Psychologies*, ed. K. P. Monteiro. Dubuque, IA: Kendall Hunt.

Padilla, A. M., and Ruiz, R. A. (1973). *Latino Mental Health: A Review of the Literature*. Washington, DC: U.S. Government Printing Office.

Paine, T. (1944). *Representative Selections*. New York: American Books.

Paredes, A. (1978). The problem of identity in a changing culture: popular expression of culture conflict along the lower Rio Grande border. In *Views Across the Border: The United States and Mexico*, ed. S. Ross. Albuquerque: University of New Mexico Press.

Parfit, M., and Harvey, A. D. (1994). Powwow. *National Geographic*, June, pp. 88–113.

Parham, T. A. (1989). Cycles of psychological nigrescense. *Counseling Psychologist* 17:187–226.

Paz, O. (1961). *The Labyrinth of Solitude*. New York: Grove.

———— (1972). *The Other Mexico: Critique of the Pyramid*. New York: Grove.

Peal, E., and Lambert, W. E. (1962). The relation of bilingualism to intelligence. *Psychological Monographs* 76(27):1–2.

Phinney, J. (1989). Stages of ethnic identity development in minority group adolescents. *Journal of Early Adolescence* 9:34–49.

———— (1990). Ethnic identity in adolescents and adults: a review of research. *Psychological Bulletin* 108:499–514.

Phinney, J., and Alepurea, L. L. (1996). At the interface of culture: multiethnic/multiracial high school and college students. *Journal of Social Psychology* 136:139–158.

Phinney, J., and Devich-Navarro, M. (in press). Variations in bicultural identification among African American and Mexican American adolescents. *Journal of Research on Adolescence.*

Piaget, J. (1966). Necessité et signification des recherches comparatives en psychologie genetique. *International Journal of Psychology* 1:3–13.

Pick de Weiss, S., and Diaz-Loving, R. (1986). Applied psychology in Mexico. *International Review of Applied Psychology* 35:577–598.

Pike, K. (1954). *Language in Relation to a Unified Theory of Structure of Human Behavior* (Part 1). Glendale, CA: Summer Institute of Linguistics.

Ponterotto, J. G., and Casas, J. M. (1991). *Handbook of Racial Ethnic Minority Counseling Research.* Springfield, IL: Charles C Thomas.

Price-Williams, D. R. (1975). *Explorations in Cross-Cultural Psychology.* San Francisco, CA: Chandler and Sharp.

Ramirez, A. (1977). Chicano power and interracial group relations. In *Chicano Psychology*, ed. J. L. Martinez. New York: Academic.

────── (1988). Racism toward Hispanics: the culturally monolithic society. In *Eliminating Racism: Profiles in Controversy*, ed. P. A. Katz and D. A. Taylor. New York: Plenum.

Ramirez, M. (1967). Identification with Mexican family values and authoritarianism in Mexican Americans. *Journal of Social Psychology* 73:3–11.

────── (1969). Identification with Mexican family values and psychological adjustment in Mexican-American adolescents. *International Journal of Social Psychiatry* 11:151–156.

────── (1977). Recognizing and understanding diversity: multiculturalism and the Chicano movement in psychology. In *Chicano Psychology*, ed. J. L. Martinez. New York: Academic.

────── (1978). A mestizo world view and the psychodynamics of Mexican-American border populations. In *Views Across the Border: The United States and Mexico*, ed. S. Ross. Albuquerque: University of New Mexico Press.

────── (1980). *A neighborhood-based, culture-responsive mental health model for Mexican-American children and adolescents.* Unpublished manuscript.

────── (1983). *Psychology of the Americas: Mestizo Perspectives in Personality and Mental Health.* New York: Pergamon.

────── (1987). The impact of culture change and economic stressors on the physical and mental health of Mexican Americans. In *Mental Health Issues of the Mexican-Origin Population in Texas*, ed. R. Rodriguez and M. T. Coleman. Austin, TX: Hogg Foundation for Mental Health.

────── (1994a). *Hacia una psicologia mestiza: Investigaciones transculturales con familias* (*Toward a psychology of the mestizo peoples: transcultural family research*). Proceedings of the Mexican Society of Social Psychology and of the International Association of Transcultural Psychology, pp. 13–17, Merida, Mexico.

────── (1994b). *Psychotherapy and Counseling with Minorities: A Cognitive*

Approach to Individual and Cultural Differences. Needham Heights, MA: Allyn & Bacon.

Ramirez, M., and Carrasco, N. (in press). *Revision of the Family Attitude Scale.* Austin, TX: University of Texas at Austin.

Ramirez, M., and Castañeda, A. (1974). *Cultural Democracy, Bicognitive Development and Education.* New York: Academic.

Ramirez, M., Cox, B. G., and Castañeda, A. (1977). *The psychodynamics of biculturalism.* Unpublished technical report to Office of Naval Research, Arlington, VA.

Ramirez, M., Cox, B. G., Garza, R. T., and Castañeda, A. (1978a). *Dimensions of biculturalism in Mexican-American college students.* Unpublished technical report to Office of Naval Research, Arlington, VA.

Ramirez, M., Diaz-Guerrero, R., Hernandez, M., and Iscoe, I. (1982). *Coping with life stress in families: a cross-cultural comparison.* Unpublished manuscript.

Ramirez, M., and Doell, S. R. (1982). *The traditionalism-modernism inventory.* Unpublished manuscript.

Ramirez, M., Doell, S. R., Rodriguez, N., and Kim, D. (in press). *Revision of the Traditionalism–Modernism Inventory.* Austin, TX: University of Texas at Austin.

Ramirez, M., Garza, R. T., and Cox, B. (1978b). *Multicultural leader behaviors.* Unpublished technical report to Organizational Effectiveness Research Programs, Office of Naval Research, Arlington, VA.

———— (1980). *Multicultural leader behaviors in ethnically mixed task groups.* Unpublished technical report to Office of Naval Research, Arlington, VA.

Ramirez, M., and Gonzalez, A. (1973). Mexican Americans and intelligence testing. In *La Causa Chicana: The Movement for Justice* (*The Chicano Cause: The Movement for Justice*), ed. N. M. Mangold. New York: Family Service Association of America.

Ramirez, M., and Price-Williams, D. R. (1974a). Achievement motivation in Mexican-American children. *Journal of Cross-Cultural Psychology* 7:49–60.

———— (1974b). Cognitive styles of children of three ethnic groups in the United States. *Journal of Cross-Cultural Psychology* 5:212–219.

Ramirez, M., Taylor, C. M., and Petersen, B. (1971). Mexican American cultural membership and adjustment to school. *Developmental Psychology* 4:141–148.

Ramos, S. (1934). *Profile of Man and Culture in Mexico.* Austin, TX: University of Texas Press, 1975.

Rappaport, J. (1977). *Community Psychology: Values, Research, and Action.* New York: Holt, Rinehart & Winston.

Redfield, R. (1930). *Tepoztlan—A Mexican Village*. Chicago: University of Chicago Press.

———— (1950). *A Village that Chose Progress: Chan Kom Revisited*. Chicago: University of Chicago Press.

Reid, A., and Aguilar, M. A. (1991). Constructing community social psychology in Mexico. *Applied Psychology: An International Review* 40: 181–199.

Reigel, K. F. (1972). Influence of economic and political ideologies on the development of psychology. *Psychological Bulletin* 78:129–141.

Reiser, M. F. (1975). Changing theoretical concepts in psychosomatic medicine. In *American Handbook of Psychiatry*, vol. 4, 2nd ed., ed. S. Arieti. New York: Basic Books.

Rodriguez, N., and Ramirez, M. (in press). *Procedures for Assessing Acculturation in Latinos: A New Perspective*. Claremont, CA: Pitzer College.

Rodriguez, N., Ramirez, M., and Korman, M. (in press). The transmission of values across generations of Mexican, Mexican-American, and White families. In *Racial-Ethnic Identity and Human Development: Implications for Schooling*, ed. E. Hollins and R. Sheets. Hillsdale, NJ: Erlbaum.

Rogler, L. H., and Cooney, S. R. (1984). *Puerto Rican Families in New York City: Intergenerational Processes*. Hispanic Research Center Monograph No. 11. Maplewood, NJ: Waterfront.

Rogler, L. H., and Cortes, D. E. (1993). Help-seeking pathways: a unifying concept in mental health care. *American Journal of Psychiatry* 150: 554–561.

Rogler, L. H., Cortes, D. E., and Malgady, R. G. (1991). Acculturation and mental health status: convergence and new directions for research. *American Psychologist* 46:585–597.

Rogler, L. H., Malgady, R. G., and Rodriguez, O. (1989). *Hispanics and Mental Health: A Framework for Research*. Malabar, FL: Krieger.

Roheim, G. (1932). The psychoanalysis of primitive cultural types. *International Journal of Psycho-Analysis* 13:1–224.

Romanell, P. (1971). *Making of the Mexican Mind*. Notre Dame, IN: University of Notre Dame Press.

Romano, O. (1964). *Don Pedrito Jaramillo: the emergence of a Mexican-American folk saint*. Unpublished Dissertation, University of California at Berkeley.

———— (1973). The anthropology and sociology of the Mexican-Americans. In *Voices*, ed. O. Romano. Berkeley, CA: Quinto Sol Publications.

Root, M. P. P., ed. (1992). *Racially Mixed People in America*. Newbury Park, CA: Sage.

———— (1996). *The Multicultural Experience*. Thousand Oaks, CA: Sage.

Rubel, A. (1966). *Across the Tracks: Mexican Americans in a Texas City.* Austin: University of Texas Press.

Ryan, W. (1971). *Blaming the Victim.* New York: Random House.

Salazar, J. M. (1975). Actitudes de estudiantes venezolanos de secundaria y de sus padres, hacia la patria, los simbolos nacinonales y el estado (Attitudes of Venezuelan parents and secondary school students toward their country, national symbols, and the state). In *La psicologia social en latinoamerica*, ed. G. Marin. Mexico, D. F.: Editorial Trillas.

———— (1981). *Research on applied psychology in Venezuela.* Paper presented at XVII Interamerican Congress of Psychology, Dominican Republic, June.

———— (1985). Ideology, economic change, and psychological intervention. In *Cross-Cultural and National Studies in Social Psychology*, ed. R. Diaz-Guerrero. Amsterdam: North Holland.

Sanchez, E. (1995). La psicologia social commutaria desde la perspectiva de la psicologia social. (Social community psychology from a social psychology perspective.) *Interamerican Journal of Psychology* 29(2):227–242.

Sanchez, G. I. (1932). Group differences and Spanish-speaking children—a critical review. *Journal of Applied Psychology* 16:549–558.

———— (1934). Bilingualism and mental measures: a word of caution. *Journal of Applied Psychology* 18:756–772.

———— (1948). *The People: A Study of the Navajos.* Washington, DC: United States Indian Service.

———— (1967). *Forgotten People: A Study of New Mexicans.* Albuquerque: Calvin Horn.

Sarason, S. B. (1974). *The Psychological Sense of Community: Prospects for a Community Psychology.* San Francisco, CA: Jossey-Bass.

Saunders, L. (1954). *Cultural Difference and Medical Care: The Case of the Spanish-Speaking People of the Southwest.* New York: Russell Sage Foundation.

Scopetta, M. A., and Szapocznik, J. (1980). *A comparison of brief strategic family therapy approaches in the treatment of Hispanic children.* Unpublished manuscript. Spanish Family Guidance Clinic, University of Miami, School of Medicine.

Segall, M. (1996). Individualism and collectivism: Description or explanations? *Contemporary Psychology* 41(6):540–542.

Sen, A. (1995). *Inequality Reexamined.* Cambridge, MA: Harvard University Press.

Shockley, W. (1965). Population control or eugenics. *U.S. News and World Report*, November 22, pp. 68–71.

Shore, J. H., and Nicholls, W. M. (1975). Indian children and tribal group homes: new interpretations of the Whipper Man. *American Journal of Psychiatry* 132:454–456.

Sommers, V. S. (1964). The impact of dual cultural membership on identity. *Psychiatry* 27:332–344.

Speck, R., and Attneave, C. L. (1974). *Family Networks*. New York: Vintage.

Spencer, H. (1897). *The Principles of Biology*. New York: Appleton.

Spindler, G. D. (1952). Personality and peyotism in Menomini Indian acculturation. *Psychiatry* 15:151–159.

Stephan, C. W. (1992). Mixed-heritage individuals: ethnic identity and trait characteristics. In *Racially Mixed People in America*, ed. M. P. P. Root. Newbury Park, CA: Sage.

Stone, J., and Mennell, S. (1980). *Alexis de Tocqueville on Democracy, Revolution, and Society*. Chicago: University of Chicago Press.

Stonequist, E. V. (1964). The marginal man: a study in personality and culture conflict. In *Contributions to Urban Sociology*, ed. E. Burgess and D. J. Bogue. Chicago: University of Chicago Press.

Storm, H. (1972). *Seven Arrows*. New York: Ballantine.

Sue, D. W., and Sue, D. (1990). *Counseling the Culturally Different: Theory and Practice*. New York: Wiley.

Sue, S., and Zane, N. (1987). The role of culture and cultural techniques in psychotherapy: a critique and reformulation. *American Psychologist* 42:37–45.

Sumner, W. G. (1906). *Folkways*. Boston: Gin.

Szapocznik, J., and Kurtines, W. M. (1993). Family psychology and cultural diversity: opportunity for theory, research and application. *American Psychologist* 48:400–407.

Szapocznik, J., Kurtines, W. M., and Fernandez, T. (1980). Biculturalism and adjustment among Hispanic youths. *International Journal of Intercultural Relations* 4:353–375.

Szapocznik, J., Scopetta, M. A., and King, O. E. (1978a). Theory and practice in matching treatment to the special characteristics and problems of Cuban immigrants. *Journal of Community Psychology* 6:112–122.

Szapocznik, J., Scopetta, M. A., Kurtines, W. M., and Arnalde, M. A. (1978b). Theory and measurement of acculturation. *Interamerican Journal of Psychology* 12:113–130.

Telles, C., Karno, M., Mintz, J., et al. (1995). Immigrant families coping with schizophrenia. Behavior family intervention vs. case management with a low-income Spanish-speaking population. *British Journal of Psychiatry* 167:473–479.

Teske, R., and Nelson, B. H. (1973). Two scales for the measurement of Mexican American identity. *International Review of Modern Sociology* 3:192–203.

Thomas, W. I., and Znaniecki, F. (1927). *Polish Peasants in Europe and America*, vol. 2. New York: Knopf.

Tocqueville, A. de (1835). *Democracy in America*. Paris: Michel-Levy Frères.

Torrey, E. F. (1973). *The Mind Game: Witchdoctors and Psychiatrists*. New York: Bantam.

Triandis, H. C., and Marin, G. (1983). Etic plus emic versus pseudoetic: a test of a basic assumption of contemporary cross-cultural psychology. *Journal of Cross-Cultural Psychology* 14:489–500.

Triandis, H. C., Vassiliou, V., Vassiliou, G., et al. (1972). *The Analysis of Subjective Culture*. New York: Wiley.

Trickett, E. J., Watts, R. J., and Birman, D., eds. (1994). *Human Diversity*. San Francisco: Jossey-Bass.

Trimble, J. E. (1981). Value differentials and their importance in counseling American Indians. In *Counseling Across Cultures*, 2nd ed., ed. P. P. Pedersen et al. Honolulu: University of Hawaii Press.

Tuck, R. (1946). *Not with the Fist*. New York: Harcourt Brace.

United States Kerner Commission (1968). *Report of the National Advisory Commission on Civil Disorders*. Washington, DC: U.S. Government Printing Office.

Valentine, C. A. (1971). Deficit, difference, and bicultural models of Afro-American behavior. *Harvard Educational Review* 41:131–157.

Vasconcellos, J. (1925). *La raza cosmica: Mision de la raza iberoamericana (The Cosmic Race: Mission of the Iberoamerican Race)*. Mexico, D. F.: Espasa-Calpe Mexicana S.A., 1976.

——— (1927). *Indologia: Una interpretaction de la cultura iberoamericano (The Study of Indian Cultures: An Interpretation of Iberoamerican Culture)*. Barcelona, Spain: Agencia Mundial de Liberia.

Vega, W. A. (1992). Theoretical and pragmatic implications of cultural diversity for community research. *American Journal of Community Psychology* 20:375–391.

Vigil, D. (1983). *Barrio Gangs*. Austin, TX: University of Texas Press.

Weatherford, J. (1988). *Indian Givers: How the Indians of the Americas Transformed the World*. New York: Fawcett Columbine.

——— (1994). *Savages and Civilization: Who will Survive?* New York: Ballantine.

Witkin, H. A., and Berry, J. W. (1975). Psychological differentiation in cross-cultural perspective. *Journal of Cross-Cultural Psychology* 6:4–87.

Witkin, H. A., Dyk, R. B., Faterson, H. F., et al. (1962). *Psychological Differentiation*. New York: Wiley.

Wyman, L. C., and Kluckhohn, C. (1938). Navajo classifications of their song ceremonials. *Memoirs of the American Anthropological Association*, no. 50.

Yang, Z. L. (1989). Acupuncture and emotion: the influence of acupuncture anesthesia on the sensory and emotional components of pain. *Journal of General Psychology* 116(3):247–259.

Zea, L. (1945). *En torno a una filosofia americana (Toward a Philosophy of the Americas)*. Mexico, D. F.: El Colegio de Mexico.

―――― (1974). *Dependencia y liberacion en la cultura latinoamericana (Dependence and Liberation in Latin American Culture)*. Mexico, D. F.: Editorial Joaquin Mortiz, S.A.

❖ I N D E X ❖